Performing the Self

Edited by
Karen Junod and Didier Maillat

SPELL

Swiss Papers in
English Language and Literature

Edited by
The Swiss Association of University Teachers of English
(SAUTE)

General Editor: Lukas Erne

Volume 24

narr VERLAG　francke VERLAG　attempto VERLAG

Narr Francke Attempto Verlag GmbH + Co. KG, Dischingerweg 5, D-72070 Tübingen

To the members of

Swiss Association of University Teachers of English (SAUTE)

Gunter Narr Verlag

02.12.2010

DELIVERY NOTE

Junod, Karen / Maillat, Didier (eds.)
Performing the Self
Swiss Papers in English Language and Literature 24
2010, 196 Seiten,
€[D] 49,00/SFr 69,50
ISBN 978-3-8233-6613-3

1 free copy

Narr Francke Attempto
Verlag GmbH + Co. KG

Dischingerweg 5
D-72070 Tübingen

Postfach 2527
D-72017 Tübingen

Fon +49 (0)7071 9797 0
Fax +49 (0)7071 9797 11

info@narr.de
www.narr.de

info@francke.de
www.francke.de

info@attempto-verlag.de
www.attempto-verlag.de

Handelsregisternummer
Amtsgericht Tübingen,
HRA 1449

USt-IdNr. DE 234182960

Geschäftsführer
Dr. Gunter Narr

Volksbank Tübingen

Konto 55 300 006
BLZ   641 901 10

IBAN: DE09 6419 0110
           0055 3000 06
BIC: GENODES1TUE

Postbank Stuttgart

Konto 168 770 706
BLZ   600 100 70

IBAN: DE39 6001 0070
           0168 7707 06
BIC: PBNKDEFF600

Performing the Self

Edited by
Karen Junod and Didier Maillat

narr
VERLAG

Bibliografische Information der Deutschen Nationalbibliothek

Die Deutsche Nationalbibliothek verzeichnet diese Publikation in der Deutschen Nationalbibliografie; detaillierte bibliografische Daten sind im Internet über <http://dnb.d-nb.de> abrufbar.

Publiziert mit Unterstützung der Schweizerischen Akademie der Geistes- und Sozialwissenschaften.

© 2010 · Narr Francke Attempto Verlag GmbH + Co. KG
Dischingerweg 5 · D-72070 Tübingen

Internet: http://www.narr.de
E-Mail: info@narr.de

Einbandgestaltung: Martin Heusser, Zürich
Druck und Bindung: Laupp & Göbel, Nehren
Printed in Germany

ISSN 0940-0478
ISBN 978-3-8233-6613-3

General Editor's Preface

SPELL (Swiss Papers in English Language and Literature) is a publication of SAUTE, the Swiss Association of University Teachers of English. Established in 1984, it first appeared every second year, was published annually from 1994 to 2008, and now appears three times every two years. Every second year, SPELL publishes a selection of papers given at the biennial symposia organized by SAUTE. Non-symposium volumes are usually collections of papers given at other conferences organized by members of SAUTE, in particular conferences of SANAS, the Swiss Association for North American Studies and, more recently, of SAMEMES, the Swiss Association of Medieval and Early Modern English Studies. However, other proposals are also welcome. Decisions concerning topics and editors are made by the Annual General Meeting of SAUTE two years before the year of publication.

Volumes of SPELL contain carefully selected and edited papers devoted to a topic of literary, linguistic and – broadly – cultural interest. All contributions are original and are subjected to external evaluation by means of a full peer review process. Contributions are usually by participants at the conferences mentioned, but volume editors are free to solicit further contributions. Papers published in SPELL are documented in the *MLA International Bibliography*. SPELL is published with the financial support of the Swiss Academy of Humanities and Social Sciences.

Information on all aspects of SPELL, including volumes planned for the future, is available from the General Editor, Prof. Lukas Erne, Département de langue et littérature anglaises, Faculté des Lettres, Université de Genève, CH-1211 Genève 4, Switzerland, e-mail: lukas.erne@unige.ch. Information about past volumes of SPELL and about SAUTE, in particular about how to become a member of the association, can be obtained from the SAUTE website at http://www.saute.ch.

Lukas Erne

Acknowledgements

During the elaboration of the present volume we were lucky to be able to count on the support, help, feedback and friendship of several colleagues whose expertise was called for on various levels. In particular, we wish to single out Indira Ghose, to whom we are grateful for her time and advice in many emails and discussions. We were also glad to be able to count on an inordinately large group of reviewers whose availability and work helped us greatly during the initial stages of this project. Several persons collaborated in setting up a camera ready copy. We would like to thank Keith Hewlett for his helpful assistance in preparing all the manuscripts for publication, Yvonne Droeschel for checking some of the essays, Santiago Cruz Petersen and Marlène Leuzinger Navarrete for helping us compile an index, as well as Martin Heusser for his assistance in designing the cover. Finally, we would like to thank Lukas Erne for his support throughout. To all of them we wish to express our gratitude for making this volume better. The usual proviso applies.

Table of Contents

Introduction

And who are you? Said he. – Don't puzzle me, said I.
Tristram Shandy, Book VII, Chapter 33, 473

Tristram Shandy's bewildered reaction and his inability to give a straightforward answer to the question as to who he is may be, ironically, the most appropriate way of introducing a series of essays dealing with notions of identity. The self as a concept has always proved highly intricate, if not puzzling. In Mary Shelley's *Frankenstein*, the Creature, echoing Tristram's perplexity, pondered about his own origins and identity: "'Who was I? What was I? Whence did I come? What was my destination?'" the Creature wondered, conceding regretfully "'These questions continually recurred but I was unable to solve them'" (Shelley 104). The Creature's incapacity to provide and articulate a coherent narrative for his own existence crystallizes the vexed nature of the very concept of identity. Certainly, stories relating to how the self is defined and performed have never yielded any ultimate narrative but have constantly been questioned and revised.

One standard story, often circulated within Western culture, presents an overarching movement that sees a gradual shift from communal or collective identity to a more individual and individualistic notion of the self. This tale describes the history of selfhood as a "biography of progress" that leads towards emancipation, autonomy, and authenticity; from the "tribal mentality" of "primitive societies" to the more self-centred and autonomous nature of the modern self (Porter 1). However, scholars have shown this particular tale to be obsolete, suggesting it should be replaced by other stories whose plots complicate and subvert this seemingly progressive and emancipatory development.[1] Advances in

---

[1] The collection of essays included in Porter's edited book tries precisely to undermine and supersede the views of selfhood as a biography of (Western) progress and development.

Performing the Self. SPELL: Swiss Papers in English Language and Literature 24. Ed. Karen Junod and Didier Maillat. Tübingen: Narr, 2010. 11-20.

new technologies, to mention only one example, keep changing the parameters in which the self is approached and understood, and within
this technological frame the modern "I" is certainly not as autonomous
as is usually suggested. No doubt, the question of whether the self is
something given and unique or something made and achieved, as well as
the related issue of whether the self should be conceived in individual or
social terms, have been at the core of the identity debate for centuries
(see Culler 110-122). All the essays included in the present volume argue
against an essentialist view of the self and demonstrate in various ways
how identities – whether they are defined as national, sexual, gendered,
cultural, professional, virtual, linguistic or in some other way personal –
are the products of multiple constructions and interconnected performances. "Performing" a self is indeed here shown to be an act of constant
questioning and staging, a relentless process which one perpetually re-
vises and readjusts.

Performing the Self was the title of the SAUTE conference held at the
University of Fribourg in May 2009 and attended by Swiss and international scholars of English literature and linguistics. The present volume
contains a selection of the papers presented during this event, offering
multifarious perspectives on the debate about selfhood and identity. The
diversity of approaches among the contributions, however, should not
obscure the degree of similarity and convergence among them. Despite
engaging with the topic in contrasting ways, literary and linguistic scholars concern themselves with very similar questions. Both in language
and literature, identities are the subject of renewed negotiation and ma-
nipulation, of ceaseless confirmation and contestation. Thus this volume
has to be read as a cross-disciplinary dialogue about fundamental issues
related to identity construction and identity performance. Among the
numerous subjects raised here, three in particular have drawn our attention as they offer an ideal platform for interdisciplinary discussion. First,
the postmodernist notion of fluidity and multiplicity, already hinted at
above, emerges as one central tenet in all the present essays. Unsurpris-
ingly, in an age in which virtual reality, instant communication and rapid
travelling regulate the vast majority of our actions and situations, the
idea and the experience of a self in perpetual motion, with no fixed centre, is stronger than ever before. Interestingly, the concepts of fluidity
and multiplicity can be approached both synchronically and diachroni-
cally: one particular identity trait – for example, womanhood – may shift
from context to context, while the values associated with it may fluctu-
ate over time. Another issue addressed by several papers is the relationship linking identity with notions of nationality and geography: to which
extent is one's identity shaped by the assimilation or denial of na-
tional(istic) features? More generally, how is one's personal identity geo-

graphically and culturally located? By which means do individuals construct and define themselves between the local and the global? While these notions of personal and cultural geography are closely connected with concepts of fluidity and multiplicity, they also intersect with ideas of authenticity, performance and staging, which constitute the last major themes of this volume. The idea that the world is a stage on which individuals perform the comedies and tragedies of human life goes back to antiquity. "All the world's a stage," Jaques says to Duke Senior in Shakespeare's *As you Like It*, "And all the men and women merely players: / They have their exits and their entrances; / And one man in his time plays many parts" (II.7.139-142). The negotiation of the fluid boundaries between an authentic and a staged self is a main concern for performance studies which, like postmodernism, emphasize mobility, alteration and dynamism. Indeed, performance studies propose a self that is constantly reconstructed and recreated – the latter term containing within it the idea of recreation both as regeneration as well as play and amusement.

Although the essays contained in this volume have been chosen to represent specific themes, doubtless each article could have been inserted within a different section. We believe that our thematic choice, while ensuring some structural principle, is sufficiently loose to allow for fruitful cross-questioning and intersecting exploration. In this regard, the introductory piece in this volume is symptomatic of the multi-layered dimensions of identity as it simultaneously combines notions of fluidity, nationality, and staging. In "Performing Identities in Byron and Bourdieu," Angela Esterhammer explores the modern performance of identity in Byron's poem *Beppo* (1817), an anecdote recounted by an expatriate English narrator about the customs of Venetian society. Highlighting the continuity between the early nineteenth century and the modern period, her piece shows how Byron's depiction and treatment of characters anticipates certain notions of postmodern sociology, and especially Pierre Bourdieu's theory of *habitus*. The performative and improvisatory aspects of identity construction characterizing the three main protagonists' individual experiences are enhanced in the poem by the Carnivalesque setting in which Byron's story takes place, a setting in which the boundaries between true, real, and disguised are explicitly blurred and put on show. At the same time, the highly symbolic status of Venice's cultural history, embracing as it does both Western and Oriental mores, further complicates the characters' perspective on their immediate and foreign environment, as well as on themselves.

In their essay, Adrian Pablé and Marc Haas take this same notion of fluidity as exposed in Byron's poem to heart and claim that the very existence of multiple identities for a single individual – that is, the fact that

identity is in constant flux and is contextually and dynamically constructed – calls for a different appraisal of identity-related phenomena
within the field of linguistics. In "Essentialism, Codification and the
Sociolinguistics of Identity," they argue that even the most radical socio-
constructionist linguistic analysis cannot avoid a certain form of essentialism in its approach to identity, which is difficult to reconcile with the
extreme degree of fluidity displayed in everyday communication. Instead
the authors propose that this apparent paradox requires a fundamentally
different approach which literally integrates the complex, online and
sometimes contradictory aspects of identity construction in language,
namely integrationism. Interestingly, by rejecting the more scientifically
grounded generalizations expressed in sociolinguistics, integrationism
claims a less radical – "lay" – position for itself on the continuum which
unites language and literary scholars on these questions regarding the
performance of the self.

Alexa Weik's essay, closer to the literary end of the continuum, explores the same inner tension that arises from conflicting identities. Her
piece, "From the Great Plains to the Red Apple Country: Identity and
Ecology in Zitkala-Ša's *American Indian Stories*" examines the personal,
linguistic, and ideological conflicts experienced by a woman born on a
reservation in the prairies of South Dakota and subsequently educated
in Quaker mission schools in Indiana. Weik shows how the protagonist's geographical journey is accompanied by an equally unsettling personal journey which forces her continually to question, renegotiate, and
ultimately accept the lessons learned from her conflicted identity. Re-
vealingly, Zitkala-Ša's experience of "double consciousness" translates
into her using the English language in order to narrate her biographical
experience; yet her account also shows that she continually fights to retain key aspects of her Indian identity – a personal struggle, Weik shows,
which ultimately turns into a public and political fight for Native American civil rights and environmental justice.

Touching on the fundamental relation extant between one's language
and the identity one performs, Weik thus emphasizes one of the central
ideas of the scientific approach which characterizes the linguistic investigation of identity construction. As is already apparent in the seminal
work of their forefathers, variationist studies – which focus on systematic patterns of language variation – linked the variability of linguistic
features to a number of predicting external factors (see Labov). Interestingly, the list of factors responsible for such variation has outgrown the
original geographical focus to include typical components that are often
regarded as identity traits: socio-economic background, age cohort, educational profile, professional occupation, gender, ethnicity, sexuality,
etc., thereby extending the notion of dialect to social categories or

communities. In this linguistic tradition, language is assumed to function as an index of these geographical and social parameters. That is to say that language is considered a mirror in which a speaker's identity is reflected and revealed. This is a direction which has also been explored by literary authors as they create a voice for their characters. In this respect, the presence of non-standard, prototypically insular features in the language of the youth living on Martha's Vineyard – a popular tourist destination off the coast of Massachusetts – in the 1960s, against the general trend towards standard American English, is analyzed by Labov as differentially asserting a local identity against the seasonal onslaught of tourists coming from the continent. This type of scientific investigation is echoed directly in the prose of an author like MacDiarmid who finds stylistic features to index the Scottish identity of his characters, or in Shakespeare's rendering of the "mechanicals'" social identity in *Midsummer Night's Dream*. Already in the early stages of sociolinguistic investigation, however, scholars also considered the other side of the causal relationship which was taken to hold between social and regional factors and the presence of certain linguistic traits in the speech of individuals. Thus, in the wake of social constructionist critique, language scholars started to consider how language could be used to *perform* an identity, thereby effectively reversing the causal relationship and claiming that language could be used to construct one's self/oneself. As they focus on the intricate connections that obtain between geographical and national identities and their traces in language – be it *of* an individual or *about* that individual – the contributors in this volume explore the complex and various aspects of this issue.

Céline Guignard's essay, "Recovering and Reshaping a Lost Identity: The Gael's Linguistic and Literary Struggle," forms another bridge between linguistic and literary studies and articulates the complex interconnections between language and national/local identity. Guignard's discussion adds another dimension to the debate about the political and cultural call for a literature produced in indigenous languages. Indeed, addressing this debate from a different perspective, Guignard shows how three twentieth-century Scottish authors – William Sharp, Neil Munro and Fionn Mac Colla – negotiate various ways of writing about Gaelic identity and culture in the English language. Thus, rather than seeing language as a marker of national and cultural distinction, these three authors paradoxically appropriate the very language which threatens to hasten the decline of their own culture. Their literary techniques, some of which Guignard analyzes closely, have a political impetus as they allow these writers to present and share a distinctly local and native spirit within a wider, global, environment.

In "Negotiating identities and *Doing* Swiss," Kellie Gonçalves looks into the subtle ways in which, on the one hand, a new national identity may be constructed (*"doing* Swiss"), and, on the other, how a national identity might be maintained in the heterogeneous environment of an intercultural couple. In a clear parallel with the kind of linguistic positioning discussed by Guignard regarding Scottish writers, Gonçalves shows for instance how language is perceived as an inherent, core component of a person's identity (see Pavlenko and Blackledge). She illustrates how, from a pre-theoretical point of view, the essential relationship which prevails between language and a national as well as cultural identity, is unambiguously assumed: one of Gonçalves' expats exclaims that she feels like she "jumped out of [her] culture!" and doesn't want her "house to be in a foreign language." The article also builds on Buchholtz and Hall's sociolinguistics of identity construction, as it discusses the crucial idea that identity work is "negotiated," i.e. the result of a *joint* performance between the various participants of the talk exchange. In this context, Gonçalves' notion of negotiation is reminiscent of the work carried out in the 1960s by sociologist Erving Goffman in a series of writings that were to have a long lasting impact on research into identity performance. It is this same interactional perspective, where national and cultural identity is regarded as co-constructed, which is taken up in the next paper as well.

Indeed, Amit Chaudhuri's piece, "Ray and Ghatak and Other Filmmaking Pairs: the Structure of Asian Modernity," puts into question the whole "East" versus "West" dichotomy that has characterized the vast majority of postcolonial studies. Citing the example of Satyajit Ray's reading of the Japanese filmmaker Akira Kurosawa – thus replacing the traditionally East-West dialectic by one between two Asian contexts – Chaudhuri maintains that modernity should rather be defined as the "culmination" of "a series of interchanges and tensions" between differing cultural contexts not necessarily existing in polar opposition to one another. For Chaudhuri, modernity and modern identity surface and materialize within a global network of exchanges, influences, transformations and what he calls "recognitions." The modern self is one that results from, and belongs to, a universal platform of individuals who all live in the historical moment of the present.

In "Falstaff in Switzerland, Hamlet in Bavaria: Expatriate Shakespeare and the Question of Cultural Transmission," Michael Dobson tackles similar issues of cultural dissemination and appropriation. His essay explores the reception of Shakespeare in two different national and cultural contexts: the one in Geneva in the aftermath of the Napoleonic wars, the other in Bavaria during World War II. Drawing on a wide range of different documents, Dobson's piece shows how the plays of Britain's canonical poet were re-adapted and re-adjusted into the fabric of two distinct modern stages. His essay examines the ways in which the idea of "Britishness" – here incarnated in the figure of Shakespeare – was transmitted and re-interpreted on the Continent. Essentially, Dobson's article investigates the intricate ways in which a historical past is transmitted to, and re-constructed by, a modern present. At the same time, Dobson's analysis engages with the personal implications of theatrical performance, showing how interpreting Shakespeare literally becomes part of the process of identity and gender construction for those who perform his plays.

Dobson's illustration of the fluid connections between national identity and cultural performance on the one hand, and between personal identity and theatrical performance on the other hand, crystallizes the ways in which performance studies have developed over recent decades. Indeed, performance studies were originally related to theatre studies; however, the notion of performativity has since been adopted in many different fields of research, including philosophy, cultural studies, anthropology, literature and linguistics, among others. In his paper, Nikolas Coupland also focuses on what constitutes the definitional traits of an identity, for instance "national," when he writes, like Dobson, about "Britishness." In his criticism, Coupland shows that traditional research carried out in sociolinguistics, following the work done by Labov, relies on the assumption that there exists a correlation between certain fixed social factors – e.g. age, gender, socio-economic background, educational level, ethnicity, etc. – and linguistic features. Coupland argues against the viability of this model on two distinct grounds. First, identity traits or social factors are not necessarily a property that one has but can also be the result of construction processes through language, i.e. of a (linguistic) performance. But if the relationship between language and identity can thus be reversed, the initial sociolinguistic assumption, it is argued, needs to be reconsidered. Interestingly, it is this shift of direction in the relation that holds between social parameters and linguistic markers that is also responsible for introducing a more fluid and multifaceted view of identity, in which performance creates coherence. Second, his paper "Language, Ideology, Media and Social Change" also questions the temporal fluidity of any kind of identity category. Thus, echoing the POW's performances of Shakespeare discussed by Dobson, Coupland shows that while "Britishness" is a World War II concept, its meaning and associated connotations have evolved through time, effectively referring to different social constructs. The same condition of constant flux holds true of the linguistic markers, for instance of "Standard English" features, whose indexing function changes through time. Contrary to Pablé and Haas, the author argues that a more subtle sociolinguistic approach can be found which factors in this type of inherent fluidity and maintains the scientific validity of this type of research.

Part of Coupland's linguistic investigation into "Language, Ideology, Media and Social Change" rests on an exploration of the popular-culture British television show *Strictly Come Dancing* – a programme featuring celebrities competing in Ballroom and Latin dances, and whose performances are rated by the public and four judges who are "typologically dispersed" and whose "class-related voices" differ from one another. The next article, "'There are many that I can be': The Poetics of Self-Performance in Isak Dinesen's 'The Dreamers'" by Barbara Straumann, represents an attractive literary variation on the theme of staged presentation and orchestrated performance. In line with theories of identity construction and gender performance (Butler), Straumann's essay explores the many transformations of Pellegrina Leoni, a celebrated opera singer who loses her voice in a tragic accident. Leoni's personal resurrection, the author shows, rests on assuming a variety of shifting roles that highly contrast with the "rigid star persona" for which she was initially known. The various masks that Leoni puts on allow her to perpetually construct and deconstruct herself. Significantly, it is precisely when Leoni is being asked "who she is" by one of the other characters in the narrative that she dies – thus offering a postmodern and decidedly more macabre version of Tristram Shandy's response quoted at the beginning of this introduction. The issue of making and unmaking is further complicated in the narrative by the fact that Leoni's continuous rebirths into new selves echo the many personal and artistic resurrections of Isak Dinesen herself, also known as Karen Blixen. The ever elusive relationship between truth and fiction is thus given a new literary platform, with "The Dreamers" functioning as a manifesto for Dinesen's own artistic (self)construction.

Issues of self-making, perpetual transformation and updating, as well as the complex relationship between authenticity and anonymity, are once again pursued in the next and final contribution by Brook Bolander and Miriam Locher. These two scholars investigate how computer mediated communication, in this case the Internet and more specifically the social networking website Facebook, has redefined the sort of identity construction work that speakers engage in. In doing so they show how the recent development of such online social interfaces gives us an exceptional opportunity to observe identity performance as it unfolds through a medium that categorises and re-organises identity-building acts. In "Constructing Identity on Facebook" the authors show that by offering a clean slate, that is, perfect anonymity, online space also requires that a new, possibly fictional, identity be constructed within the materiality of the medium itself. Online network participants engage in complex performances of their online selves which exploit the various dimensions of the medium (language, image, links). Through a close scrutiny of the data they collected, they reveal the specific linguistic strategies that determine online identity performance.

Clearly, many other aspects relating to identity construction and identity performance could have been raised: this volume touches upon only a few of them. Addressing the question of identity in all its various and contradictory aspects is a Herculean, if not impossible task. The aim of *Performing the Self* is, perhaps more modestly, to bring together two different fields of scholarship and to enable a cross-disciplinary dialogue among all the various papers. The two voices of this introduction, co-authored by a literary scholar and a linguist, reflect such a dialogue. We hope that our exchange will encourage further exploration, leading to further fruitful interdisciplinary discussion on the performance of self-hood and identity.

Karen Junod
Didier Maillat

References

Bucholtz, Mary and Kira Hall. "Identity and Interaction: a Sociocultural Linguistic Approach." *Discourse Studies* 7:4-5 (2005): 585-614.
Butler, Judith. *Gender Trouble: Feminism and the Subversion of Identity.* New York, London: Routledge: 1990.
Culler, Jonathan. *Literary Theory. A Very Short Introduction.* Oxford, New York: Oxford University Press, 1997.
Goffman, Erving. *Interaction Ritual: Essays in Face-to-Face Behavior.* New Brunswick, New Jersey: Aldine Transaction, 2005.
Labov, William. *Sociolinguistic patterns.* Philadelphia: University of Pennsylvania Press, 1972.
Pavlenko, Aneta, and Adrian Blackledge, eds. *Negotiation of identities in multilingual contexts.* Clevedon: Multilingual Matters, 2004.
Porter, Roy, ed. *Rewriting the Self. Histories from the Renaissance to the Present.* London, New York: Routledge, 1997.
Shakespeare, William, *As You Like It.* Ed. Alan Brissenden. Oxford: Clarendon Press, 1993.
Shelley, Mary. *Frankenstein or The Modern Prometheus* (1818). Oxford: Oxford University Press, 1993.
Sterne, Laurence, *The Life and Opinions of Tristram Shandy, Gentleman.* Ed. Melvyn New and Joan New. London: Penguin, 2003.

Performing Identities in
Byron and Bourdieu

Angela Esterhammer

In order to explore the distinctively modern performances of identity found in the later poetry of Byron, this paper focuses on *Beppo*, the hundred-stanza poem that Byron wrote in Venice in October 1817. *Beppo* is well known as Byron's first use of the serio-comic, conversational narrative voice that came to characterize his later poetry; but the "plot" of this poem, an anecdote related by an expatriate English narrator about the habits of Venetian society, has received relatively little attention. By exposing interpersonal relationships and the construction of identities as performative and improvisatory processes, this anecdote intriguingly anticipates the perspective of postmodern sociology. Pierre Bourdieu's theory of *habitus* as the disposition inculcated in individuals by their socio-economic environment is a particularly relevant model for reading the behaviour of Byron's Venetian characters and their interactions within a Carnivalesque setting. *Beppo* throws open questions about individual and national identities: how fixed or durable they are, whether they are conceptual or embodied, how they are negotiated in interpersonal situations. Adopting an ironically sociological perspective, Byron depicts social role-playing as a conjunction of environmental determinism with individual improvisation.

Separately and – especially – together, Lord Byron's life and his poetry manifest processes of identity-construction on multiple intersecting levels. The performance of identity is arguably the main structuring principle of *Childe Harold's Pilgrimage* (1812-1818), in which the wandering Byron/Harold assembles a self by accumulating performative responses to European historical landscapes. In a different way, the performance of identity underlies Byron's mock-epic masterpiece *Don Juan* (1819-1824), whose rambling cantos are tenuously held together by the protag-

Performing the Self. SPELL: Swiss Papers in English Language and Literature 24. Ed. Karen Junod and Didier Maillat. Tübingen: Narr, 2010. 21-31.

onist Juan's adaptive performances of national, local, (cross-)gendered, professional, social, and relational identities as history and fortune drive him around Europe. *Don Juan* thereby represents a more sociological perspective on identity-construction than the egocentric self-performance of the brooding, conflicted, remorseful, yet great-souled Byronic hero that goes on in *Childe Harold's Pilgrimage*. The more social and cosmopolitan performative identities of Byron's later poetry are the focus of this essay, which takes as its main point of reference *Beppo: A Venetian Story*, the hundred-stanza poem that he wrote in Venice in October 1817. *Beppo* is significant for Byronists and Romanticists because it marks Byron's first use of the serio-comic, conversational narrative voice that came to characterize his later poetry. Yet the "Venetian story" promised in Byron's sub-title – an anecdote told by a dandyish, expatriate English narrator about the habits of Venetian society – has received relatively little interpretation.[1] I will propose that, by exposing interpersonal relationships and the construction of identities as performative and improvisatory processes, this anecdote intriguingly anticipates the perspective of postmodern sociology.

A similar "improvisational turn" can be identified in late-twentieth-century sociological theory and in late-Romantic literature.[2] In Byron's *Beppo*, the notion of improvisation is explicitly evoked through the setting of the story in the midst of the Venetian Carnival, and on the narrative level by the haphazard style of the storyteller. More generally, Byron, along with many of his early-nineteenth-century contemporaries, manifests an understanding of the relation among individual agency, social practice, temporality, and identity that finds distinct resonances in the work of twentieth-century social theorists who recognize improvisation sometimes as an analogy for, and sometimes as an actual component of, social practice. Claude Lévi-Strauss' notion of *bricolage*, Erving Goffman's analysis of interpersonal "interaction rituals," Victor Turner's anthropological study of rituals developed by cultures to deal with crisis situations, and Harold Garfinkel's "ethnomethodological" study of the way ad-hoc decisions get codified into official procedures are examples of a wide-ranging shift of attention from *structure* to *process* in the modern social sciences (see Lévi-Strauss; Goffman; Turner; Garfinkel). While these approaches already incorporate various forms of "adhocism" (to use the architectural term coined by Charles Jencks), postmodern theorists like Pierre Bourdieu and Michel de Certeau go a

---

[1] A notable exception is Paul Elledge's "Divorce Italian Style," which makes substantial use of the story of Beppo in exploring Byron's poetics of discontinuity.

[2] For a much more extensive development of this hypothesis, see Esterhammer, *Romanticism and Improvisation*.

step further. They explicitly identify improvisation as an element that complicates theories based on notions of ritual, script, or game (such as those mentioned above). Thus, Certeau demonstrates in *The Practice of Everyday Life* that subjects use improvisational "tactics" to assemble a social identity in defiance of the "strategies" pursued by institutions. Interpersonal relations, according to this improvisation-based anthropology, depend on separate moments of contingent behaviour and a web of connections among these moments that is tenuously woven by human subjects or derived from social processes. This interpretive web conceals the discontinuities between contingent moments and provides a fragile basis for the fiction of a continuous, underlying "essential self."

For a reading of social behaviour in Byron's *Beppo*, the work of Pierre Bourdieu provides especially apt terms of reference. Bourdieu negotiates between the two poles of environmental determinism and individual improvisation, or social conditioning and individual creativity, primarily through his reorientation of the term *habitus*. Inheriting different inflections of this originally Aristotelian term from medieval scholasticism (which translated Aristotle's *hexis* into *habitus*) and later from twentieth-century sociologists like Marcel Mauss and Norbert Elias, Bourdieu redefines it as a concept that mediates between objective structures and subjective behaviour, as well as between ideology and the materiality of the body. As a set of dispositions acquired from social institutions such as family, school, and religion that become physically inculcated in a subject's body, *habitus* does not determine or programme behaviour, but rather inclines the subject to act and react in systematic ways, although the details of each reaction are as unpredictable as the contingent circumstances that call it forth. "The *habitus*," Bourdieu writes,

> a product of history, produces individual and collective practices – more history – in accordance with the schemes generated by history. . . . Because the *habitus* is an infinite capacity for generating products – thoughts, perceptions, expressions and actions – whose limits are set by the historically and socially situated conditions of its production, the conditioned and conditional freedom it provides is as remote from creation of unpredictable novelty as it is from simple mechanical reproduction of the original conditioning. (54-5)

To cite examples equally relevant to Bourdieu and Byron, *habitus* may encompass ways of speaking, dressing, or eating, semi-ritualized social behaviour such as gift-giving, and the manner in which one has learned to make (or avoid) eye contact. In Bourdieu's theoretical formulation as in Byron's narrative depiction, *habitus* is "embodied history" (56), the product of "economic and social processes" (50) beyond the individual's control, yet it manifests itself in unpredictable behaviour called forth by the unforeseeable contingencies of everyday life. In this sense, as Bourdieu explicitly suggests, everyday behaviour is comparable to the "regulated improvisations" (57) of music or poetry that are played out in time and generate variations on a theme.

Bourdieu insists that understanding social practice demands more than the static structures identified by traditional sociology; it demands a *narrative* description that takes full account of temporality. Such a description reveals that social practice is discontinuous: rather than following mechanical sequences or rigid rituals, it is full of temporal gaps that admit apparent spontaneity and uncertainty into the structures of everyday life. "The most ordinary and even the seemingly most routine exchanges of ordinary life," Bourdieu writes, "presuppose an improvisation, and therefore a constant uncertainty, which, as we say, make all their *charm*, and hence all their social efficacy" (99). An example of a "routine exchange of ordinary life" that will be germane to *Beppo* is the promise and its more ritualized form, the marriage vow. The temporal gap between utterance and fulfillment in the marriage vow, as in any promise, opens up a space for improvisation, admitting the possibility of unforeseen behaviour that may or may not respect the expectations aroused by the promise. Improvisation, therefore, is not merely a useful analogy for the ongoing interaction of a person's *habitus* with new situations; rather, improvisation actually and constantly occurs in social practice. In Bourdieu's postmodern sociology, the view of society as a set of rigid structures and durable relations gives way to a practice-oriented description of social relations as time-bound behaviour interrupted by gaps of indeterminacy that call forth improvised responses. Identities and relationships are therefore circumscribed by what Bourdieu calls "sincere fiction[s]" (112): on the one hand, ordinary individuals uphold a fiction that their actions are free and unconstrained, while, on the other hand, social scientists who study them maintain an equally fictitious belief that rituals and relationships are durable, stable, and inevitable.

The best description of social practice, according to Bourdieu, negotiates between the sincere fictions of subjectivity and objectivity – and I would like to suggest that the nameless English narrator in Byron's *Beppo* anticipates this Bourdieusian perspective. Both an expatriate observer and a participant in the social practices of Venice, the narrator represents himself as a pseudo-scientific analyst, yet presents his observations in a storytelling mode. The "Venetian story" he relates is circumscribed by the structuring rituals of Venetian society, from Christian marriage to the masquerades of the Carnival season, but its action hinges on interruptions and moments of uncertainty, including a long, unexplained absence on the part of one marriage partner and an unconventional encounter at a masked ball. In other words, this story of a love triangle among three characters called "Beppo," "Laura," and "the Count" (Laura's lover) centres on a discontinuity in social relations, a disruption to which all three characters react spontaneously yet in a way that manifests the *habitus* inculcated in them by their Venetian environment. Reading this anecdote with Bourdieu's terminology in mind highlights a new sociological-anthropological orientation that enters Byron's poetry at this juncture, along with the insights it generates into the performative nature of individual and collective identity-construction.

From the beginning, an epistemological undercurrent runs through this lighthearted poem. Thematically and rhetorically, *Beppo* highlights the theme of knowing and not knowing, whereby not-knowing takes a variety of forms that include misunderstanding, misrecognition, superficial observation and jumping to conclusions. These terms prove equally relevant to the characters' relations with one another, and the narrator's relation to his subject matter. With his jaunty opening words – "'Tis known, at least it should be, that throughout / All countries of the Catholic persuasion . . ." (stanza 1) – the narrator embarks on an underlying parody of the enormously popular nineteenth-century genre of travel literature that purports to convey knowledge of foreign customs. But the passive formulation "'Tis known" evokes the same ironic response as another famous opening sentence about universal knowledge penned by Byron's contemporary Jane Austen: "It is a truth universally acknowledged . . ." (Austen 1). Both these claims immediately trigger questions about the reliability of universally acknowledged cultural information: known by whom? On what authority? How objectively? *Who knows?*

Beppo's assertion of knowledge is countered by the literal and epistemological obscurity that pervades the poem's setting in the midst of the Venetian Carnival, the season of masks and disguise. Much in this world is literally dark and unreadable: black eyes, black hair, black clothing. The "dusky mantle" of night (stanza 2) offers concealment, as does the gondola, a "coffin clapt in a canoe, / Where none can make out what you say or do" (stanza 19). Names themselves serve to conceal, rather than to reveal identity. The trio of main characters is made up of a protagonist known only by his nickname "Beppo," the Italian equivalent of "Joe"; an unnamed Count, whose dandyish description identifies him with the stereotypical Italian social role of *cavaliere servente* or acknowledged lover of a married woman; and "Joe"'s estranged wife, of whose name the narrator is entirely ignorant. Calling her "Laura" only "because it slips into my verse with ease" (stanza 21), the narrator conceals her behind a pleasant-sounding pseudonym just as she conceals herself behind costume and make-up when attending the Carnival festivities.

Rather than one of the traditional disguises of Carnival-goers, however, the "Laura mask" recalls Petrarch's Laura, the ideal, chaste love-object, an association that becomes more and more obviously misleading as this lady's physicality and her cavalier approach to marriage become more apparent.

Laura, the Count, and Beppo are sketched as blatant products of the social and economic processes of Venetian society (to echo Bourdieu's formulation); they wear their *habitus* as if it were a Carnival mask. The plot, such as it is, turns on the meeting of the three characters at the Ridotto masked ball, an unexpected encounter that demands a spontaneous reaction within the constraints of each character's ingrained disposition. It is an encounter triggered by the unconventional behaviour of one of the characters in the midst of an otherwise conventional Venetian setting. Instead of meeting and greeting other masked revellers, "one person" draws Laura's attention by staring at her in a manner deemed "rather rare" by those who frequent the Ridotto:

> While Laura thus was seen and seeing, smiling,
>   Talking, she knew not why and cared not what,
> So that her female friends, with envy broiling,
>   Beheld her airs and triumph, and all that;
> And well dress'd males still kept before her filing,
>   And passing bow'd and mingled with her chat;
> More than the rest one person seem'd to stare
> With pertinacity that's rather rare.
>
> He was a Turk, the colour of mahogany;
>   And Laura saw him, and at first was glad,
> Because the Turks so much admire philogyny,
>   Although their usage of their wives is sad . . . (stanzas 69-70)

That is to say, a moment of unconventional behaviour renders conventional Venetian social practice discontinuous and thus gets the action underway on the level of the characters as well as on the level of narrative. The narrator promptly turns *his* attention to this staring stranger with the identifying affirmation "He was a Turk." What can "He was a Turk" possibly mean, however – given a setting where everyone is in disguise – except "He *was not* a Turk"? 'Tis known only that the stranger is dressed to look like a Turk, which is as much as to say that he must "really" be something or someone else. Yet the appearance of Turkishness leads Laura into a significantly mistaken assumption, and the narrator into a significantly lengthy digression, about the disposition associated with "being a Turk."

The crucial ambiguity here is between interpreting the stranger's Turkish appearance as his *habitus* – that is, as an ingrained disposition rightly or wrongly understood to be produced by Turkish social and religious institutions – and interpreting it merely as a Carnival mask. The poem has already provided a coy hint that Turkishness should be seen as a removable mask: at the outset, when describing the Venetian Carnival for English readers, the narrator actually names "Turks" first among the masks to be found there, even before the traditional *commedia dell'arte*-inspired costumes of "harlequins and clowns":

> And there are dresses splendid, but fantastical,
> Masks of all times and nations, Turks and Jews,
> And harlequins and clowns, with feats gymnastical,
> Greeks, Romans, Yankee-doodles, and Hindoos . . . (stanza 3)

So, in all likelihood, the "Turk" who stares so egregiously at Laura is *not* a Turk – but, in a further twist, it turns out he is not a stranger dressed up as a Turk to celebrate Carnival, either. Rather, he is the concealed title character Beppo, returning after years of absence from his native Venice, wearing and performing one of many identities he has improvised over the years in order to survive captivity in Turkey and piracy at sea. As the narrator eventually explains,

> he got off by this evading,
> Or else the people would perhaps have shot him;
> And thus at Venice landed to reclaim
> His wife, religion, house, and Christian name. (stanza 97)

Thus the Turk is unmasked as a Venetian pretending to be a Turkish merchant in order to safeguard his life and property, whom his wife Laura and the reader mistake, first for a real Turk, then for a Venetian stranger dressed up as a Turk while revelling in the Carnival. The process of peeling back these layers, however, generates lingering uncertainty about what it means to be or not to be a Turk, a Venetian, or, by extension, an English expatriate in Venice.

The recognition scene between Beppo and his wife is a *tour de force* that perpetuates the confusion between assumed masks and embodied cultural identity. Beppo's disguise is thoroughgoing enough that Laura, even after recognizing him, does not know whether to treat him as her returning husband or as a visiting stranger. Once she has got over her initial shock enough to recover her voice, she mixes both forms of address indiscriminately:

And are you *really*, *truly*, now a Turk?
  With any other women did you wive?
Is't true they use their fingers for a fork?
  Well, that's the prettiest shawl – as I'm alive!
You'll give it me? They say you eat no pork.
  And how so many years did you contrive
To – Bless me! did I ever? No, I never
Saw a man grown so yellow! How's your liver?

Beppo! that beard of yours becomes you not;
  It shall be shaved before you're a day older:
Why do you wear it? Oh! I had forgot –
  Pray don't you think the weather here is colder?
How do I look? You shan't stir from this spot
  In that queer dress, for fear that some beholder
Should find you out, and make the story known.
How short your hair is! Lord! how grey it's grown!   (stanzas 92-93)

In the course of this tirade, Beppo is addressed as a returning traveller who can report on the foreign customs of the Muslims ("Is't true *they* use their fingers for a fork?"), but also as a Muslim himself ("They say *you* eat no pork"). Besides shifting pronouns, Laura jumps erratically between domestic concern about her husband's health and appearance, and the nervously polite small talk she would exchange with a foreign visitor ("Pray don't you think the weather here is colder?"). She alternately registers Beppo's Turkishness as external and as internal. It is in some respects an embodied state, signalled by his yellow skin, his diet, and the condition of his internal organs, but at the same time it is a "queer dress" that he can throw off along with shaving his beard. Harebrained as it is, Laura's diatribe worries the question of whether Beppo's Turkish disguise – or, for that matter, her own painted Venetian one – is a consciously removable covering like a Carnival mask, or an embodied identity akin to Bourdieusian *habitus*. Even the narrator cannot, or will not, resolve this ambiguity. He affirms that Beppo "threw off the garments which disguised him," but, in the same breath, that Beppo was rebaptized on his return to Venetian society (stanza 98), suggesting that his assumed Muslim identity is thoroughgoing enough to require a ritual re-naming and re-admission to European Christendom.

Nevertheless, the other speech-act ritual (besides Christian baptism) that structures the three characters' social identities – that is, the classic performative of the marriage ceremony – remains ironically intact when Beppo returns after years of absence to reclaim his wife. After their encounter, he, Laura, and the Count fall into an improvised lifestyle, apparently a happy enough *ménage à trois* in which Beppo and Laura resume their married state without disruption to the Count's place in the house-hold. Indeed, Beppo and the Count, who borrow each others' clothes and are "always friends" (stanza 99), seem to get along better than Beppo and his wife. The moment of recognition and choice on which Byron centres his anecdote of Venetian mores opens up the performative ritual of marriage to the possibility of improvisation. His "Venetian story" thereby becomes a sociological observation, cast in a narrative mode, about the collective improvisation on monogamy that Venetian society is already practising, with its general tolerance of a *cavaliere servente* as part of the marital household. Despite a gap of many years that admits absence, infidelity, and Beppo's radically altered bodily appearance as well as his dubious ethnic-religious identity, the marriage vow that underlies Beppo's and Laura's social identities as husband and wife miraculously survives. Its openness to improvisatory variation forestalls the complete breakdown of social relationships and prevents this charming mini-drama of *anagnorisis* or discovery from being followed by a tragic *peripeteia* or reversal.

On several levels, then, Byron's parodic Venetian story throws open questions about individual and collective identities: how fixed or durable they are, how far they penetrate the body, how they are acknowledged or negotiated anew in interpersonal situations. Through characters who are part Carnival masks, part manifestations of Venetian *habitus*, and part unpredictable improvisers, Byron's poem explores the extent to which identity is performative, and questions whether Turkish, Venetian, and English identities are equally so. On the narrative level, the narrator's long-term absence from his native England gives rise to improvisatory accommodations that parallel those of Beppo and the Venetians in the inset story. The expatriate condition creates a similar discontinuity and necessitates a similar re-negotiation of relationships that manifests itself in the narrator's rhetoric, particularly his forms of address and his allusions to his native culture. Externally, he dons Italian costume and adopts an Italian verse-form – yet he reinforces his underlying affiliation with an English readership by consistently using the pronouns "we" and "our." He adapts to Venetian custom by eating fish during Lent, yet makes it palatable by importing his fish-sauce from England (stanza 8). This and other evocative details show the narrator and the characters responding to dislocations and discontinuities while reaffirming the *habitus* inculcated in them by nationality and history. As a literary text, finally, *Beppo* constitutes an especially good example of Bourdieu's claim that written texts should not be regarded as static objects, but instead – by bearing in mind the temporality of writing – as "irreversible oriented sequences of relatively unpredictable acts" (98). In other words, improvisation inheres in written texts, since they are the result of a series of choices made in response to a series of contingencies. Stylistically speaking, *Beppo* wears its construction out of choices and contingencies on its sleeve; the narrator's haphazard logic and rhetoric give the impression that the choices are still being made and the contingencies are still intruding even as the pen touches the paper. Byron's *Beppo* thus portrays both poetic and social practice as "sincere fictions" – as sequences of partially determined, partially improvisatory moments that make up relationships and identities.

References

Austen, Jane. *Pride and Prejudice*. Ed. James Kinsley. Intro. Fiona Stafford. Oxford: Oxford University Press, 2004.

Bourdieu, Pierre. *The Logic of Practice*. Trans. Richard Nice. Cambridge: Polity Press, 1990.

Byron, Lord [George Gordon]. *Beppo: A Venetian Story*. *Lord Byron: Selected Poems*. Ed. Susan J. Wolfson and Peter J. Manning. Harmondsworth: Penguin, 1996. 573-98.

Certeau, Michel de. *The Practice of Everyday Life*. Trans. Steven Rendall. Berkeley: University of California Press, 1984.

Elledge, Paul. "Divorce Italian Style: Byron's *Beppo*." *MLQ* 46 (1985): 29-47.

Esterhammer, Angela. *Romanticism and Improvisation, 1750-1850*. Cambridge: Cambridge University Press, 2008.

Garfinkel, Harold. *Studies in Ethnomethodology*. [1967.] Cambridge: Polity Press, 1984.

Goffman, Erving. *The Presentation of Self in Everyday Life*. Garden City, New York: Doubleday, 1959.

Lévi-Strauss, Claude. *The Savage Mind*. London: Weidenfeld and Nicolson, 1966.

Turner, Victor. *The Anthropology of Performance*. New York: PAJ Publications, 1987.

Essentialism, Codification and the Sociolinguistics of Identity

Adrian Pablé and Marc Haas

This paper critically examines the work and discourse of two American anthropologists and linguists, Mary Bucholtz and Kira Hall, from the vantage point of an integrational critique of linguistics. The focal point of our critique is the conviction that "identities," as first-order communicational phenomena, cannot be the object of scientific empirical research because doing so presupposes that indexical values are viewed as micro-contextually determined and available to outsiders with an "insider view" (i.e. the ethnographer). As a consequence, Bucholtz and Hall's insistence that they are not "fixed-code" linguists seems little credible, precisely because, unlike integrationists, they cannot subscribe to the view that signs are radically indeterminate: ethnography of communication, after all, relies on data collection and data analysis. The integrationist, in turn, sees "identity" as a metadiscursive label used by lay speakers to cope with their everyday first-order experience: the focus, therefore, ought to be on lay (and professional) discourses about such labels.

1. Introduction: (Socio)linguistics and the "Language Myth"

Since the publication of his book *The Language Myth* in 1981, Roy Harris has launched a relentless critique of linguistics as a "science," arguing that professional linguists have deluded themselves into believing that establishing linguistic "facts" was their particular domain of expertise. Harris' criticism makes crucial reference to the "language myth" (e.g. Harris, *Integrational Linguistics* 32), i.e. the thesis that (i) speech is a form of *telementation* (a means of conveying thoughts from one mind to another) and the thesis of (ii) *linguistic determinacy* (languages are "fixed codes"). In turn, Harris maintains that (i) communication is an "integra-

Performing the Self. SPELL: Swiss Papers in English Language and Literature 24. Ed. Karen Junod and Didier Maillat. Tübingen: Narr, 2010. 33-46.

tional," time-embedded process involving many different kinds of in-
separably bound and situationally contingent mental and physical activities (the strictly *verbal* component being only one of them) and that (ii)
this process is "private" (in the sense that the integrational process depends on an individual's biography and is unpredictable). With its emphasis on the uniqueness of situations and utterances, *integrational linguistics* is sceptical about both universal and culture-specific generalizations.

The linguistics envisaged by Harris is thus a "lay-oriented" one,
which acknowledges that linguistic "facts" cannot be reconstructed
"truthfully" by an impartial scientist: as a consequence, the professional
linguist's reconstruction of what was *really* uttered (or of how something
was *really* understood, etc.) merely becomes a particular kind of discourse (itself worthy of attention) which is, qualitatively speaking, on a
par with how laypeople retrospectively establish linguistic "facts:"

> As far as the integrationist is concerned, any linguistics worth having will be
> "essentially lay-oriented" [. . .] and the facts it deals with will be facts of the
> kind that have to be dealt with in everyday linguistic communication by
> those who engage in it.   (Harris, *Integrational Linguistics* 146)

This is not to claim that verbal communication has no *social* component,
or that individuals (and their ways of behaving) are not influenced by
social phenomena: what the integrationist rejects is the idea that individuals can be categorized, by an objective outsider, as belonging to certain social groups with particular linguistic codes. This is where integrationists disagree with sociolinguists, who believe that situated linguistic
behaviour is amenable to scientific observation.[1] While traditional sociolinguistics (an offspring of dialectology) is dedicated to producing descriptions of systems of varieties of languages (in the tradition of a Saus-
surean structuralism), and hence strongly relies on the *determinacy thesis*,
more recent, ethnographically-inspired sociolinguistic work has shown
little sympathy towards operating with notions such as "fixed codes,"
arguing instead that communication is a *cultural practice* that is best observed in micro-group activities, where the question of a shared com-
munity-wide *code* is of no consequence in order to understand "what is
going on:" the latter school is often referred to as "sociocultural linguistics," and its preferred research focus lies on "identity practices."

---

[1] Examples of integrational empirical studies on how speakers in concrete (social) situations establish "facts" (and the methodology adopted for the purpose) can be found in
Pablé ("Socio-Onomastics;" "Integrationist on Name Variation").

The present paper is meant as an *integrational* critique of sociolinguistic (meta)theory, in particular as presented within the sociocultural framework of analysis. Our critique is directed towards the work of two American linguistic anthropologists, Mary Bucholtz and Kira Hall, because they are strong adherents to the view that sociocultural linguistics in general – and the sociolinguistics of identity in particular – do not adhere to the "fixed-code" fallacy, or to an essentialist view of language and society (e.g. Bucholtz and Hall, "Theorizing Identity"). Bucholtz and Hall (ibid.) also claim that pursuing political interests (here defending the rights of members of sexual minority groups) does not prevent one from carrying out research on sexual identities impartially and objectively. In turn, we would like to argue that sociocultural linguistics is no different from any other branch of orthodox linguistics, in that its main goal is ultimately to establish "facts" based precisely on verbal output. What is more, we believe that sociolinguistics is not done just for the sake of "science," but ultimately has political-ideological goals, which is why its claim to "scientific impartiality" is little credible. It is important to notice that Bucholtz and Hall have already been criticized for their work on previous occasions, notably by Deborah Cameron and Don Kulick (e.g. Cameron and Kulick; Kulick); however, we believe that this criticism does not go far enough, and is, moreover, inconsistent when viewed against the background of Cameron and Kulick's own work on identity.

2. The sociolinguist *qua* essentialist

Rom Harré (323) once distinguished "linguistic essentialism," i.e. "the thesis that there is something which a word *really* means" from "material essentialism," i.e. "the thesis that each kind of material being has a constituent structure, whose particular manifestation in this or that instance of the kind is causally responsible for the manifest properties of its sample realizations." Harré (ibid.) went on to add: "I take it that linguistic essentialism is false and that material essentialism is true, at least in some restricted domains as inorganic chemistry." As Roy Harris (*Semantics of Science* 65) justly remarks, this distinction allows Harré to make the claim that it is possible to discover what x (say, copper) really is, without claiming that it has also been discovered what the word x (*copper*) really means.

In sociolinguistics, the question *what word x really means* is generally treated as a question of socio-regional variation: for instance, who qualifies as a "Yankee" varies among the different speech areas and/or social groups, as investigated in numberless studies of "perceptual dialectology." No sociolinguist, in turn, would like to claim that there is a way of scientifically ascertaining the properties constituting a true "Yankee." In this respect, there is a difference between finding out what, say, "copper" is and finding out what a "Yankee" is. But what about sociocultural phenomena like "languages" or "dialects," whose essence cannot be material (as in the case of "copper")? Again, we agree with Harris (*Semantics of Science* 65) when he says that definitions as they stand in the latest version of the "dictionary of science" *must* be essentialist definitions, including any attempt at defining "variety of language x" in terms of its properties.[2] Essentialism in traditional sociolinguistics has been noted, with respect to William Labov's work, both by theorists (e.g. Figueroa 92) and interactional sociolinguists (e.g. Bucholtz and Hall, "Identity and Interaction"), the latter criticizing Labov's macro-social categorizations of informants as conveying the impression that identities (e.g. "social class," "ethnicity," "sex," and "age") are given prior to actual communication, and that they are objectively verifiable and classifiable as real. In ethnographically-inspired sociolinguistic theory, in turn, identities are claimed to be analyzed in *non-essentialist* terms. Thus, Bucholtz and Hall are interested in gathering the interactional "facts" on the basis of what informants display (i.e. how they make their practices *accountable* to each other) in their attempts at claiming or imposing an "authentic" identity or when perceiving an identity as such. According to Bucholtz and Hall, sociocultural linguists merely state that identities can be "real" for certain people at certain moments, which does not mean that these identities have an ontological existence outside the contingent episode of communication, or that they exist as a stable part of a person's self.

This article takes the position that essentialism, i.e. the assumption that there is a set of properties that truly characterize someone or something as being x or y (whether in a specific context or generally), is a pervasive everyday human phenomenon: Bucholtz and Hall ("Theorizing Identity" 499) equally "recogniz[e] the importance of essentialism as an identity tactic for social subjects." It seems to us, however, that to claim, as sociocultural linguists do, that there is something (e.g. a set of linguistic and paralinguistic properties) to which identity x corresponds at

---

[2] Hence, what a *language name* really means is not treated by the professional linguist on a par with what an ethnic nickname ("Yankee") means: even though varieties of language have names originating within folk usage, the linguist (*qua* sociolinguist or dialectologist) believes these varieties to have an ontological existence, i.e. the "language names" have a *true* meaning (its true "referent" presumably being the native speakers of that language), which scientists can ultimately detect (or at least get closer to) as they discover new "facts" (like, for instance, the fact that Standard British English and Standard American English are not the only varieties to deserve the label "Standard English").

point y in time is precisely to *reify* this identity (and therefore to essential-ize it), notwithstanding that the sociocultural linguist is merely taking his/her informants' perspective: in fact, the analyst claims to be in a po-sition to say that an identity is perceived as, or claimed to be, "authen-tic" (or "inauthentic") by one or more interactants on the very basis that the linguistic and paralinguistic features x, y, z were employed during the interaction. It matters little on that score whether the analyst believes that the identity exists as such (e.g. a "social class identity" in realist so-ciolinguistics) or is merely discursively constructed in the *here-and-now* (as in social constructionist models). The problematic lies in the very claim that it is possible to prove that identity x is "real" (or claimed to be real) for one or more persons, and that the key to proving it lies in analyzing language use.

3. Reiterating the "anti-identity position" (Cameron and Kulick)

In their 2004 article, Bucholtz and Hall see fit to address some of the points directed against their language and sexuality framework of analy-sis by Cameron and Kulick, who espouse a desire-centred view of sexu-ality. According to Bucholtz and Hall, their reply to Cameron and Ku-lick's critique has a wider scope than merely defending the sociocultur-ally-oriented approach to sexuality, as identity research in general is un-der attack:

> And although the anti-identity position is framed in terms of language and sexuality, it is consequential for the sociocultural study of language more generally. The fields of sociolinguistics, linguistic anthropology, and dis-course analysis have increasingly recognized that the study of the linguistic construction of society and culture requires the study of linguistically con-structed subject positions [. . .] discarding this fundamental insight in any area of socially oriented linguistics could set back progress in other areas as well. (Bucholtz and Hall, "Theorizing Identity" 472)

Bucholtz and Hall (474) reject Cameron and Kulick's critique that "lin-guistic research on minority sexual identities [is] concerned with the search for a linguistic code," i.e. "a distinctive way of speaking and/or writing which serves as an authentic expression of group identity" (Cameron and Kulick xiii-xiv). This kind of focus Bucholtz and Hall regard as essentialist, and concede that indeed some of the earlier stud-ies on language and sexuality were carried out in this spirit. In turn, cur-rent scholarship within sociocultural linguistics views identity "as a vari-able and indexical phenomenon" (Bucholtz and Hall, "Theorizing Identity" 474). From that it follows that Bucholtz and Hall link essentialism in sociolinguistics with the search for "fixed codes," i.e. the assumption that members of social groups share a "register" (or "dialect") which precedes actual usage: on the other hand, the description of "language use in particular contexts" (ibid.), which is what sociocultural linguistics is concerned with, has nothing to do with a view of language as "coded" and "fixed."[3] They hasten to add that terminology in the field suggesting adherence to a "fixed-code" view of language, e.g. terms like "lesbian speech" or "gay men's English," should be seen as "nominal construction[s]" expressing "the uncontroversial proposition that 'lesbians speak'" (ibid.) and – it might be added – that gay men whose native language is English speak "English". On these grounds, they caution language and gender researchers to "select their terms with greater care to avoid misconstruals and charges of overgeneralization," adding that "broad wording frequently gave rise to bitter accusations of essentialism" (ibid. 508, fn. 8).[4] On the other hand, Bucholtz and Hall *do* associate social groups with "particular ways of speaking," at least potentially, as they themselves claim:

> If "masturbators" or "wine enthusiasts" are indeed salient social categories in a particular culture that are associated with particular ways of speaking, then linguists might indeed do well to study them.   (Bucholtz and Hall, "Theorizing Identity" 478)

---

[3] Bucholtz and Hall ("Theorizing Identity" 475) profess their belief in "the fundamental heterogeneity of even the smallest social group." In turn, it is speakers who adhere to an "ideology of linguistic homogeneity," and this is what interests the sociocultural linguist, i.e. the fact that this "ideology [. . .] may become salient in social interaction across lines of individual difference." On this and similar points, see section 5.

[4] Bucholtz and Hall ("Theorizing Identity" 490/475) highlight the term "queer" (and "queerspeak") as evidence against a "fixed code" view of language: "Queer linguistics follows queer theory in refraining from assigning a fixed, categorical meaning to 'queer.' In specific situations, the (temporary and situated) meaning of 'queer' emerges at the excluded margins of historically and culturally variable heteronormative systems. This meaning is arrived at analytically through principles established by sociocultural approaches to language, such as ethnography, that foreground the importance of local understandings and contexts." It seems to us, however, that Bucholtz and Hall still have to presuppose that "queer" has a fixed (i.e. intersubjectively shared) meaning, namely a fixed contextual meaning. Nor is it convincing to argue, as Bucholtz and Hall (ibid. 490) do in their attempt at adducing evidence that "queer" has no fixed, categorical meaning, that heterosexuals may also be "positioned as queer when they fall outside normative structures of sexuality." In fact, to argue that "queer" is not only used as shorthand for "lesbian, gay, bisexual, and transgender," but also in some cases for heterosexuals does not undermine a fixed-code semantics – on the contrary, it only reaffirms the concept of "polysemy."

Note that the linguist is not to study the discourse *about* these salient social categories, i.e. what others believe masturbators or wine enthusiasts say, but the groups themselves (and respectively, their particular ways of speaking). Again, Bucholtz and Hall do not mean to say that "masturbator language" exists (as that would be tantamount to admitting that they believe in "codes"), but rather that the sexual practice of masturbating might have consequences for the practitioners' language.[5]

Bucholtz and Hall's claim that they do not essentialize social identities (by linking them to atemporal "fixed codes") chiefly relies on the concept of "indirect indexicality." In their defense of a *sociocultural* approach to minority sexual identities they write:

> Critics have objected to researchers' analyses of linguistic features as markers of lesbian and gay identities. They [the critics] note that other kinds of speakers may also use the same features; thus, such features cannot be said to be distinctively lesbian or gay. This position rests on the fallacy that linguistic forms must be uniquely assigned to particular identities in order to be socially meaningful. A simple solution to this apparent problem is offered by the semiotic concept of INDEXICALITY [. . .] Specific linguistic forms can come to be ideologically associated with particular social identities indirectly [. . .] This kind of indirect indexicality allows for the creation of multiple indexical links to a single linguistic form [. . .] the discovery that different groups may use similar linguistic resources for identity construction, far from vitiating the concept of identity, demonstrates the robust capacity to create new social meanings from existing linguistic practices.
> (Bucholtz and Hall, "Theorizing Identity" 475-6)

What are we to do with Bucholtz and Hall's firm rejection of the "code view" and their emphasis on the phenomenon of *indexicality* instead? If we examine their studies with greater care (e.g. Bucholtz, "Why be Normal;" "Whiteness of Nerds;" Bucholtz and Hall, "Identity and Interaction"), it is indeed hard to believe that their conception of languages (or varieties of languages) is not one of "fixed codes." Or else

---

[5] Bucholtz and Hall ("Theorizing Identity" 477) clearly reject Kulick's (270) and Cameron and Kulick's (102) suggestion that lesbians' or gay men's linguistic practices could be compared to the "specialized registers" of stamp collectors and wine enthusiasts, thus to linguistic resources that are in principle available to *any* speaker; according to Bucholtz and Hall (ibid.), lesbian and gay identity must not be trivialized by being put on the same level as "upper class leisure activities." Understandably, the authors wish to underline that being "lesbian" is more identity-building than being a "stamp collector," however fervently one does it. But still, the question remains as to which kinds of social identity are consequential for one's language use (i.e. are more than merely superficial "expert talk"); it seems that minority group identities automatically fall in that category, while upper-class activities (being a "wine connoisseur") do not necessarily do so.

how could Bucholtz have determined that the female teenagers at Bay City High School, California, investigated by her in the mid-1990s, displayed a "nerd identity" via the linguistic, prosodic and paralinguistic features $a,b,c,$ at time x (as reconstructed on the basis of tape-recorded material)? The features at issue are, among other ones, words assigned by her to the "formal register," as well as certain phonological and syntactic patterns, some of which are part of a variety which Bucholtz terms "Superstandard English" (Bucholtz, "Whiteness of Nerds"). The very fact that Bucholtz can make such statements is proof that she herself adheres to a coded view of language, for being able to say that for speaker A variant x is indexical of value y at time b presupposes fixity insofar as the analyst is in a position to state that variant x is unmistakably intended by speaker A as projecting value y, and not any other value. It is evident that the indexical value of a variant is shared intersubjectively: otherwise what use would it be to project, say, a "nerd identity" by means of linguistic features $a,b,c,$ if their local indexical value (e.g. "nerdiness") could not be recognized as such by the other members of the local group? To argue that these indirect indexical links attached to linguistic features are created as part of the interaction (and are therefore not given in advance) still presupposes that they are "coded" (or become coded in a specific context, i.e. as signs of identity y): how else could they be recognized as what they are? In other words, the social practices that bring these indexical values into being in specific microsocial contexts must exist as abstractions in some way to be recognizable at all. Even those paralinguistic features which a traditional linguist would classify as "not system-related" (in English, for instance, a rise in pitch, a change in voice quality, etc.) must be treated as subject to mutually shared underlying rules of interpretation in the sociocultural framework of analysis. Saying that the indexical values attached to actual linguistic and paralinguistic forms are recognizable among interactants in one particular local context (and in no other) begs the question of how the researcher knows that these values are recognized as such by all interactants for whom intersubjectivity is claimed.[6]

---

[6] Bucholtz and Hall ("Theorizing Identity" 495-496) stress the fact that "intersubjectivity" is only about "sufficient similarity": ". . . much of the time what is sufficient is merely partial identification or similarity between social subjects." It must be added at this point, however, that in order to link linguistic features with a social identity as done within the sociocultural framework of analysis, there must be at least *some* overlap (in the sense of "identicality") of intersubjective interpretations of signs (or indexicality) in context that is presupposed, or else no reliable statements could be made by researchers concerning the emergence of a specific identity through features x,y,z. Moreover, if "intersubjective agreement" merely consists of an approximation to the same meaning, the

On top of that, by clinging to the notion of "indexicality" in their defense of language and social identity research, Bucholtz and Hall become an easy target for criticism, precisely because they conflate two quite different metalinguistic uses of the term "indexical," with the consequence that the very notion of a "social identity" becomes nonsensical: (i) *indexicality* as a feature of what is commonly called "social marker," which, being "social," requires multiple occurrences, i.e. extending beyond the single speaker and the single occasion of utterance (otherwise how could it be "social" at all?); (ii) *indexicality* as "deixis," i.e. indicating context-bound reference to a particular person, time and place, which is not socially marked (like the words *I* or *yesterday*) and refers to a single context only. Bucholtz and Hall, however, make this very claim when it comes to the indexical value of linguistic features, namely that they are "social" (i.e. going beyond a single occurrence) but at the same time analyzable only in terms of one specific local context.

4. To be or not to be an essentialist

An important factor to consider in the discussion about essentialism in language and identity research is the political dimension inherent in the programme. Sociolinguists study minority groups with the goal of contributing to the latter's "cause": for instance, showing that a "gay identity" or "lesbian identity" is not something stable but is enacted interactionally in local contexts is hardly helpful in the activists' fight for equal rights. Bucholtz and Hall ("Theorizing Identity" 476-7) themselves approve of so-called "strategic essentialism", which they regard as a "powerful intellectual and political tool [. . .] to remedy the historical underrepresentation of social groups;" they go on to add that "temporary overgeneralizations [. . .] are often necessary in the establishment of sociopolitical institutions such as research fields and political movements." It is clear that only by considering social groups in an essentialist perspective, can one succeed politically. In fact, it is noticeable that, despite everything, sociocultural linguists cling to essentializing labels to describe identities which they claim to be studying in a non-essentialist way, which is why their insistence on not being essentialists *qua* sociolinguists is unconvincing. What matters ultimately is to foreground a group as having its own "identity", and showing that this identity is not "objectively verifiable and classifiable as real," as Bucholtz and Hall believe (but a discursive phenomenon which emerges out of the contin-

---

question arises as to when meanings are "sufficiently similar" so as not to cause serious misunderstandings or even communication breakdowns.

gent situation), is hardly helpful in fostering recognition and equal rights for minority groups.[7] We suspect that the thesis of identities as "fluid and situationally constructed" serves to underpin the image of the sociolinguist *qua* "scientist," who shows a concern for ascertaining the "truth" about language-related sociocultural phenomena, while not refraining from essentializing these phenomena when deemed profitable. While we do not contest the right for political action, it is not clear how a "science" of linguistics can help minority groups not (primarily) discriminated against on the basis of their "improper" use of language (like gays and lesbians).[8] In our view, it is problematic when politically committed sociolinguists profess themselves to be unaffected by their own interests as they are conducting research and analyzing data, thereby drawing a sharp line between the sociolinguist *qua* professional and the sociolinguist *qua* political activist, who – just like others – tends to overgeneralize. In our view, the political activist's sense of justice should not be confused with the scientist's quest for "truth."

A criticism raised against sociocultural linguistics in this article concerns precisely the linguist's claim to "superior insight": hence, the professional linguist knows whether an identity was (or was not) essentialized by a specific interactant. This *mind-reading ability* with which the linguist is apparently endowed is manifest in Bucholtz and Hall's discussion of sex phone workers, whose clients essentialize (i.e. take as authentic) the sexualized identity on the other end of the line, while the analyst knows (of course) that the identity is only *performed* by the worker: "Thus, while phone sex workers' performances cannot be interpreted by analysts as authentic – given that they cross lines of race, ethnicity, and even gender – their clients are not usually so *enlightened*" ("Theorizing Identity" 499, italics ours). In a similar vein, the sociocultural linguist's belief that more adequate frameworks of analysis (like the advent of ethnomethodology and the ethnography of speaking) will en-

---

[7] To be sure, the "identity as fluid and constructed" thesis can be used profitably by politically active scientists as evidence that members of minority groups do not conform to the essentializing stereotypes encountered in everyday lay (including the politicians') discourse.

[8] In what way the innumerable sociolinguistic studies "proving" that the dialects spoken by ethnic minority groups are systematic (and thus just as "grammatical" as Standard varieties) have helped the cause of these groups is another question, which, it seems to us, deserves attention on the part of the professional linguists (but must involve the minority groups themselves as well). In spite of the fact that most linguists (at least all sociolinguists) would have no doubts as to the beneficial impact that these studies (and future ones) will have on linguistically discriminated groups, there are also those who precisely fear that by essentializing these groups one may actually go against the will of at least some of its members. This, however, does not mean that we believe sociolinguists should engage in spreading the "Myth of Standard varieties."

able social scientists ultimately to discover the "truth" about sociocultural phenomena parallels the position of the natural scientist, who subscribes to essentialism in his attempts at finding the "true nature" of his object of study. In language and identity research, the very focus on the micro-level of society (i.e. the community of practice), requiring an anthropological approach to participant observation, turns out to be the veritable "eye-opener." One is indeed reminded here of Rom Harré's creed (302), i.e. "the limitations of my equipment are the limits of my world."

5. An alternative view of sign-making

One reason why Bucholtz and Hall cannot accept Cameron and Kulick's critique seems to be grounded in the fact that the desire-centred approach to sexuality itself depends on a "code" view of language, and therefore on "decontexualized interpretations of linguistic data" (Bucholtz and Hall, "Theorizing Identity" 478):

> Another way in which the desire framework sets aside social context, at least in some of its manifestations, is in its reliance on the very "code" view claimed to be characteristic of research on sexual identity. In the most extreme formulation of this view, the linguistic expression of desire is represented as necessarily distinctive in form [. . .] Whereas Kulick forcefully and repeatedly argues against the possibility of associating any distinctive formal features with sexual identities, he willingly accepts the assumption that distinctive formal features attach to sexual desires. [. . .] Our own view, as suggested above, is that language use need not be distinctive to construct sociocultural meanings. (ibid. 480)

It should be clear by now that any credible critique of sociocultural linguistics must take as its starting-point the rejection of the sign (linguistic or other) as "intersubjectively shared." Only if signs are regarded as "private," i.e. as inextricably bound to an individual's personal experience with them, is it consistent to argue against the notion of "indirect indexicality," which is the key concept underlying sociocultural approaches to language in use. In other words, there is simply no way of finding out whether the indexical value I attach to feature x is identical to how the other interactants interpret it (not even if I ask my conversational partners retrospectively). Of course, individual A and individual B may have experienced the linguistic features x,y,z in similar ways (i.e. in conjunction with speakers they both regard as "belonging to social group X"), but given the uniqueness of each and every interactional episode, individuals A and B will never actualize these experiences with x,y,z in the same way; it could be, for instance, that just prior to a communicational episode involving A and B, speaker A has encountered features x,y,z as part of the speech of somebody who, A knows with certainty, does not "belong to social group X." There is simply no way for interactional sociolinguists to control these biographical factors concerning their informants, which is why researchers focus on a clearly delineated tape-recorded sequence, thereby treating a given episode as autonomous rather than seeing it as part of an *open-ended continuum*. Since no two people share exactly the same range of experiences with a certain sign, a "God's truth" perspective (if anything like that were humanly possible) would determine that in fact interactants (as well as the researcher) do not interpret the "same" sign (as present in the *here-and-now*) alike – it is a different sign for each of them.

In this perspective, signs are indeed looked upon as context-bound, but we see no reason why the interpretation of signs can only be *socioculturally meaningful* if undertaken as part of interpersonal communication. Sign-making does not presuppose interaction, as experiential actualization (attaching a "meaning" to a form in context) does not only concern social interaction but also self-communication and reflection. Obviously, to interpret signs in context while alone in our office or sitting at a table with colleagues requires different mechanisms of integrating the sign, namely along parameters that Roy Harris has termed "biomechanical," "macrosocial" and "circumstantial" (Harris, *Integrational Linguistics* 29).

"Indexicality" is indeed a phenomenon that each of us is familiar with from our own experience as communicating beings endowed with the gift of meta-reflexivity. While communicating with others, we notice certain features more than others, some of which we retrospectively assign to certain characteristics ("identities?") we associate with a particular person. On that score, the layperson's method of inquiry (e.g. concerning evidence that speaker A, "who is known to be x," displayed "identity x") is the same as the sociocultural linguist's, albeit without the aid of the tape-recorder. As a layperson I can – again retrospectively – exchange opinions with others in order to check whether they noticed the very same features and took them to mean "A is indeed x," but whatever the result of that inquiry, it is not possible to gain insight into the original state of mind of individuals experiencing the "same" communicational episode: in other words, how can the researcher claim, on the basis of "scientific" evidence, whether identity x was perceived as authentic (i.e. essentialized) by speaker A, but not by speaker B? In our view, the student of discourse had better take an interest in pursuing the various "glossing practices" (Harris, *Integrational Linguistics* 76-77) re-sorted to by speakers to clarify their verbal exchanges.

If one adheres to a philosophy of language and linguistics along the parameters outlined above, there is no justification for language and identity research as conceived by sociocultural linguists: "identity" be-comes a mere label one encounters in discourse (as used by laypersons and experts alike), which has no identifiable referent (whether existing independently of the contingent moment or not). Hence, it is simply humanly impossible to objectively observe the emergence of "an iden-tity" by means of analyzing language use; the firm belief that this is fea-sible is an illusion triggered by the linguist's adherence to "fixed codes" and a simplistic view of how language and "reality" interconnect.

The authors wish to thank Roy Harris, Christopher Hutton and the two anonymous reviewers for their helpful comments on the article, and Didier Maillat for raising important questions concerning the confer-ence paper.

References

Bucholtz, Mary. "Why be Normal?": Language and Identity Practices in a Community of Nerd Girls." *Language in Society* 28 (1999): 203-223.

———. "The Whiteness of Nerds: Superstandard English and Racial Markedness." *Journal of Linguistic Anthropology* 11(2001): 84-100.

———. "Identity and Interaction: a Sociocultural Linguistic Approach." *Discourse Studies* 7:4-5 (2005): 585-614.

——— and Kira Hall. "Theorizing Identity in Language and Sexuality Research." *Language in Society* 33:4 (2004): 469-515.

Cameron, Deborah and Don Kulick. *Language and Sexuality*. Cambridge: Cambridge University Press, 2003.

Figueroa, Esther. *Sociolinguistic Metatheory*. Oxford: Pergamon, 1994.

Harré, Rom. "Exploring the Human Umwelt." In Bhaskar, R. (ed.). *Harré and his Critics*. Oxford: Blackwell, 1990. 297-364.

Harris, Roy. *Introduction to Integrational Linguistics*. Oxford: Pergamon, 1998.

———. *The Semantics of Science*. London: Continuum, 2005.

Kulick, Don. "Gay and Lesbian Language." *Annual Review of Anthropology* 29 (2000): 243-85.

Pablé, Adrian. "The 'Dialect Myth' and Socio-Onomastics. The Names of the Castles of Bellinzona in an Integrational Perspective." *Language & Communication* 29:2 (2009): 152-165.

———. "Language, knowledge and reality: The integrationist on name variation". *Language & Communication* 30:2 (2010): 109-122.

From the Great Plains to the Red Apple Country: Identity and Ecology in Zitkala-Ša's *American Indian Stories*

Alexa Weik

Identity and ecology are closely interwoven in the autobiographical texts of Lakota writer Zitkala-Ša. Born on a reservation in the prairies of South Dakota, Zitkala-Ša was educated in Quaker mission schools in the "Red Apple Country" of Indiana, and later became a teacher at Carlisle Indian Industrial School in Pennsylvania. Interpellated by strongly conflicting ideologies from a very young age, Zitkala-Ša gradually developed her own, Native-American version of W. E. B. Du Bois's famous concept of "double consciousness." While the Western, American aspect of her identity is expressed not least in the fact that she wrote all of her essays and stories in English, her Indian self-understanding was anchored in her special relationship to nature. In my essay, I demonstrate how representations of the imperiled ecological space of the Great Plains are of central importance to Zitkala-Ša's autobiographical texts, and how her Native-American double consciousness aided her in her political fight for Native American civil rights and environmental justice.

Zitkala-Ša was a woman of many names. Registered as Gertie Felker when she was born on the Yankton Sioux Reservation in the winter of 1876, she would later take on the Lakota word for "Red Bird" – Zitkala-Ša – as her Indian name and use it alongside her married American name Gertrude Bonnin, depending on the context. The ambiguity in naming mirrors the ambiguity of Zitkala-Ša's identity: born into the confined landscape of an Indian reservation, she was educated in Quaker mission schools in Indiana, and later became a teacher at the Carlisle Indian Industrial School in Pennsylvania. Interpellated by strongly conflicting ideologies from a very young age, Zitkala-Ša could not help but

Performing the Self. SPELL: Swiss Papers in English Language and Literature 24. Ed. Karen Junod and Didier Maillat. Tübingen: Narr, 2010. 47-59.

develop a Native American version of the dual and conflicted identity
that W. E. B. Du Bois has called "double consciousness." Referring to
the "souls" of oppressed African Americans, Du Bois famously explains
that these are necessarily shaped by "a world which yields [them] no true
self-consciousness, but only lets [them] see [themselves] through the
revelation of the other world" (Du Bois 45). The "other world" that Du
Bois mentions is of course white America: the European American citizens of the United States who at the time oppressed both black Americans and American Indians, if in different ways. While the destinies of
these two minorities were in many ways quite different, they also shared
some commonalities: both groups were labeled, by European Americans, as backward, uncivilized and pre-modern, and members of both
groups had to define and negotiate their identities over and against the
stereotypes and prejudices that were constantly imposed on them.

Born on an Indian reservation and subjected to a "modern" education at Indian boarding schools, Zitkala-Ša's experiences mirror those of
thousands of Native Americans who struggled with the psychological
consequences of dispossession and forced acculturation. As I will show
in the following, Zitkala-Ša responded to these social and cultural pres-
sures with her own version of "double consciousness": while the Western, American aspect of her identity is expressed not least in the fact
that she wrote all of her essays and stories in English, she was able to
retain important aspects of her Indian identity, expressing them predominantly through her spiritual relationship to nature. In her autobiographical writings, Indian identity always springs from the earth and is
anchored in the inseparability of humans (of all colors) and the rest of
the natural world. Representations of the imperiled ecological space of
the Great Plains pervade her texts, and when she remembers moments
of personal serenity and self-confidence they are without exception related to the natural environment of the prairies. While the forced assimilation practices at the Indian boarding schools she attended did not
leave her unchanged, Zitkala-Ša refused to let go of Indian culture and
its deep connections with nature. Making the best of her insider-
outsider status in American society she learned to use her hybrid identity
deliberately for the political fight for Native American civil and environmental rights.

Whoever speaks or writes about American Indians and the environment is quickly suspected of embracing that romanticizing image that
Shepard Krech III has called the "Ecological Indian." As Krech points
out in his influential book of the same title, published in 1999, the Ecological Indian is the stereotype of "a man living in and with nature who
understands the systemic consequences of his actions, feels deep sympathy with all living forms, and takes steps to conserve so that earth's

harmonies are never imbalanced and resources never in doubt" (*Ecological* 21). The Ecological Indian, Krech explains, is one manifestation of the stereotype of the "Noble Savage," and it was repeatedly used by European intellectuals such as Montaigne and Rousseau to laud the pureness, naturalness, and equality of Indian life and to condemn the life style of the Old World as corrupt, greedy, and unnatural.[1] The problem with "the rhetoric implicit in the image of the Ecological Indian," according to Krech, is that it "masks complex and differing realities" ("Beyond" 3). After all, environmental historians have shown that Native Americans, too, had a transformative influence on their environment, and that there have been instances in history when Native American practices actually turned out to be ecological unsustainable.[2] Our awareness of the dangers of romanticization however, as Krech also points out, should not prevent us from seeing that indigenous people in North America and elsewhere did (and do) indeed possess "extensive and precise knowledge of their environment" ("Beyond" 3). The deep spiritual connection to and direct dependence on the land manifested itself in Indian social and cultural tradition, thus shaping Indian knowledge and identity.

It is this kind of place-bound ecological knowledge and cultural tradition that we find on display in Zitkala-Ša's autobiographical *American Indian Stories* (1921), and it is striking to note how consistently the Indian component of her identity is linked to her memories of a traditional life in and with nature. In "Impressions of an Indian Childhood," the first chapter of *American Indian Stories*, Zitkala-Ša remembers her early childhood on the Yankton Sioux Reservation in South Dakota. The life of Indian children on the reservation, she makes clear, was embedded in the natural world. Not only did she drink the water from the nearby river and – at least during the summer months – eat her meals outside on the grass, but it also was plants and trees that provided both candy and entertainment. "Many a summer afternoon," Zitkala-Ša remembers,

---

[1] French intellectuals such as Montaigne and Rousseau, Krech explains, "seizing on liberty and equal access to basic resources as characteristic of 'savage life' and important virtues to emulate, were without peer over two centuries in developing an imagery of noble indigenousness" (18). The works of these writers were extremely influential, not least in the "New World." While, as Krech points out, "one train of influence runs toward and converges with the nature poetry of William Wordsworth, Samuel Taylor Coleridge, and others . . . a nearly uninterrupted path runs from Wordsworth to James Fenimore Cooper, best-selling author from the early 1820s through the 1840s and arguably the most important nineteenth-century figure for development of the Noble Indian imagery" (18).
[2] For a detailed discussion of Native American environmental practices, see Carolyn Merchant's *American Environmental History*, especially chapter 1: "The American Environment and Native-European Encounters, 1000-1875."

"a party of four or five of my playmates roamed over the hills with me. We each carried a light sharpened rod about four feet long, with which we pried up certain sweet roots" to eat it like candy (21). A few lines down in the same chapter, she recalls how

> the mere shifting of a cloud shadow in the landscape near by was sufficient to change our impulses; and soon we were all chasing the great shadows that played among the hills. We shouted and whooped in the chase; laughing and calling to one another, were like little sportive nymphs on that Dakota sea of rolling green. (*American Indian* 22-3)

In this poetic passage, Zitkala-Ša describes the natural environment of the reservation fondly, almost lovingly. "The Dakota sea of rolling green" emerges as the idyllic setting of an untroubled and happy childhood supported and protected by a tightly-knit social network and a close relationship to the land. The setting is so idyllic, in fact, that it sometimes comes unsettlingly close to the romanticized version of Native American life that we find expressed in Western notions of the Noble Savage. The only serious problem in this peaceful remembered world is what Zitkala-Ša's mother calls the "paleface," but it is a problem so multifaceted and ubiquitous that from the very first pages of the narrative it compromises and threatens the remembered childhood idyll. We learn that white Americans are not only directly responsible for the death of Zitkala-Ša's uncle and sister, but for the plight of the Sioux people in general. "We were once very happy," Zitkala-Ša remembers her mother saying, "but the paleface has stolen our lands and driven us hither. Having defrauded us of our land, the paleface forced us away" (*American Indian* 10). The "defrauding" mentioned here most likely refers to the fact that in 1858, the Yankton chief Struck-by-the-Ree and nine other Yankton headmen had reluctantly signed over 11 million acres of Sioux land to the American government. In exchange, they were guaranteed that the remaining 435,000 acres of their land was "reserved" for the tribe's own use. In addition, the US government promised to provide the newly established Yankton Reservation for fifty years with "food, livestock, lumber, plows, cash, and other services, totaling $1.6 million" (Rappaport 7). Doreen Rappaport tells us that as a result of the treaty, "the Yanktons were rounded up and force marched . . . to the reservation. When they arrived . . . they were told they could not leave without a written pass" (7).

These are the traumatic experiences that prompt Zitkala-Ša's mother to assert that "the paleface is a sham, – a sickly sham" (*American Indian* 9). Not only has the white man cheated her and her people out of their land and thus made it impossible for them to sustain themselves; he is now also in the position to exchange the badly-needed food rations for a defining influence on the education – and eventually on the identity and psyche – of their children. Zitkala-Ša's mother knows that if she does not agree to have her son and daughter schooled away from the reservation, her already insufficient food rations will be cut in half. This is why she reluctantly agrees to have both her son David and Gertrude taken to Indian boarding schools where they can learn how to be civilized and "white." From what Zitkala-Ša tells us, her mother seems to have done her best to prepare her daughter to be a traditional Yankton woman during the first seven years of her life. However, even as the little girl was educated in a traditional Indian way, we should not forget that her identity was already at that early age a hybrid one, and deeply influenced by the European conquest of the American continent. Not only did Zitkala-Ša grow up on a *reservation* on which Indian life was circumscribed and often policed by American authorities, she also was half-white herself. Her father was a white man whom her mother seems to have left after he mistreated her oldest son David (from a different father). However, while her mixed-race ancestry as well as her life in the constrained space of a reservation must have seemed entirely natural to the little girl, the experience in an Indian residential school was not. The coerced re-education and indoctrination that she experienced there, shared by hundreds of thousands of Indian children over the decades, produced a significant rupture in Zitkala-Ša's life, and had a deep impact on her identity and her relation to her native land.

Initially, we learn in Zitkala-Ša's memoir, she was eager to go. When her mother first tells little Gertrude that her brother has spoken to the "paleface missionaries," she fears that "David had forbidden them to see me and that my hope of going to the Wonderland would be blighted" (*American Indian* 40). Her friend Judéwin has told her that the missionary school is "in the East, in a land of great trees filled with red, red apples. You could reach out your hands and pick all the red apples you could eat there" (41-2). Gertrude has never seen apple trees and not "tasted more than a dozen red apples" in her life (42). A keen lover of nature, she cannot wait to see the "Red Apple Country" with its fabulous orchards and thus decides that she must go, against the wishes of her mother, who warns her that the missionaries' "words are sweet, but, my child, their deeds are bitter" (41).

The little girl insists and in the end follows the missionaries to "the wonderful Eastern land" (43); already in the train to Indiana, however, she realizes that things might indeed not be quite as wonderful as the missionaries have promised her. White children are staring at her, pointing at her moccasined feet: "Their mothers, instead of reproving such rude curiosity, looked closely at me, and attracted their children's further notice to my blanket. This embarrassed me, and kept me constantly on the verge of tears" (*American Indian* 48). The embarrassing incident foreshadows the humiliating and painful experiences that Gertrude will make at the school, where the sole aim of her teachers will be to erase every possible trace of her Indian identity to make her a civilized member of the "modern" American world.

Throughout the period of their existence – roughly from 1870-1990 – the expressed aim of Indian residential schools all over the United States was the complete transformation of American Indian children into assimilated working-class Americans. Shepard Krech reminds us that despite frequent romanticization of Indian culture "nineteenth-century anthropologists and sociologists positioned savages on the earliest and lowest rungs of human society" in their theories of social evolution (*Ecological* 17). Most white Americans viewed traditional Indian culture and education as backward and worthless if not dangerous, and they acted accordingly. Richard Henry Pratt, captain in the US Army and the founder of the notorious Carlisle Indian Industrial School in Pennsylvania, was one of the most influential people in terms of Indian education and federal Indian policy at the turn of the twentieth century. "It is a great mistake to think that the Indian is born an inevitable savage," Pratt explained in a paper read at the Nineteenth Annual Conference of Charities and Correction in Denver in 1892 (Pratt). "Transfer the savage-born infant to the surroundings of [modern] civilization, and he will grow to possess a civilized language and habit" (Pratt). Pratt's infamous battle-cry, "Kill the Indian in him, and save the man," formulated with perfect clarity the goal of Native American re-education.

In his confrontational book of the same title – *Kill the Indian, Save the Man* (2004) – Ward Churchill gives a detailed and often heart-wrenching account of the practices at Indian residential schools in the USA and Canada. The regimen at such schools, Churchill explains, was "deliberately and relentlessly brutal," not least in psychological terms (19). "From the moment the terrified and bewildered youngsters arrived at the schools . . . a comprehensive and carefully-calibrated assault on their cultural identity would commence" (Churchill 19). The children, who had often been taken forcefully from their native reservations, were forbidden to speak indigenous languages or practice native spirituality and instead "educated" in modern Western mores and forcefully converted to Christianity. In Churchill's view, the ruthless and brutal "Americanization" of Native Americans by forced cultural assimilation was nothing less than a genocidal practice, one that aimed at destroying the very cultural foundations of a people by systematically erasing that culture from the identities of their children.[3]

This seems to have been exactly what happened to Zitkala-Ša in what she calls the Josiah White Institution's "civilizing machine" (*American Indian* 66). "I had arrived in the wonderful land of rosy skies," she writes about her first days at the Institute, "but I was not happy, as I had thought I should be" (51). Her description of the confined and lifeless space of the school contrasts sharply with the "Dakota sea of rolling green." Arriving in Indiana in early February, she finds no rosy skies or red apples. Instead, everything in the "massive brick building" of the school seems cold and dead to her, and "the constant clash of harsh noises" and "the annoying clatter of [western] shoes on bare floors" (*American Indian* 53) frighten and bewilder the young girl, who feels like "the captured young of a wild creature" (45). The process of "civilization" begins almost immediately, and in the next few days Gertrude looses her soft moccasin shoes, her beloved blanket, her long braids, and her very humanness: "Not a soul reasoned with me, as my own mother used to do; for now I was only one of many little animals driven by a herder" (*American Indian* 56). From now on, the employees of the school will be doing their best to kill the Indian inside of the little girl.

Because of its central importance in the process of identity formation, language is one of the top priorities of the teachers. Like all the students at Indian residential schools Gertrude and her companions are severely punished for speaking in their native tongues. Since she does not speak a word of her "new" language, it takes Gertrude a year before she is able to communicate with her teachers in what is still broken English. Slowly, though, she begins to adjust. She stops throwing herself lengthwise into the snow to look at her own impression, she learns how to move in clunky shoes and tightly fitting clothes, she learns to wait for the bell before sitting down on a wooden chair for lunch, and she learns to pray correctly – all of this to avoid the ever-looming punishment. She does not, however, allow her teachers to completely erase her Indian identity. Early on, she decides that she "will not submit" (*American Indian* 54), and one of the first English words she learns to speak is "no"

---

[3] In his application of the term "genocide," Churchill goes back to what he calls "the *actual* definition of the word" (xlv). This definition was given by Raphaël Lemkin, who coined the term in 1944. Lemkin explained that "generally speaking, genocide does not necessarily mean the immediate destruction of a nation, except when accomplished by a mass killing . . . . It is intended rather to signify a coordinate plan of different actions aiming at the destruction of the essential foundations of the life of national groups, with the aim of annihilating the groups themselves" (79). In Churchill's view, European American practices in their interaction with American Indian nations fit this original definition of genocide quite perfectly.

(57). She scrutinizes Christian ideology through the lens of Indian spirituality, and, like many other Indian children, she now and then even resists or subverts the strict school regime, thus "actively testing the chains which tightly bound my individuality like a mummy for burial" (*American Indian* 67). When, as a punishment, she is ordered to mash turnips for dinner (which she resents), she hits the masher with so much rage into the bottom of the jar that she destroys it. At another moment, she scratches out with a pencil the wicked yellow eyes of the feared and abhorred "white man's devil" in one of the school's editions of *The Stories of the Bible*, thereby destroying the book thoroughly (*American Indian* 64). In both cases, she feels like having taken revenge; and the scolding she receives for her deeds gives her nothing but deep satisfaction.

Caught between the forcefully assimilationist policy of the school and her residual Indian identity, Gertrude thus develops the "twoness" that W. E. B. Du Bois sees at the basis of a "double consciousness": the "sense of always looking at one's self through the eyes of others, of measuring one's soul by the tape of a world that looks on in amused contempt and pity" (45). For Du Bois, the dilemma of double consciousness is at the very foundation of the African American experience: as members of a discriminated and oppressed minority, black people in the United States cannot help but look at themselves through the eyes of others who deeply disapprove of them. Trying to be an American and a "Negro" at the same time, Du Bois argues, leads to a mighty conflict between "two warring ideals in one dark body, whose dogged strength alone keeps it from being torn asunder" (45). The continuous nature of this deep self-conflict gives white stereotypes an unhealthy power over black self-perception, and there is always the danger that it eventually leads to the complete adaptation of a person's identity to the perceptions of disapproving others.

The dilemma that Du Bois describes seems to have been a common experience not only for African Americans but also for the students of Indian residential schools. Ward Churchill quotes one former student who states that "long before [I had] completed [my] schooling, [I had] learned to hate, not simply the people who oppressed [me], but [my]self and [my] race as well" (24). Zitkala-Ša similarly remembers how her "education" at the White Institute made her feel deeply ambivalent and insecure about her own identity and culture. When in the narrative Gertrude returns to her native reservation for the first time after three years of schooling, she feels estranged not only from her mother and her people, but even from the rolling green hills that she used to love so much. "Even nature seemed to have no place for me," she writes, "I was neither a wee girl nor a tall one; neither a wild Indian nor a tame one" (*American Indian* 69). What becomes evident here is one of the greatest problems of hybrid and transcultural identities: that of not feeling at home *anywhere*. Neither in the (in this case forced) host culture, nor in the original home culture.

Despite these painful moments of seeming rejection and estrangement, however, Zitkala-Ša continues to connect the Indian component of her identity to the natural environment of the Great Plains. She recalls how "the cloud shadows which drifted about on the waving yellow of long-dried grasses thrilled me like the meeting of old friends" (*American Indian* 86). In a moment of sudden desperation, her younger self steals her brother's pony and gallops into the prairie. When the pony races with her across the level lands, she happily notices that

> There was nothing moving within the great circular horizon of the Dakota prairies save the tall grasses, over which the wind blew and rolled off in long, shadowy waves. Within this vast wigwam of blue and green I rode reckless and insignificant. (70)

Here, the natural space of the prairie becomes Gertrude's "wigwam" and thus her spiritual and emotional home. Evoking the "Dakota sea of rolling green" of her earlier memories, Zitkala-Ša sharply contrasts the confined, artificial environment of the residential school to the openness and sheer vastness of the prairie, the place where she feels at home. Lovingly, she describes the beauty of the grassland, an ecological space at least as much endangered by the advance of the white man as her own culture and identity. At this moment, she seems to be one with the landscape and even if this return and reunification is not permanent – she will enroll in another Indian boarding school only a few months later – the deep spiritual connection with nature displayed here will remain a defining feature of the Indian component of her identity throughout all of Zitkala-Ša's autobiographical texts. "Perhaps," she writes tellingly

> my Indian nature is the moaning wind which stirs [my memories] now for their present record. But, however tempestuous this is within me, it comes out as the low voice of a curiously colored seashell, which is only for those ears that are bent with compassion to hear it. (*American Indian* 67-8)

Equating her own literary voice to the natural sound of a seashell, Zitkala-Ša addresses her (white) reader directly, suggesting to him to listen more carefully to hear what both she and nature might have to tell him.

As in the passage quoted earlier, Zitkala-Ša asserts her Indian identity through a depiction of an indigenous life in harmony with nature. And like in that earlier passage, she relies on what we cannot help but read as a somewhat romanticized representation of Native American life. Must we thus suspect Zitkala-Ša herself of embracing the problematic image of the "Ecological Indian" that I discussed earlier in this essay? And if yes, was she doing it on purpose? I would argue that the answer to both questions is yes and no. It is crucial to keep in mind that in the clutches of the American "civilizing machine," Zitkala-Ša's memories of the prairies, and of her people's spiritual relationship to them, were one of the few things she could cling to in order to maintain at least part of her Indian identity. Quite possibly, some of these memories became ever more precious to her in the process, and she increasingly romanticized them as a result. However, this should not preclude the fact that, like many American Indians, Zitkala-Ša and her people *did* have a spiritual relationship to nature and what Shepard Krech calls an "extensive and precise knowledge of their environment" ("Beyond" 3).

Secondly, one must remember that one of Zitkala-Ša's main purposes as an adult became to educate white Americans about the beauty and intrinsic value of Indian culture – and to ask for some understanding. Not by coincidence her second important text, *Old Indian Legends* (1901), is a translation, transcript, and re-telling of traditional Sioux legends. Marketed as a children's book, *Old Indian Legends* foregrounds even more pronounced than *American Indian Stories* Native American spirituality and its close connection to nature. While this connection most certainly is something that Zitkala-Ša experienced as true and real in her own life, she might nevertheless have used it rhetorically to make the Indian world she described more attractive to white American readers.

Zitkala-Ša's attempt to bridge cultures, and the sometimes perilous balancing act it implied, was of course always grounded in her own "double" and transcultural identity. Some scholars criticize Zitkala-Ša's attempts to reconcile the conflicting parts of her identity in her writing as a weakness or even failure. Dexter Fisher, for example, argues that the texts' "oscillations between two diametrically opposed worlds" lead to a lack in overall cohesion (237). Other critics, like Martha Cutter, Sandra Stanley, or Jeffrey Myers, see this interpretation as somewhat misguided, as it seems to call for a kind of coherence and closure that Zitkala-Ša's life (and that of many other American Indians who shared her destiny) simply did not offer. As Jeffrey Myers explains, "to let go of Lakota-Dakota culture and embrace the dominant culture's ways [would have been] cultural suicide. But to fail to engage with Euroamerican culture [would have amounted to a tacit acceptance of] cultural genocide" (116). The only practicable way out of this situation was to work within the force field of both cultures and thus with a hybrid identity. Zitkala-Ša's texts show, argues Myers, that she was well aware that white identity was a construction, constructed "not only against 'blackness' but against the ecological and racial Other containing all people of color and the nonhuman world" (129). And she thus used her writing to construct her own fragile and hybrid identity over and against white supremacy, using images of Native life and nature to affirm and ground the Indian component of her self. "For the white man's papers," writes Zitkala-Ša in *American Indian Stories*, "I had given up my faith in the Great Spirit . . . had forgotten the healing in trees and brooks. . . . Like a slender tree I had been uprooted from my mother, nature, and God" (96). However, she makes clear, this was not the end of her story: "A day would come when my mute aching head, reared upward to the sky, would flash a zigzag lightning across the heavens . . . a new way of solving the problem of my inner self" (97). This new way, for the adult Zitkala-Ša, was to leave her teaching position at Carlisle Indian School and use her hybrid identity in order to do something more meaningful for herself and her people.

While her time in Indian residential schools left Zitkala-Ša with a number of physical and psychological problems, it also thus helped her to develop the cross-cultural literacy and competence that would be of central importance for her later political work. In her autobiographical writings she developed a spirit of resilience that allowed her to be both Zitkala-Ša and Gertrude Bonnin for the remainder of her life. In 1902, three years after leaving her teaching position at the Carlisle Indian School, *The Atlantic Monthly* published her controversial essay "Why I Am a Pagan." In this essay she powerfully affirms her Indian spirituality and her close connection to nature, and sharply criticizes the brutal practices of Christian missionaries. "Still," she adds at the end of her essay,

> I would not forget that the pale-faced missionary and the hoodooed aborigine are both God's creatures, though small indeed their own conceptions of Infinite Love. A wee child toddling in a wonder world, I prefer to their dogma my excursions into the natural gardens where the voice of the Great Spirit is heard in the twittering of birds, the rippling of mighty waters, and the sweet breathing of flowers. If this is Paganism, then at present, at least, I am a Pagan. ("Why I Am a Pagan" 803)

All beings in the world are related, Zitkala-Ša affirms here and elsewhere in her writings; and the insights of Indian tradition and spirituality are in fact of great value for the co-existence of humans and the rest of the natural world, and should thus be preserved and appreciated. Her cross-cultural literacy and double consciousness thus, in the end, served her to better understand the fatal problems inherent in Western approaches to both cultural otherness and the planet as a whole. A few months after the publication of this essay, Zitkala-Ša returned to South Dakota, to spend the rest of her life as a committed political activist, fighting for civil and environmental rights for American Indians, and the preservation of Native American culture and history.

References

Churchill, Ward. *Kill the Indian, Save the Man: the Genocidal Impact of American Indian Residential Schools.* San Francisco: City Light Books, 2004.

Cutter, Martha J. "Zitkala-Sä's Autobiographical Writings: The Problems of a Canonical Search for Language and Identity." *MELUS* 19:1 (Spring 1994): 31-44.

Du Bois, W. E. B. *The Souls of Black Folk.* 1903. New York: Signet Classic, 1995.

Fisher, Dexter. "The Evolution of a Writer." *American Indian Quarterly* 5:3 (August 1979): 229-238.

Harkin, Michael Eugene, ed. *Native Americans and the Environment: Perspectives on the Ecological Indian.* Lincoln and New York: University of Nebraska Press, 2007.

Krech, Shepard, III. *The Ecological Indian: Myth and History.* New York: Norton and Co., 2000.

———. "Beyond the Ecological Indian." *Native Americans and the Environment: Perspectives on the Ecological Indian.* Ed. Michael Eugene Harkin. Lincoln: University of Nebraska Press, 2007. 3-31.

Lemkin, Raphaël. *Axis Rule in Occupied Europe: Laws of Occupation, Analysis of Government, Proposals for Redress.* Washington, D.C.: Carnegie Endowment for International Peace, 1944.

Merchant, Carolyn. *American Environmental History.* New York: Columbia University Press, 2007.

Myers, Jeffrey. *Converging Stories: Race, Ecology, and Environmental Justice in American Literature.* Athens and London: University of Georgia Press, 2005.

Pratt, Richard Henry. "Kill the Indian, Save the Man." Paper at the Nineteenth Annual Conference of Charities and Correction, at Denver, Colorado in 1892. Accessed on 26 August 2009. Available online: <http://socrates.bmcc.cuny.edu/bfriedheim/pratt.htm>.

Rappaport, Doreen. *The Flight of Red Bird: the Life of Zitkala-Ša.* New York: Dial Books, 1997.

Stanley, Sandra Kumamoto. "Claiming a Native American Identity: Zitkala-Sa and Autobiographical Strategies." *Pacific Coast Philology* 29:1 (September 1994): 64-69.

Zitkala-Ša. *Old Indian Legends.* 1901. Boston: Elibron Classics, 2006.

———. "Why I Am a Pagan." *Atlantic Monthly* 90 (1902): 801-803.

———. *American Indian Stories.* 1921. Lincoln and London: University of Nebraska Press, 1985.

Recovering and Reshaping a Lost Identity: The Gaels' Linguistic and Literary Struggle

Céline Guignard

Language has long been considered to be at the heart of the concept of national identity and the relationship between language and identity was at the centre of the literary debate that took place at the beginning of the twentieth century in Scotland. In the context of such a debate, three authors in particular - William Sharp, Neil Munro and Fionn MacColla - believed that it was possible to write about Gaelic identity and culture in the English language, despite the fact that English was seen as the very language which threatened to hasten the decline of Scottish Gaelic. This essay examines the literary techniques which they developed in order to make the Gaelic nature of their texts shine through their English prose. Part of the essay will also focus on the way the two languages are represented in the three authors' fiction and on the relationship their Gaelic and English protagonists entertain with the language.

> The man who loses his language
> loses his world.
> The Highlander who loses his language
> loses his world.[1]

These lines from Iain Crichton Smith's poem "Shall Gaelic Die?" (68-69) refer to the existence of a link between national, or ethnic, identity and language. The belief in the existence of such a link is by no means new. John E. Joseph, in *Language and Identity*, quotes from Ep-

---

[1] "Am fear a chailleas a chànan, // caillidh e a shaoghal. // An Gàidheal a chailleas a chànan, // caillidh e an saoghal."

Performing the Self. SPELL: Swiss Papers in English Language and Literature 24. Ed. Karen Junod and Didier Maillat. Tübingen: Narr, 2010. 61-73.

icurus of Samos (341-270 BC) and the Book of Genesis to show that the debate over the relationship between identity and language is indeed ancient (Joseph 42-43, 95-96). In the Scottish context, the idea that language is central to the formation of an identity has long been part of nationalists' discourse. Attempts by the British government in the nineteenth century to enforce the use of English to the detriment of the native Gaelic were perceived by Highlanders, rightly or not, as so many attacks against Gaelic identity. Likewise, any nationalist programme tends nowadays to focus on the reintroduction of the ancient language as an essential part of the restoration of a Highland identity.

The purpose of the present essay is neither to confirm, nor to refute, the existence of a link between language and ethnic identity, as this would be the domain of linguists and ethnologists.[2] It focuses, rather, on the works of three Scottish authors who believed that language was an essential part of Scottish Gaelic identity and analyses the use they made of the Gaelic and English languages in their prose. William Sharp (1855-1905), Neil Munro (1863-1930) and Fionn MacColla (1906-1975) chose to write their fiction in English while retaining the Gaelic language at the centre of their work. They deliberately chose to blend Gaelic prose within an English foundation in an attempt to reassert their own Highland identity.[3] The period in which Sharp, Munro and MacColla wrote spans over the last decade of the nineteenth century and the first half of the twentieth century, from what is often referred to as the "Celtic Twilight" to the "Scottish Renaissance" of the 1930s. It was a period of heated debates among the Scottish literati over such issues as the existence and essence of a Scottish national literature. The choice William Sharp, Neil Munro and Fionn MacColla made of selecting for their prose the very language that threatened the Gaelic with annihilation can only be understood within a certain cultural context which I propose to sketch briefly.

---

[2] For a discussion on the relationship between ethnic or national identity and language, see Hobsbawm's *Nations and Nationalism* and Silverstein's contribution to Kroskrity's *Regimes of Language*. On the same topic but with a particular focus on the Scottish case, see Joseph's *Language and Identity* and McColl Millar's *Language, Nation and Power. Language in the British Isles*, edited by David Britain, and *Languages in Britain and Ireland*, edited by Glanville Price, both provide a useful insight into the complex linguistic situation in Scotland.

[3] William Sharp was born in Paisley and was therefore not a Highlander by birth. Yet, his love for and knowledge of Highland culture, together with his frequent stays in the Highlands make him a Gael by adoption. Fionn MacColla was also born in the Lowlands of Scotland, on the East coast. His father was a Highlander though and MacColla became familiar with the Gaelic language from an early age. MacColla lived for over twenty years in the Western Isles.

At the time of the Scottish literary Renaissance, many issues that were taken up by Scottish nationalists at the end of the twentieth century were already at the centre of debates. If most protagonists tended to agree on the importance of a distinct national literature for the formation of a national identity, the question whether this literature was to be written in a Scottish national language or whether a distinctively Scottish literature could be written in English became of primary importance. The Irish success in creating a literature that was distinct from the so-called English literature in which, traditionally, Anglo-Irish works had been included, led the Scots to wonder whether a similar feat was feasible in Scotland. Those who, in the 1920s and 1930s, maintained that Scottish authors could both write in English *and* express their Scottish identity were often designated as the successors of the Anglo-Celtic literary movement that was at its height in the 1890s. The writers who belonged to the so-called Anglo-Celtic movement argued that, as descendants of the British Celts, the Scots could bring valuable assets to British literature and culture to complement the Saxon characteristics of English. They argued that as Anglo-Celts they successfully combined the imagination, the creativity, and the sensitivity that were said to characterise the Celtic mind, with the pragmatism, the force and precision of the Saxon character.

In Scotland, the choice of a traditional, ancient tongue that could be considered a national language was between two contenders only: Gaelic, a Q-Celtic language spoken mainly in the Highlands and Islands of Scotland, and Scots, a Germanic-based language spoken in Lowland and North-East Scotland. The debate over the choice of a national tongue for Scotland and its literature triggered three types of reactions: Some, like Gordon Leslie Rayne or Edwin Muir, thought that it was too late to save either Gaelic or Scots and turn them into national languages (Rayne 109-110; Muir 823). The two languages, they argued, had got stuck in the past through disuse and neglect and had, as a result, stopped their evolution. They could not, therefore, be used to express the present in all its complexity and diversity, and thus had no future as literary media. Other writers, including Fionn MacColla, thought that it was still possible to save the Gaelic language, but that it was essential to preserve and restore its linguistic purity. A third group, led and sustained mainly by the poet Hugh MacDiarmid and his friends, thought that it was possible to use Scots as a national language to write a distinctive Scottish literature but that such use necessitated an update of the vocabulary, together with a few alterations, so that the language could be used to express anything a modern man might wish to express.[4] John E. Joseph argues that the coexistence of two potential national languages in Scotland has impeded the development of linguistic nationalism, as the partisans of Gaelic and Scots have spent much energy combating the claims of the rival group, rather than the hegemony of English. He also mentions that a majority of Scots "consider the strategic economic value of using a world language as greatly outweighing the political, cultural and sentimental value of the 'heritage' languages. A case might be made that the eternal struggle between Gaelic and Scots is an intelligent way of keeping the nationalist flame burning while making sure that it does not set fire to the bank" (Joseph 94).

In the context of such a debate, William Sharp, Neil Munro and Fionn MacColla chose to write in English and believed that specifically Gaelic and Scottish features could be expressed despite the use of a non-Scottish medium and that a quality Scottish literature could be created. A closer analysis of these authors' texts reveals a series of literary techniques which they developed in order to make the Gaelic tongue and culture shine through the English superstrate. Moreover, Gaelic as a language also plays a part in these authors' fiction that goes beyond the formal level of the text; the issue of the relationship the Gaels entertain with their native and adopted languages is often developed as a theme on its own, as will be shown later.

One of the first writers who succeeded in blending the two languages in his fiction was William Sharp (1855-1905). A poet, biographer, playwright and novelist who met and befriended the greatest literary figures of his day, he is now best remembered for his writings under the pseudonym of Fiona Macleod. He succeeded in leading two separate literary careers without revealing the true identity of the female author who was hailed worldwide as a Celtic visionary. It was William Sharp's wish to give expression in his "Fiona Macleod" writings to what he felt was the Highland half of his personality. He was not a Highlander himself, but he felt close to Highland culture and spent much of his time in the northern and western parts of Scotland. As a reporter and a writer he had a keen interest in local folk tales and legends, and he tried, in his fiction, to offer an accurate rendering of life in the Highlands as he had experienced it. Whether his writings are close to reality or whether they correspond to a phantasmagoric vision he had of Gaelic society and life is subject to debate. What cannot be questioned, however, are his efforts to confer a Gaelic flavour to his texts.

---

4 For a first-hand account of the debate over the use of Scots and Gaelic in literature, see McCulloch's *Literature and Society in Scotland*.

The first technique employed by William Sharp in order to add a Gaelic flavour to his English prose consists in inserting Gaelic place-names, terms of endearment ("m'eudail"[5]), curses and exclamations ("mo chreach", "O Dhia!", "Ochone!"[6]). These insertions provide authenticity and exoticism without hindering the understanding of the text. Short sentences in Gaelic are also inserted into the English prose; phrases like "Tha e agam"[7] or "Sin agad!"[8] add local colour without being essential to the understanding of the text itself. Sharp did not, of course, invent this technique. Walter Scott already inserted words and names in Gaelic into his prose when dealing with Highland scenes. He took care, however, to Anglicise the spelling of Gaelic terms so as to allow non-Gaelic readers to reach a fairly good approximation of the way they were pronounced. Scott replaced, for example, the commonly used consonant combination "mh" with the letter "v," or used the letter "w" (unknown in the Gaelic alphabet) or accents to render in English the original Gaelic pronunciation. Thus, the name of the Highland clan chief whom Edward Waverley meets in the eponymous novel is transformed from the original "Fearghus Mac Iomhair Mhic Iain Mhóir" to the Anglicised form of "Fergus Mac-Ivor Vich Ian Vohr" (Fergus MacIvor Son of John the Great) (75). Another example of Scott's alteration of Gaelic spelling in *Waverley* is his mention of a "Saxon Duinhé-wassal" (English gentleman) instead of the original "duine-uasal" (75).[9]

Beside the insertion of Gaelic terms, William Sharp developed another technique consisting in juxtaposing Gaelic and English sentences, with the English sentences featuring as translations of the Gaelic originals. Such juxtaposition allows his prose to flow naturally. The following extract from *Pharais*, Sharp's first text as Fiona Macleod, illustrates the advantages of such "juxtaposition" technique. In this passage, the heroine Lora is worried about her husband's late return from the mainland. Her husband had an important appointment with a doctor, and the last ferry he could possibly be on before the night is about to pass their island without stopping. Lora therefore begs her friend Ian to row her to the ferry so that she can inquire about her husband:

---

[5] "My love."
[6] "My Goodness," "Oh, God" and "Alas!"
[7] "I have it" or "I have him." Literally, "it is him that is on me."
[8] Probably short for "Sin agad e," meaning "There you have it."
[9] Neil Munro and Fionn MacColla also frequently inserted into their own prose place-names, expressions and phrases in Gaelic, yet, unlike Scott, they kept the original Gaelic spelling.

A dark figure rose from beside the ferry-shed.

"Is that you, Ian? 'Am bheil am bhata deas? Is the boat ready? Bi ealamh! bi ealamh! Mach am bhata: quick! quick! out with the boat!"

In her eager haste she spoke both in the Gaelic and the English: nor did she notice that the old man did not answer her. . .

"Oh, Ian, bi ealamh! bi ealamh! Faigh am bhata deas! rack a stigh do'n bhata!"

Word for word, as is the wont of the people, he answered her:

"Why is it that I should be quick? Why should I begin getting the boat ready? For what should I be going into the boat?"

"The Clansman! Do you not see her? Bi ealamh; bi ealamh or she will go past us like a dream!"

. . . "There is no good in going out, Lora bhan! The wind is rising: ay, I tell you, the wind goes high: we may soon hear the howling of the sea-dogs."

But Lora, taking no notice, had sprung into the boat. . . Ian followed, grumblingly repeating, "Tha gaoth ruhbr am! Tha coltas stairm' air!"

(*Pharais* 26-27)

This passage offers an illustration of different techniques of juxtaposition. In the second paragraph, whatever phrase Lora utters in Gaelic gets directly translated into English in the following sentence. The fourth paragraph shows a slightly different approach: It is entirely in Gaelic, and the reader only gets to know what Lora has said (to Ian) when Ian's answer is given. In the seventh and eighth paragraphs, the process is inverted; Ian's words are first given in English in the text and their Gaelic translation is given slightly later in the text. The overall result of such juxtapositions of the two languages is effective. The comprehension of the text is by no means hindered by the insertion of sentences in Gaelic and the prose remains fluid. The interweaving of sentences in both languages adds the required touch of Gaelic atmosphere, while simultaneously reflecting Lora's own tendency to mix the two languages in her own worried speech.

The technique that consists in telling in a paragraph in English what is about to be said by a character in Gaelic was used relatively often by Sharp at the beginning of *Pharais*, although it is dropped later in the tale as the story focuses on the two main characters – the lovers. The reason for dropping the device as the story unfolds might have been that it proved too heavy to be carried on throughout the whole tale. Moreover, it would probably have hindered both the flow of the prose and the establishment of the poetic and mystic atmosphere for which Fiona Macleod became famous. The following examples show how heavy and ungainly a device this technique proved to be:

Rapidly he gave his directions to Lora to take the helm and to keep the boat to windward:
"Gabh an stiuir, Lora: cum ris a' ghaoth i!" (*Pharais* 28)

In the middle of the cove she stopped, waved her hand, and, in a dull voice bidding goodnight, wished sound sleep to him:
"Beannachd leibh! Cadal math dhiubh!" (*Pharais* 33)

In later texts written under the Fiona Macleod pen-name, Sharp made more extensive use of footnotes to provide translations. They sometimes included phonetic guides to the pronunciation of the Gaelic expressions. Sharp was not really a native speaker of Gaelic, and this might have rendered him attentive to the difficulty of pronouncing the Gaelic words and names correctly. *The Mountain Lovers*, Fiona Macleod's second novel, contains several passages in Gaelic in the main body of the text, with translations and linguistic remarks in footnotes. These are indeed informative, especially to non-Gaelic readers, but they prove disruptive in the long run and not so successful a device as the techniques mentioned above. William Sharp was criticised by his friend Grant Allen for inserting too many Gaelic expressions and words into his prose, and he seems to have heeded his friend's opinion, for he stopped mixing passages in Gaelic with his prose after his second novel as Fiona Macleod (E. A. Sharp 229).

Another author, who was nearly contemporary with Sharp and whose work the latter greatly admired (E. A. Sharp 326), took Sharp's process of mixing Gaelic and English prose one step further. This author was Neil Munro (1863-1930), a talented writer of Scottish fiction born in Inveraray in Argyllshire and, unlike Sharp, a native speaker of Gaelic. Nowadays he is best remembered for the humorous Para Handy tales, which he wrote under the pen-name of Hugh Foulis.

One of Munro's innovations concerned the rendering of dialogues. Unlike Walter Scott and James Hogg, who represented spoken words of Gaels and Scots phonetically, thus often creating a comical effect to the detriment of the speakers, Munro chose to have his characters converse in English but often with a Gaelic syntax and with no indication of any particular accent. This technique avoids comic effects and presents the Gael in a new light. Thus in Munro, the Gaels are not rustics who murder English in order to express with difficulty their rather primitive thoughts, but persons with an adequately complex mind who give expression to their thoughts in a language which they master. If the characters happen to be speaking English according to the context, then their Gaelic syntax stresses their Gaelic origins, rather than a particular rusticity or lack of education. If the context indicates, on the other hand, that they are currently conversing in Gaelic, then the Gaelic turn of phrase reminds the readers of the actual language in which the conversation is taking place. Examples of Munro's adoption of a Gaelic turn of phrase for his English prose can be found in such sentences as "hunger's on us" (*The New Road* 193) and "It is I that am in it" (*Children of Tempest* 156). Indeed, since Gaelic has no equivalent for the English verb "to have," possessions, feelings and bodily manifestations *are* either *at*, *on*, or *in* us. The use of such Gaelic turn of phrase is at once simple and economical.

Munro's prose skilfully mixes Gaelic turns of phrase with word-for-word translations of Gaelic idioms into English ("the mouth of the night" for the English "twilight" or "dusk"),[10] Gaelic place-names, proverbs, names of tunes and songs, together with a few Gaelic first names. The overall effect is that of creating the illusion that the reader is initiated into the language. Munro also inserts many common words in Gaelic, for the understanding of which he provides a Gaelic glossary of his own making at the end of his volumes of tales. The glossary, however, is not complete, and a thorough reader might have wished for a guide to Gaelic pronunciation. For a reader with no previous knowledge of Gaelic, such a glossary is, however, of great help, for the Gaelic words Munro chose to insert into his prose are less common than, for example, the expressions of endearment or surprise that regularly appear in William Sharp's prose. Here are some examples of sentences in which words in Gaelic are inserted:

> "[H]e was *duin'-uasal*[11] who carried the sword."
> "The *biodag*[12] went flying into the grass at Calum's feet . . . From Kilmune to Uchdanbarracaldine the red fellows were passing, or playing with the *clachneart* or the *cabar*[13] . . . "
> "With luck and a good *sgian-dubh*[14] a quick lad could do some gralloching."
> (Munro, "Black Murdo" 36, 42)

Another feature of Munro's style is his inclusion in his prose of a wide range of words in Scots. This technique is both historically accurate, as many such words from the Scots dialect would have infiltrated the

---

[10] "Beul na h-oidhche" in Gaelic (see Munro, *John Splendid* 197).
[11] "A gentleman."
[12] "The food."
[13] "Clachneart" literally means "stone of strength". The throwing of the "clachneart" and the tossing of the "cabar" are two disciplines of the Highland Games.
[14] Literally "a black knife." A traditional knife used in the Highlands and now part of the Highland dress, its name might come from the fact that it was kept hidden and secret, either under the armpit or in the hose.

Highland speech, and effective, as it reinforces the Scottish nature of the prose. Typographically speaking, the fact that the words in Gaelic are set out in italics facilitates the reader's progression through the text, but it also stresses the foreignness of the terms with regards to the English language. As will be shown below, Fionn MacColla deliberately renounced the use of italics and Gaelic and English words mingle freely in his prose. Munro developed another device to help the narrator introduce his reader into a Gaelic world: he has a Lowland character take part in the conversations. This allows expressions in Gaelic to get translated and explained for the benefit of the character, and of the reader, of course.

A third author well-worth focusing upon in this context is Fionn MacColla (1906-1975). Fionn MacColla, the pen-name of Thomas Douglas MacDonald, was born in Montrose in 1906. A life-long nationalist and a friend of Hugh MacDiarmid, he is the author, amongst other works, of *The Albannach* (1932) and *And the Cock Crew* (1945), a powerful account of the Presbyterian clergymen's role in the social disaster of the Highland Clearances.

MacColla's technique of interaction between Gaelic and English recalls that of Munro, although it is to be noted that the Gaelic words and sentences are not highlighted by any typographic device like italics – they mingle freely with the English prose. This might indicate the author's will to stress that for characters the mixing of Gaelic and English words is just a normal way of speaking, without one language being subordinate to the other. Often, as with Sharp and Munro, one sentence in Gaelic is followed by its translation in the same paragraph. MacColla also uses a specifically Gaelic word order in his English prose.

A notable feature of MacColla's prose is the particular attention he pays to the Gaelic names of people and places and to their correct spelling. He puts greater emphasis than any of his predecessors on the way Gaelic names characterise the person or the place they refer to, and on the fact that Gaelic as a language has no equivalent.[15] This is particularly apparent when MacColla deals with the theme of the Highland Clearances in *And the Cock Crew*, where he stresses the fact that the Gaels were not only robbed of their lands and culture by the English, but also of their names (and, therefore, of their identity), as these were Anglicised by the government for official matters.

Thus, MacColla's use of genuine Gaelic names goes beyond a desire to restore the names' correct spelling; it makes the question of names and identity an issue which he develops in his fiction. MacColla pays particular attention to the relationship the Gaels have with their native

---

[15] A dramatisation of this issue can be found in MacColla's *The Albannach* (70-71).

language. In Munro and Sharp's fictions, Gaelic is recurrently depicted as the language of truth and emotion. It is a particularly poetic language to be used only among friends and decent company.[16] English, on the other hand, is tellingly used by Gaels when plotting and lying, or when they wish to hide their feelings from their interlocutors.[17] The English language is also recurrently referred to in its Gaelic translation, as "the Beurla." As such, it is robbed of its name, swallowed up by the very language whose existence it appears to threaten.

Fionn MacColla goes beyond Munro and Sharp's rather dichotomic representation of the two languages and addresses the issue of the link between language and personal identity. His prose writings feature characters whose relationship with their native Gaelic language is complex and often uneasy. Some are seen making efforts to drop their Gaelic altogether for English in order to sound more genteel and educated. Other characters are so ashamed of their Gaelic origins that they deny having any knowledge of Gaelic at all (*The Albannach* 150). In *The Albannach*, Murdo marries a young woman whom he very soon comes to despise, partly for the airs that she puts on which are inspired by the English tales of romantic love that she reads. Murdo particularly dislikes her imitation of the genteel English discourse that is to be found in her reading and recurrently accuses her of negating her origins. MacColla deliberately stresses the awkward pronunciation of such characters who use English to communicate with other Gaels. However, as he does so, one cannot help feeling that the attack is directed less against English as a language than against the characters themselves, who are guilty of both negating their origins and roots and betraying their community.

With regard to characters who insist on speaking a language that is not theirs and which, it is implied, they do not master, MacColla was especially intent on stressing the appalling irony of the situation in which many Gaels found themselves as they struggled to master a foreign language in order to sound more genteel and learned, with their often poor performances having in fact the opposite effect of what they sought to achieve. In *The Albannach*, the hero is told off by his schoolmaster for using the Gaelic language instead of English. And yet the schoolmaster's own English is shown to be poor and clumsy (102). At a later stage in the novel, the hero's mother tries her best to write to her son in what she thinks is a proper language, i.e. English (104-105). Although she apparently finds it difficult and apologises to her son for the

---

[16] See, for example, the interview Lora has with her abductors in Munro's *The Children of Tempest* (161).
[17] See, for example, the several instances when Munro's hero Col plots in English with his pirate accomplices in *The Children of Tempest* or in *The New Road* (193-4).

poverty of her prose, she does not seem to have considered the option of writing in her own mother tongue. Thus, MacColla ironically depicts the awkward situation in which a literate Gaelic woman finds herself to be willingly handicapped, for propriety's sake, in her private correspondence with her own son. All such characters are guilty, for MacColla, of betraying their roots and native culture, and several scenes of *The Albannach* are symbolic of a breach in Gaelic identity.

All three writers succeed in providing an air of Gaelic authenticity to their prose by means of Gaelic words, names, idioms and turns of phrase. Munro and MacColla, especially, give their readers the impression of being part of the Gaelic community they describe. They have achieved a balance between the English language that enables the reader to have easy access to both the plot and the themes of their novels, and the Gaelic vocabulary that gives the texts their special flavour. The choice of Sharp, Munro and MacColla to write in English about Gaelic culture enables non-native speakers of Gaelic to have access to a world which might otherwise have remained hermetic and daunting. In doing so, such authors did much to rescue a culture that might otherwise have been in its death-throes. The assertion that "It's a dead language that is in the Gaelic," which recurrently features in MacColla's *The Albannach* is to be belied.

References

Britain, David, ed. *Language in the British Isles.* Cambridge: Cambridge University Press, 2007.

Crichton Smith, Iain. "Am faigh a' Ghàidhlig bàs? // "Shall Gaelic Die?". *Taking You Home: Poems and Conversations.* Derick Thomson, Iain Crichton Smith, Andrew Mitchell. Glendaruel: Argyll Publishing, 2006. 65-69.

Hobsbawm, E. J. *Nations and Nationalism since 1780: Programmes, Myth, Reality.* Cambridge: Cambridge University Press, 1990.

Joseph, John E. *Language and Identity: National, Ethnic, Religious.* Basingstoke: Palgrave Macmillan, 2004.

MacColla, Fionn. *And the Cock Crew.* London: Souvenir Press, 1977.

———. *The Albannach.* Edinburgh: Reprographia, 1971.

MacLean, Malcolm and Theo Dorgan, eds. *An Leabhar Mòr: The Great Book of Gaelic.* Edinburgh: Canongate Books, 2002.

McColl Millar, Robert. *Language, Nation and Power.* Basingstoke: Palgrave Macmillan, 2005.

McCulloch, Margery, ed. *Modernism and Nationalism: Literature and Society in Scotland 1918-1939 – Source Documents for the Scottish Renaissance.* Glasgow: Association for Scottish Literary Studies, 2004.

Muir, Edwin. "Literature in Scotland." *Spectator* 25 (May 1934): 823.

Munro, Neil. *The Children of Tempest: A Tale of the Outer Isles.* Isle of Colonsay, Argyll: House of Lochar, 2004.

———. *John Splendid: The Tale of a Poor Gentleman, And the Little Wars of Lorn.* Edinburgh: Black and White Publishing, 1994.

———. *The New Road.* Edinburgh: Black and White Publishing, 1994.

———. *The Lost Pibroch and Other Sheiling Stories.* Isle of Colonsay, Argyll: House of Lochar, 1996.

———. "Black Murdo." *The Lost Pibroch and Other Sheiling Stories.* Isle of Colonsay, Argyll: House of Lochar, 1996. 34-44.

Price, Glanville, ed. *Languages in Britain and Ireland.* Oxford: Blackwell, 2000.

Rayne, Gordon Leslie. "This Scottish Tongue: The Renascence and the Vernacular." *Scots Magazine* 19:2 (May 1933): 107-110.

Scott, Walter. *Waverley; Or, 'Tis Sixty Years Since.* Ed. Claire Lamont. Oxford: Oxford University Press, 1998.

Sharp, Elizabeth A. *William Sharp – Fiona Macleod: A Memoir, Compiled by His Wife.* New York: Duffield and Company, 1910.

Sharp, William. *Pharais; A Romance of the Isles.* Vol. I of *The Works of "Fiona MacLeod."* Arranged by Mrs William Sharp. Uniform Pocket Edition. London: William Heinemann, 1927.

Silverstein, Michael. "Whorfianism and the Linguistic Imagination of Nationality." *Regimes of Language: Ideologies, Polities, and Identities.* Ed. Paul V. Kroskrity. Santa Fe: School of American Research Press, 2000. 85-138.

Negotiating Identities and *Doing* Swiss in Intercultural Couples

Kellie Gonçalves

This article adopts a post-modern approach to identity construction as multiple, dynamic, performed and discursively co-constructed in social interaction. Data collected in 2006 from nine intercultural couples, namely Anglophone women married to native German-speaking Swiss men indicate a discrepancy between implicit and explicit identity claims and see them as multiple and hybrid. The informants' rejection, acceptance and embracing of a Swiss identity based on language use and other socio-cultural practices often correlates to negative and positive assessments and stereotypes attached to the reification of Swiss as well as individuals' first-order perceptions of their stable, fixed and essential selves. Linguistic devices such as reference, adjuncts, and stance markers are used to index individuals' attitudes concerning their identities and what it means to *do* Swiss. A discourse analytic approach is taken to scrutinize individuals' first-order perceptions of themselves by considering their essentialist stances, emerging identities, and various modes of positioning within the context of a recorded conversation. Although post-modern definitions of identity are understood as multivalent, I argue that any discussion of identity should not discard the notion of essentialism since individuals more often than not discursively construct themselves and each other as stable and unitary beings.

Introduction

Living in a mixed marriage can be an *intimate performance* of *juggling identities* and the *ideologies* associated with them, a dance sometimes threatening to perform as well as to behold. It is sometimes enriching, but always calls into question *deeply held assumptions* about the nature of *one's own identities*, and those of *one's reference groups*. (Breger and Hill 28, italics added)

Performing the Self. SPELL: Swiss Papers in English Language and Literature 24. Ed. Karen Junod and Didier Maillat. Tübingen: Narr, 2010. 75-89.

For Breger and Hill living in a mixed marriage connotes images of a close, intimate relationship between individuals as well as their ideologies or beliefs they live with and live through on a daily basis. The use of the metaphor *dance* in this quote reveals that this particular action or performance can be done privately or publicly and it is also movable. Moreover, their use of the adverb of frequency *sometimes* suggests that living in a mixed marriage is not always enriching but perhaps difficult, demanding and frustrating as well. This passage underscores the main themes in this study such as positioning, performativity, identity construction, language ideologies and widely held beliefs about one's culture. I analyze the discourse of nine intercultural couples, consisting of Anglophone women married to native German-speaking Swiss men who reside in the geographic region of Interlaken, located in central Switzerland where a diglossic situation prevails. In scrutinizing their discourse, I consider *how* and *if* these individuals come to terms with their multiple or hybrid identities and what it means for them to *do* Swiss. I analyze the various discourses produced regarding their language ideologies, beliefs (Blommaert) about the self and other, their assumptions about these discourses, as well as the cultural practices and performances they make reference to (Bourdieu; Butler; Fenstermaker and West; Zimmerman).[1] In doing so, I also take a close look at linguistic features such as reference, adjuncts and stance markers individuals employ to construe their assumptions and identities. A focus on these linguistic devices has been chosen since these features emerge within the context of spoken discourse.

Scrutinizing individuals' first-order perceptions (Watts et al.) of themselves by taking an ethnomethodological perspective inevitably entails being encountered with essentialist views of identities as stable or what Bucholtz and Hall have termed an "ethnographic fact" ("Language and Identity" 375). The data in this study reveal that participants are constantly positioning and re-positioning themselves as certain types of individuals who perform or carry out particular local and socio-cultural practices within specific contexts. Discourse about their past practices and thus former selves is juxtaposed to the discourse produced of their current practices, which means that any account of *doing* Swiss becomes a collaborative discursive practice. Refusing, accepting or embracing multiple or hybrid identities based on what *Swiss* means emerges as a site of the negotiation of meaning, which led to the following three research questions:

---

[1] I understand the term practice to be the "habitual social activity, the series of actions that make up our daily lives" (Bucholtz and Hall, "Language and Identity" 377) while performance is "highly deliberate and self aware social display" (ibid. 380).

1) How do individuals understand who they are as a result of living in an intercultural marriage abroad?

2) How is *doing Swiss* discursively co-constructed and negotiated?

3) How do individuals position themselves and each other in discourse and what linguistic devices are used to accomplish this?[2]

In a recent paper Bucholtz and Hall state that

> [a]s researchers, we need to start with what speakers are accomplishing in-teractionally and then build upward to the identities that thereby emerge. At the same time, in order to ensure that our analyses are cognizant of the rich intertextual layers that resonate between these different levels, we need to ground our interactional analyses both in the ethnographic specificities that endow interactions with social meaning and in the broader social, cultural, and political contexts in which social actors are imbricated. In short, neither identity categories nor interactional analyses alone are enough to account for how social positioning is accomplished through language; the two levels of analysis are most effective when they work in unison, and in conjunction with a focus on the larger social, cultural, and political contexts in which identity work is carried out. ("Finding identity" 154)

It is precisely "the two levels of analysis," namely the categories-and-labels approach to identity, which considers individuals' essentialist stances of their inherent selves as well as interactional analysis, and more specifically, interactional positioning, which is focused on in this paper. The first research question correlates to individuals' first-order perceptions of themselves as well as their overt identity claims. The second question considers how individuals discursively construct and negotiate the reification of Swiss. In talking about Swiss vis-à-vis other national identity labels such as "American," "British," or "South African," other labels such as "local," "foreigner," and "native" notably emerge. According to Eckert and McConnell-Ginet such

> [r]eifications structure perceptions and constrain (but do not completely de-termine) practice, and each is produced (often reproduced in much the

---

[2] Harré and van Langenhove discuss 9 modes of positioning, 4 of which I focus on in this paper. First order positioning "refers to the way persons locate themselves and others within an essentially moral space by using several categories and storylines" (20). Second order positioning occurs when first order positioning of self or other is rejected and needs to be renegotiated. Deliberate positioning is intentional and explicit while tacit positioning is implied.

same form) through the experience of those perceptions and constraints on day-to-day life. (470)

And finally, the third question is concerned with how individuals position themselves and each other in discourse by employing particular linguistic devices such as:

- reference – *nouns, pronouns, determiners*
- adjectives – *denote features, qualities of entities and their actions*
- tense – *past, present progressive, present perfect, simple present*
- adjuncts – *manner, time, indefinite frequency*
- stance markers – *actually, certainly, hopefully, I think, really*

Data collection and corpus

Engaging in qualitative research means "capturing people's stories and weaving them together to reveal and give insight into real-world dramas" (Patton xiii, as quoted in Rossman and Rallis). As a result, capturing stories and listening to individuals' experiences, interpreting and analyzing their thoughts in the form of various discourses is not meant to be representative. I conducted informal "conversations with a purpose" (Burgess 108) with all couples, which were carried out over a six-month period from January to May 2006.[3] Conversations lasted between one and one and a half hours and altogether 15.5 hours of recorded material was collected. Broad transcriptions resulted in a corpus of 125,395 words which I manually color-coded and subdivided into 5 thematic categories labeled as follows:

- language choice and language practices
- couple discourse
- 4 types of positioning
- overt mentions of identity
- cultural practices

An interdisciplinary theoretical approach

I draw on Bucholtz and Hall's ("Language and Identity;" "Identity and interaction;" "Finding identity") sociocultural linguistic approach to identity and the social psychological theory of positioning (Davies and Harré; Harré and van Langenhove). Bucholtz and Hall's model underscores the role of interaction in identity construction and emphasizes

---

[3] The extracts used throughout this study are from the recorded conversations.

that identity is emergent and gains social meaning in conversation, while positioning theory outlines specific ways individuals are positioned or located as certain types of individuals in discourse.

Recent investigations concerning the correlation between language and identity (Benwell and Stokoe; Bucholtz and Hall "Language and Identity;" "Identity and interaction;" "Finding identity"; Joseph; Pavlenko and Blackledge; Piller; Schüpbach) align themselves with post-structuralist and socio-constructionist views of identity as emergent, multiple, negotiated and discursively constructed and embedded in relations of power. These reject earlier accounts of identity as stable, fixed and assigned to certain social categories. Nevertheless, the notion of essentialism should not be disregarded within ethnographic studies.

Benwell and Stokoe claim that "it is assumed that although people present themselves differently in different contexts, underneath that presentation lurks a private, pre-discursive and stable identity" (3). This view correlates to earlier psychological studies that placed the concept of identity within the "broader area of 'personality,, and viewed identity as 'a person's essential, continuous self, the internal, subjective concept of oneself as an individual'" (Reber 341, as quoted by Bhavnani and Phoenix 8). I understand and use the term identity throughout this study as "the social positioning of self and other" (Bucholtz and Hall, "Identity and Interaction" 586). Despite post-structuralist and socio-constructionist approaches of identity, individuals more often than not align themselves with the assumption of pre-discursive and stable identities as one female informant, Tanya, states in the first extract from my data:

(1)
1. Tanya: you know, i've been here for so long and i just know that there are certain
2.   things that i do different than other people do . . . i don't know if that's
3.   american or if that's just who i am [. . .]

From this extract it becomes obvious that although Tanya is indeed aware of the different practices she engages in (line 2), she admits to being uncertain when it comes to identifying these dissimilarities as culturally based or due to her inherent self.

For Bucholtz and Hall, "a non-essentialist approach to identity within linguistic anthropology cannot dispense with the ideology of essentialism as long as it has salience in the lives of the speakers we study" ("Language and Identity" 375-6). In other words, the notion of essentialism should not be ignored when investigating discourse concerning individuals' identities (for a different view cf. Antaki and Widdicombe). Similarly, Joseph maintains that

[t]he analyst who refuses any truck with essentialism risks missing a factor of the highest importance in the identity's construction. In other words, essentialism versus constructionism is not as mutually exclusive a distinction as it is normally taken to be [. . .] there must remain space for essentialism in our epistemology, or we can never comprehend the whole point for which identities are constructed. (90)

Making room for individuals' notion of "having" stable identities based on who they construct themselves to be or act inherently while simultaneously scrutinizing how they are co-constructed and emergent entails fusing these two epistemological paradigms. This means that individuals' first-order perceptions of who they say they are or think they are must be considered in any account of identity. This study therefore illustrates that essentialist accounts of identity should not be viewed against social constructionist or post-structuralist accounts of identity, but that they all simultaneously work together in order to account for the complex notion of identity and the convoluted performances of *doing* identity work.

Situated and situational identities

Despite the fact that many individuals regard their identities as stable, psychological attributes as was exemplified by Tanya in extract (1), their discourse reveals that *doing* Swiss becomes an inter-subjective collaboration of social, cultural, gendered, and linguistic practices. Individuals' first-order perceptions of themselves and what it means to *do* Swiss relies on their beliefs of their past and current selves that are based on their past and current practices. In order to clarify this distinction between past and present, I introduce the terms *situated* and *situational identities* to depict the fixed, transient and ephemeral positions individuals take up or find themselves in, through and in discourse.[4]

Within the context of this study, a *situated identity* can be understood as a) an individual's sense of self, which is often characterized as "stable," "fixed" and "unchanged" in that it is how individuals consider

---

[4] The terms situated and situational identities are used differently from Zimmerman's notions of discourse identities, situational identities and transportable identities. For Zimmerman all three "have different home territories" (90). Discourse identities are understood as "integral to the moment-by-moment organization of interaction. Participants assume discourse identities as they engage in the various sequentially organized activities: current speaker, listener, story teller [. . .]. Situated identities come into play within the precincts of particular types of situation [and] transportable identities travel with individuals across situations and are potentially relevant in and for any situation" (ibid.).

themselves to be or act inherently; and b) it can also refer to how they are "seen," placed or situated by others as certain individuals within a specific context. One way in which individuals index a situated identity correlates with the verb tense used to describe themselves, which often means employing the auxiliary verb *be*. Situated identities differ from *situational identities* in that the latter is more flexible, dynamic, temporary and can be constructed by oneself or co-constructed by others. Such situational identities are referred to by individuals when they describe themselves or others as being or acting in a way with reference to particular circumstances or conditions. What is important to keep in mind is that both types of identities are intertwined and always encompass social aspects. Just because one individual situates him/herself as being a certain type of person does not mean that the depiction he or she has of him/herself is not connected to the larger social world.

Moreover, both situated and situational identities can be simultaneously revealed within a single utterance as is exemplified in the following extract between Clara and her husband Timo:

(2)
1. Clara: [. . .] that way- and also i don't like driving, i've never liked driving that
2.   much, i love taking trains, yeah, there are certain swiss things
3. Timo: mhm [or riding the bike, just walking
4. Clara: [but my personality i think is still american

In this extract we see that Clara does not like certain practices such as *driving*, she enjoys *taking trains*, a practice she perceives as Swiss. Despite engaging in *certain Swiss things* (line 2), making reference to her *personality* as *American* (line 4), indexes her first-order perception of her self based on her inherent personality she regards and constructs as stable by employing the auxiliary verb *is*, the stance marker *I think* and the adverb *still*. According to Carter and McCarthy (144) *still* could mean that, "something is true in spite of something else or in contrast to it." In other words, despite living in Switzerland for over twelve years and liking and doing *Swiss things*, Clara inevitably feels as though she has not changed, thus positioning her self and situated identity as stable. For Clara, her situational identity is discursively co-constructed as Swiss in several ways by both Clara and her husband. First, she admits that when it comes to means of transportation, she prefers *taking trains* rather than driving implying that since her move to Switzerland, *taking trains* is a practice she not only perceives as Swiss, but one she has willingly adopted. Moreover, her husband Timo also positions his wife as changed concerning means of transportation when he makes reference to *riding the bike, just walking* (line 3), two other activities he perceives as Swiss and which he feels his wife has taken on.

Rejecting Swiss based on language practices

The notion of *having* a Swiss identity or engaging in Swiss practices often correlated to individuals' first-order perceptions of their competence and ability to speak the local Bernese dialect. Language practices, however, are just one way in which individuals come to understand and hold onto their past selves or situated identities although engaging in various local and socio-cultural practices of everyday life. The various discourses found within my data about these practices are listed below:

- competence in and ability to speak a Bernese dialect
- social arrangements/socializing
- working
- housekeeping
- cooking/eating
- child-rearing
- shopping

For the purposes of the present study, I limit the discussion to competence and ability to speak a Bernese dialect as well as social arrangements.

Extract (3) highlights the saliency of the local Bernese dialect. It begins with Conny's positioning of herself and her husband concerning L2 learning within a diglossic area:

(3)
1. Conny: i was taking a german class in berne when i first met peter and he was so
2.   arrogant about that, i'd say, "ok i have huusaufgabe (homework), you
3.   wanna help me?" and he says, "oh just- christ! learn the swiss german, it's
4.   so stupid to be learning german!" which i think nowadays, i'm so proud
5.   that i
6. Peter: so again, you put it on [me that you didn't learn german
7. Conny: [no, but i'm glad- i'm glad that you did that
8.   because i agree, i- for me personally to have children living in a small
9.   town the size of a cat's forehead
10. Kellie: @@@
11. Conny: it's much more comfortable to speak the local language than to
12.   speak high german

In deliberately positioning her husband as *arrogant* (line 2) regarding learning standard German by using the past tense *was*, Conny tacitly positions herself as a willing language learner when she first came to Switzerland. Conny's use of direct quotation together with the predicative adjective *stupid* (lines 3-4) to convey her husband's language ideologies tacitly positions him as unsupportive of his wife's initial L2 efforts. This first order positioning of Peter is not accepted, but questioned when he states, *so again you put it on me that you didn't learn German* (line 6) thus calling for a second order positioning of him. Conny then re-positions her husband and herself since Peter's former behavior and attitude is presented as ultimately beneficial for Conny's current Bernese dialect performance by employing the adjective *glad* and the simple present verb *be* to index her situational identity in *I'm glad that you did that because I agree* (lines 7-8). When asked about her current language practices with her family at home, the rejection of Swiss emerges in the following extract:

(4)
1. Conny: i already feel like i jumped out of my culture! my language! my
2.   everything! to live here, i don't want my house to be in a foreign language,
3.   i don't feel comfortable enough about that, i'm not- i don't feel like living
4.   as a foreigner

For Conny language practices within her family are intentional and correlate with her sense of "having" a Swiss identity, one she ultimately rejects. She accomplishes this by deliberately positioning herself first and foremost as the spouse who has had to sacrifice everything by making reference to her *culture*, her *language* and *everything* else that living abroad entails. Furthermore, the use of Swiss German in her house is rejected as it connotes feelings of strangeness when she explicitly states not feeling *comfortable* about using a *foreign language* and thus *living as a foreigner* (lines 3-4) in her own home. Because of her past actions and sacrifices, Conny's situated identity has been jeopardized to some degree, but her determination to hold onto it is done through language maintenance. Like Conny, Glenda also rejects a Swiss identity and makes reference to a failed *plan* in:

(5)
1. Glenda: but that was the actual plan, i didn't want to live here, i'm probably the
2.   only one with a swiss passport who doesn't want it

Glenda's use of the past tense *was* (line 1) indexes that life after marriage should have been in Ireland rather than Switzerland. Her admission that she never wanted to live in Switzerland positions her as an unfortunate victim, as a result of an economic choice. Her use of the present tense, reference to *a Swiss passport*, and the indefinite pronoun *the only one* (line 2) is a deliberate positioning of herself as an anomaly. Her utterance implies that anyone else in her position would be grateful to live in Switzerland, but she is not. When asked whether Glenda had taken on any Swiss practices, she denies it as is revealed in extract (6):

(6)
1. Glenda: but erm no, i haven't changed at all . . .
2. Michael: no- i would say it's [the other way around
3. Glenda: [no, i don't want these things
4. Kellie: what do you mean?
5. Michael: i took more on . . . of the irish way

Glenda's use of the present perfect tense in *haven't changed* positions herself and her situated identity as stable. Michael then makes a deliberate positioning of himself by claiming *it's the other way around* initially positioning himself and his situational identity as open and multiple. Employing the past tense in *I took on more of the Irish way* (line 5) suggests that his past situated identity was altered and possibly hybrid. His use of the definite article in *the Irish way*, however, indexes a certain monolithic way of being, thinking and acting, which is a deliberate positioning of himself as changed, but not necessarily dynamically.

Social arrangements as a socio-cultural practice

Reasons for rejecting a Swiss identity were based on the fact that individuals perceived themselves as unchanged, but also due to the negative evaluations attached to particular practices. One of the practices that was cast in a negative light was that of social arrangements, but more specifically making appointments to visit friends. In the next extract Glenda discusses the differences between the socio-cultural practices in Ireland and in Switzerland, which is underscored when she makes reference to the expected unwritten rules concerning friendships:

(7)
1. Glenda: i mean to go to somebody's house, i mean- all my friends- i mean, i don't
2.   phone them up and make an appointment ... i just walk in whenever i feel
3.   like it and they do the same you know what i mean?
4. Kellie: mhm
5. Glenda: you can't do that here either, it's all by appointment and when you don't
6.   grow up that way ... it's very hard

For Glenda, making appointments is discursively constructed as different and Swiss. This is accomplished by comparing the habitual activity
of planning social engagements in Switzerland to her and her friends'
ways of doing things in Ireland by using the simple present tense *don't
phone, walk in*, and the time adjunct *whenever* (lines 1-2). In doing so, she
tacitly positions herself and her Irish friends as more spontaneous and
fun. Glenda's utterance also functions as a simultaneous tacit positioning of her Swiss friends as less flexible and rigid when she asserts, *you
can't do that here* (line 5) referring to making unannounced visits. Glenda
confesses to the challenges faced concerning these Swiss cultural practices by comparing them to her Irish upbringing in the statement: *and
when you don't grow up that way, it's very hard* (line 6). Once again, reference
to Glenda's past and current practices and the respective events that
have shaped her construction of them need to be considered when ac-
counting for her first-order perceptions of both her situated and situational identities. For Glenda, the socio-cultural practices she has been
confronted with on a daily basis since moving to Switzerland have been
difficult to overcome. She regards these practices as tedious and regi-
mented compared to the Irish socio-cultural practices she grew up with.
In the next extract, Sarah attests similar views concerning social arrangements, albeit differently:

(8)
1. Sarah: i think one thing i used to really dislike- i still do, but i do it myself now, is
2.   the way you can't just sort of call on people, you don't just sort of pop
3.   round, "hey, you wanna cup of coffee?" you know? or have people calling
4.   round here, you phone first, you arrange a time and it has to be fixed! and
5.   then maybe you'll do it perhaps a week later

In extract (8) Sarah confesses to having a negative attitude towards the
way these arrangements are done by employing the past tense *used to* and
the stance marker *really*. Using the adverb *still* expresses her continual
dislike to scheduling appointments, but she admits to taking it on board
by using the simple present tense and the adverb of time *now* in *I do it
myself now* (line 1). The simple present tense and hedges used in the utterance *you can't just sort of call on people* (line 2) implies that unannounced
visits are not tolerated and as a result, not done. This deliberate positioning of the Swiss may also be accredited to the length of time Sarah
has resided in Switzerland, namely twenty-four years. Because of this,
she knows how certain Swiss practices work, thus tacitly positioning
herself as an expert. This is apparent when she lists how this specific
practice functions in a systematic way by using the quasi imperative in

you phone first, you arrange a time (line 4), which is then followed by *it has to be fixed!*

In extract (9) Tanya also perceives such social arrangements as Swiss, however, she intentionally chooses to maintain different and thus American practices:

(9)
1. Tanya: and i think that's something that we also do that now as a couple, on a
2.   sunday we'll go for a walk and we'll go ring somebody's doorbell and ...
3.   that's not very swiss, i mean- swiss- you have to call ahead and make sure,
4.   "hey, are we not bothering you and that?" and that's one of the things that
5.   i can think of that- that maybe ... is a cultural thing that i- that i have kept

In this extract Tanya makes a deliberate positioning of the Swiss with regards to this practice as organized and structured when she states, *you have to call ahead* (line 3). Despite her belief that this is indeed the Swiss way of "doing" things, she and her husband Ray intentionally do not abide by it, tacitly positioning themselves as flexible and spontaneous. This is evident when she makes use of *will* to refer to habitual events in *we'll go for a walk and ring somebody's doorbell* (line 2). For Tanya, such an action is perceived as *not very Swiss* (line 3) indexing that her situational identity within those particular circumstances is also not Swiss. And finally, Tanya refers to this practice as *a cultural thing*, one which she claims to *have kept* by employing the present perfect tense (line 5). Her utterance implies that some of her former American practices and thus situated identity have remained unchanged and therefore stable.

Conclusion

Analyzing individuals' first-order perceptions of their identities and *doing Swiss* ultimately means scrutinizing interpersonal discourse within an intimate community of practice where the positioning of self and other constantly emerges. The analysis presented not only underscored the construction and negotiation of what *doing* Swiss means, but also revealed the essentialist views individuals discursively construct of themselves and others in and through discourse. By proposing the terms *situated* and *situational identities* within ethnographic studies, my aim was to re-conceptualize the saliency of individuals' situated past identities, positions, and practices and juxtapose them to individuals' current situational identities, positions, and practices in order to facilitate individuals' rejection of hybridity.

For the participants in this study claiming a hybrid identity is an assertion that is often met with caution and uncertainty as the dramatic 4.0 second pause and stance marker *certainly* exemplify in the final extract:

(10)
1. Sarah: swiss identity? (4.0) i don't know? yes! i mean, i'm certainly no longer
2.   completely british
3. Kellie: mhm
4. Sarah: i mean, when i'm in england, i'm a bit of the swiss person

Nevertheless, a hybrid identity is a concept that individuals living in an intercultural marriage are inevitably faced with regardless if it is rejected, accepted or embraced.

Transcription conventions

,	clause final intonation ("more to come")
!	exclamation mark indicates exclamatory intonation
?	clause final rising intonation (yes-no questions)
…	three dots indicate pause length of ½ second or more
[	brackets indicate overlapping speech
[…]	omission
XXX	inaudible utterance
( )	extra information
@	laughter (one @ per syllable)
@laughingly@	utterance between the two @s is spoken while laughing
/ /	transcriber's doubt
-	incomplete word or utterance

References

Antaki, Charles and Sue Widdicombe, eds. *Identities in Talk*. London and Thousand Oaks: Sage Publications Ltd., 1998.

Benwell, Bethan and Elizabeth Stokoe. *Discourse and Identity*. Edinburgh: Edinburgh University Press, 2006.

Bhavnani, Kum-Kum and Ann Phoenix (eds). *Shifting identities, shifting racisms: a feminism and psychology reader*. London: Sage, 1994.

Blommaert, Jan. *Discourse*. Key Topics in Sociolinguistics. Cambridge and New York: Cambridge University Press, 2005.

Bourdieu, Pierre. *The Logic of* Practice. Trans. Richard Nice. Cambridge: Polity Press, 1990.

Breger, Rosemary Anne and Rosanna Hill. *Cross-Cultural Marriage: Identity and Choice*. Oxford: Berg, 1998.

Bucholtz, Mary and Kira Hall. "Language and Identity." *A Companion to Linguistic Anthropology*. Ed. Alessandro Duranti. Oxford: Blackwell Publishing, 2004.

———. "Identity and Interaction: a sociocultural linguistic approach." *Discourse Studies* 7:4-5 (2005): 585-614.

———. "Finding Identity: Theory and Data." *Multilingua* 27 (2008): 151-163.

Burgess, Robert G., ed. *Field Research: A Sourcebook and Field Manual*. Contemporary Field Research Series 4. London and New York: Routledge, 1982.

Butler, Judith. *Gender Trouble: Feminism and the Subversion of Identity*. New York / London: Routledge, 1990.

Carter, Ronald and Michael McCarthy, eds. *Cambridge Grammar of English*. Cambridge and New York: Cambridge University Press, 2006.

Davies, Bronwyn and Rom Harré. "Positioning: The Discursive Production of selves." *Journal for the Theory of Social* Behaviour 20:1 (1990): 43-63.

Eckert, Penelope and Susan McConnell-Ginet. "Think Practically and Look Locally: Language and Gender as Community-Based Practice." *Annual Review of Anthropology* 21 (1992): 461-490.

Fenstermaker, Sarah and Candace West. *Doing Gender, Doing Difference: Inequality, Power, and Institutional Change*. New York / London: Routledge, 2002.

Harré, Rom and Luk van Langenhove, eds. *Positioning Theory*. Oxford and Malden: Blackwell Publishers Ltd, 1999.

Joseph, John Earl. *Language and Identity: National, Ethnic, Religious*. Basingstoke: Palgrave Macmillan, 2004.

Pavlenko, Aneta and Adrian Blackledge, eds. *Negotiation of Identities in Mulitilingual Contexts*. Clevedon and Buffalo: Multilingual Matters Ltd., 2004.

Piller, Ingrid. *Bilingual Couples Talk: the Discursive Construction of Hybridity*. Amsterdam and Philadelphia: John Benjamins Publishing Company, 2002.

Rash, Felicity. *The German Language in Switzerland: Multilingualism, Diglossia and Variation*. German Linguistic and Cultural Studies, volume 3. Berne: Peter Lang, 1998.

Rossman, G.B. and Rallis, S.F. *Learning in the Field: An Introduction to Qualitative Research*. 2nd ed. Thousand Oaks and London: Sage Publications, 2003.

Schüpbach, Doris. *Shared Languages, Shared Identities, Shared Stories? A Qualitative Study of Life Stories by Immigrants from German-Speaking Switzerland in Australia*. Melbourne: doctoral dissertation, 2005.

Watts, Richard. J., Sachiko Ide and Konrad Ehlich, eds. *Politeness in Language: Studies in its History, Theory and Practice*. Trends in Linguistics 59. Berlin and New York: Mouton de Gruyter, 1992.

Zimmerman, D.H. "Identity, Context and Interaction." Ed. C. Antaki and S. Widdicombe. *Identities in Talk*. London and Thousand Oaks: Sage Publications Ltd., 1998.

Ray and Ghatak and Other Filmmaking Pairs: the Structure of Asian Modernity

Amit Chaudhuri

How did a cultural encounter in the time of modernity – in particular, one that involves a new artwork – actually occur? When the encounter is taking place between historically opposed, or at least different, entities, such as the "East" and the "West," is it possible to escape, as one views or experiences the artwork, the familiar language of cultural difference? Is it possible to use the parameter of modernity as a way out of that language, as well as from the notion of a universal human nature through which to understand a variety of (sometimes challenging and resistant) experiences? But, if we introduce the notion of modernity in a situation involving both "East" and "West," is it possible to avoid a narrative to do with "Western" and "non-Western" modernities, or a modernity that's engendered by the West and then transported elsewhere? Many of these questions underlie, I think, the Indian filmmaker Satyajit Ray's reflections on his first encounter with Japanese cinema, and I return to them here. I also look at the way in which major filmmakers in Asian countries often seem to emerge in pairs – pairs that, in turn, complicate the bases on which we make our distinctions between "Western" and "Eastern" sensibilities and histories.

It seems that there are all kinds of unresolved problems to do with Satyajit Ray – to do with thinking about him, with finding a language to speak about him that doesn't repeat the indubitable truisms about his humanism and lyricism. How does he fit into history, and into which history – the history of India; the history of filmmaking; some other – do we place him first? We don't ordinarily talk about Ray "fitting in," because he is an icon and a figurehead, and figureheads don't generally have to fit in; traditions, schools, and oeuvres emanate from them. Glancing toward Ray, we see, indeed, the precious oeuvre, but it's more

Performing the Self. SPELL: Swiss Papers in English Language and Literature 24. Ed. Karen Junod and Didier Maillat. Tübingen: Narr, 2010. 91-100.

difficult to trace the tradition – either leading up to Ray or emerging
from him. People closer to home will mention something called the
"Bengal Renaissance," and Tagore, when thinking of lineage; and even
those who aren't students of film know who some of the precursors are:
Jean Renoir, Vittorio de Sica, John Ford. As to inheritors of the style,
you could, with some hesitation and prudence, point to Adoor
Gopalakrishnan, and, a bit further away, to Abbas Kiarostami. But what
does this constellation of names and categories add up to? For, in the
end, we're reduced to looking at Ray as if he were alone, as someone
who possessed, as Ray said of *Rashomon*, "just the right degree of universality" (155).

   To me, it's increasingly clear – especially in the light of the changes
in politics and culture in the last quarter of a century – that Ray is the
only embodiment of an Indian "high" modernity, specifically a vernacular "high" modernity, that the world has had to deal with. The "world,"
in this instance, refers to places in Europe and America where film festivals were hosted, the great metropolitan centres in which debates to do
with "culture" were decided, and even sections of the Indian intelligent-
sia: Ray's humanism was noted in his heyday, but the encounter with
Indian modernity was hardly mentioned, or only inadvertently experienced by the viewer. And yet Ray's work did occupy the consciousness
of the second half of the twentieth century, and, to be understood, must
have required a different set of rules from those applying to the paradigmatic, "authentic" India of either the Orient or of post-coloniality –
the India of chaos, crowds, voices, irresistible self-generation, and colour. Ray's India, or Bengal, was not, in this sense, paradigmatic – but, as
with Apu's room overlooking a terrace and railway tracks in *Apur Sansar*,
it was strangely recognisable and true. Were we being shown, then, that,
it was, after all, "recognisability," rather than cultural "authenticity," that
was a feature of modernity? And how aware was the audience, as they
discovered Apu's world, of that distinction?

   Let's go back at this point to Ray's own record of his encounter with
Japanese cinema in the form of Kurosawa's *Rashomon*. Ray is writing
about this in 1963, probably a little more than twelve years after its release – for Kurosawa's film went to the Venice Film Festival in 1951,
winning the Golden Lion there, and Ray says, "I saw *Rashomon* in Calcutta soon after its triumph in Venice." He adds – for Japan seems as
far away from Bengal as it is from Venice, and Venice probably closer to
his Calcutta – "This is the point where I should confess that my knowledge of the Far East is derived largely from Waley and Lafcadio Hearn;
and that while I know my Shakespeare and Schopenhauer, I have yet to
know Murasaki and the precepts of Lao-tzu" (155). This is not just the
prototype of the colonised subject airily declaiming his allegiances; it's

the modern as revisionist, impatiently estranging himself from a fundamental constituent of his identity: that is, the Orient as a point of origin.
For Ray, I think, the prism of this revisionism is his particular understanding of "Bengaliness": Ray once offended readers of the *Illustrated
Weekly of India* – and I speak from living memory – by saying that he
didn't think of himself as a Hindu, but as a Bengali. This revisionist view
of Bengaliness is not so much a sub-nationalism, or even just a residue
of his father's Brahmoism, as an opposition to cultural identity as we
understand it today. It's an opening out onto a secular, local, even regional sense of the everyday, cohabiting, at once, with a constant pre-
monition of the international, which defines the "Bengaliness" of the
first half of the twentieth century.

In the same essay on Japanese cinema from which I've just quoted,
"Calm Without, Fire Within," Ray, still discussing *Rashomon*, makes a
shrewd observation, to do with the culture of filmmaking certainly, but
also the sort of questions that the sudden appearance of a compelling
cultural artefact raises. "It was also the kind of film that immediately
suggests," says Ray, "a culmination, a fruition, rather than a beginning.
You could not – as a film making nation – have a *Rashomon* and nothing
to show before it. A high order of imagination may be met with in a
beginner, but the virtuoso use of cutting and camera was a sort that
came only with experience" (155-156). Those first two statements are
among the cleverest statements I've read on the reception of the product of one culture into another, a cautionary reminder of how the critical language of reception simplifies and caricatures, even while occasionally applauding, the encounter with the foreign artwork or phenomenon, and ignores certain blindingly obvious problems. Remember
that Ray is not speaking here of the classic encounter with "otherness,"
with the savage or the peasant, the staple archetypes of post-coloniality,
but of something – in this case, *Rashomon* – that only occurs in the
economy and theatre of modernity, of a moment of dislocation, of revaluation, taking place within that terrain of film festivals, film societies,
and educated – maybe even cinematically educated – middle-class audiences. Why is it that, when a clearly modern non-Western phenomenon
emerges globally – say, Mandela, or Ray himself, or Arundhati Roy's
environmental activism, or a liberation movement – he or she or it is
seen as a "beginning" rather than a "fruition" or "culmination" as if
they belonged to an intellectual environment without texture or entan-
glements or process, a history composed, astonishingly, of supermen or
women who rise without explanation from the anonymity around them?
Even more than Western history after Carlyle, non-Western history still
seems, at least in the popular imagination, condemned to be an account
of exceptional men and women and events springing out of an undiffer-

entiated, homogenous landscape: the site of development. In coining the wonderful rubric, "film making nation," with its conflation of a specialist activity with a political entity, Ray is not so much being a cinema geek as he's reminding us of the nitty gritty, the materiality, the processes, of history, and of crafting history.

The opening sentences of Ray's next paragraph give us an important key to understanding the sort of encounter he's talking about, but end in a somewhat conventional formulation: "Later revelation of Kurosawa's past work and the work of other Japanese directors has confirmed what *Rashomon* hinted at: the existence of an art form, western in origin, but transplanted and taking root in a new soil. The tools are the same, but the methods and attitudes in the best and most characteristic are distinct and indigenous" (156). Is that all, however, that the encounter with *Rashomon* hints at – a transplantation of an art-form, and its subsequent indigenisation? Is the history of the modern artwork simply a history of its production in the West, and its indigenisation elsewhere? (These are questions, of course, that have been raised by historians such as Dipesh Chakraborty and others in other contexts, to do with the nature of the "modern" itself, but not, I think, in connection to the specific business of genre.) We must remember that, crucially, Ray's own response to *Rashomon* could not have come out of nowhere; we couldn't, to paraphrase his words on Kurosawa's film, have had that response and "nothing to show before it." It – that response to *Rashomon* in 1963 in Calcutta – is not so much a beginning as a "fruition, a culmination" of something; and the history from which it emerged at that moment, in the context of *Rashomon*, cannot be summed up as a history of Western origination, colonial dissemination, and, finally, indigenisation; of import and export. Yes, it's a history that involves travel, but travel as a means of unravelling meaning rather than just moving forward in a landscape; modernity, in the realm of culture, appears to consist of a series of interchanges and encounters in which the putatively initiating meeting – such as the one between Ray and Kurosawa's film – is also a "culmination, a fruition," of interchanges that have already taken place.

One is reminded of this if one thinks back to the emergence of Iranian cinema in the late Eighties. There was that initial moment of surprise when, in London and other cities, audiences viewed the films of Abbas Kiarostami and Mohsin Makhmalbaf and, in the Nineties, Jafar Panahi and others, for the first time. There was fairly widespread acknowledgement that a form of art-house cinema that was at once deeply humane and innovative was coming out of a country about which the secular middle classes around the world knew relatively little, and about which they knew already whatever they needed to know. Into this frame, the frame of preconceptions, entered, for instance, the engineers, film directors, and drifting professionals who drove through Kiarostami's tranquil but earthquake-stricken landscapes, with middle-class children sitting, often, beside them in the car, journeying towards families in houses in remote villages; also in that frame appeared Makhmalbaf's weavers, village primary schoolteachers, Afghan daily wage-earners, carnival bicyclists. Objects came into the frame as well – apples; fabrics; the blue tile on the wall of a village house; shoes in a shop window in Tehran. The audiences noted these people and things with a mixture of delight, surprise, and recognition, seeing them as elements of what they hadn't known before, as well as of the already known. The quality of the already known gave to these details their recognisability, their authenticity; viewers knew almost straightaway that what they were watching was indisputably "real" cinema; the details possessed not just universality, but the pacing and aura of the modern, particularly modernism, with certain modulations on that sensibility that these very gifted filmmakers' works introduced. So, "foreignness" wasn't the crux and core of Iranian cinema; the crux was its enlivening and dislocating recognisability. The fact that this cinema had its impact at a time when the infra-structure and *raison d'être* of the art-house cinema movement was, worldwide, being dismantled was an irony that was either not noticed, or not considered worth commenting on. Yet the most important question regarding these films still remains unaddressed. Here was a kind of cinema that "immediately suggest[ed]," as Ray had said of *Rashomon*, "a culmination, a fruition, rather than a beginning" (155-156). What was it a fruition of? What had happened, or was happening, in Iran, and, for that matter, elsewhere, that these films were powerfully hinting at – not through their subject-matter, but through the culmination of a certain practice, and all the more powerfully for that? Not knowing leaves a gap in our understanding, and dependent on that model of transplantation and indigenisation. And what happens when something that's purportedly been indigenised is carried back to the land it was transplanted from – an occurrence such as the first showing, say, of Iranian films in New York? Whatever the answer to that might be, it cannot approximate the frisson that the actual event – the New York audience watching the Iranian film – would have involved. The emergence of Iranian cinema represented not just a culmination of certain filmic styles and values, but a convergence of links, hitherto unnoticed, that came together to create a new-minted but unexpected, even unlikely, experience of the "modern," in that decade when modernity, apparently, had finally begun to wane. "Modernity" was the unlooked-for culmination through which New York and Iran momentarily came together.

And yet this experience of the "modern," which arises not from a canonical history of modernity written solely by and in the West, but through a series of interchanges and tensions (such as Ray's encounter with *Rashomon* embodies) – this continual experience of the "modern" is almost always, if it involves a non-Western artist, subsumed under the categories of "East" and "West," and within issues of cultural authenticity. Everyone collaborates in this emotive and persistent haziness to do with cultural characteristics, including the commentators and the artists themselves. That is, they fit their thoughts and justifications into one of two compartments: that either the artwork, if it was produced in the East, bears the unmistakable and ancient imprint of its cultural lineage; or that it transcends all those marks into the convenient domain of the universal. Only the artwork itself refuses to collaborate in this formula, insisting that the intersection between cultural lineage, foreignness, and recognisability must, in the time of modernity, be arrived at as, in Ray's word, a "fruition," that is, as a radical moment of awareness of underlying histories, and, at once, as an unpremeditated but considered acknowledgement of that "fruition." By "fruition" Ray means, as we have seen, not something static, not a pinnacle of development, but a sudden intimation of intelligibility, and modernity as a language dependent on, and constantly illuminated by, such intimations. But then Ray himself, in his essay, goes on to speak in the terms of the same dichotomy that I just described. "Of all the Japanese directors, Kurosawa has been the most accessible to the outside world," he says. "There are obvious reasons for this. He seems, for instance, to have a preference for simple, universal situations over narrowly regional ones. . . . But most importantly, I think, it his penchant for movement, for physical action, which has won him so many admirers in the West" (156). Ray then clarifies that he isn't overly bothered by whether the "penchant" for action is a consequence of a "strong Occidental streak" in Kurosawa, or whether it springs from something "within the Japanese artistic tradition;" for he is still "able to derive keen aesthetic pleasure" from Kurosawa's work. However, he points out that "there is no doubt that he is a man of vastly different temperament from Ozu and Mizoguchi, both of whom come nearer to my preconception of the true Japanese film maker. Here, too, I may be wrong, but a phrase of my dear old professor sticks in my mind: 'Consider the Fujiyama,' he would say; 'fire within and calm without. There is the symbol of the true Oriental artist'" (157).

Ozu and Mizoguchi are actually, as far as filmmaking temperament and subject-matter go, quite different from each other: in contrast to Ozu's subtle suburban idylls, Mizoguchi's work, in fact, shares with Kurosawa a fascination with pre-modern Japan and its distinctive artistic resources. I suppose what Ray is talking about – and the basis of the comparison he's making – has more to do with pacing: the "movement" and "action" of Kurosawa's kind of cinema, the slowness of Mizoguchi's and especially of Ozu's universe. Slowness, who knows, may well be an Oriental characteristic; it may also be part of the colonialist construction of the Orient, as well as of the response of Western critics to directors like Ozu. Ray points out, bringing his own metier, at this point, into the picture, that the "complaint is frequently heard that some Japanese films – even some very good ones – are 'nevertheless very slow'. Some of my own films, too, have drawn this comment from Western critics." (Chandak Sengoopta, in a recent issue of *Outlook* magazine, reminds us of the sort of early criticism that Ray is talking about here [Chandak Sengoopta, "Apu-In-The-World."]) Ray points out that "a slow pace is, I believe, as legitimate to films as it is to music. But as a director I know that a slow pace is terribly hard to sustain. When the failure is the director's fault, he should be prepared to take the blame for it. But it is important to remember that slowness is a relative thing, depending on the degree of involvement of the viewer" (159-160). With the phrase "a relative thing," Ray is, I think, gently refuting the "universal" cultural situation presumed by Western critics, and arguing, somewhat diffidently, for his Easternness. But he doesn't remind us that slowness is also a principal, even sacred, feature of modernism, which privileges the image over narrative, the individual moment over the overarching time-span, thus holding up the way a story ordinarily unfolds. It's possible, of course, that Ray's pacing is the result of an Oriental identity that he's usually at pains to distance himself from. For instance, the sequence in Ray's first film *Pather Panchali* (1995, based on Bibhuti Bhushan Banerjee's 1928 novel of the same name) in which the camera spends a noticeably large amount of time observing the movement of water insects upon a pond during the monsoons might be, as Max Lerner said of the Apu trilogy in the *New York Post* in 1961 (and this kind of opinion is obviously still fresh in Ray's mind in 1963), "faithful to the Indian sense of time, which is actually a sense of timelessness." Or it could, more plausibly, be at once a sideways reference to the long descriptions of Apu reading by a pond in Banerjee's novel (which Ray makes no attempt to invoke directly), as well as a homage to and a reworking of the forty seconds or so (a considerable amount of time in a film, even more considerable when the film is about half an hour long) in Renoir's *Une Partie de Campagne* (1936), given to the swirls and eddies of river-water as the holiday-makers paddle downstream. The eddies of water in Renoir's river and the agitated pool in Ray on which the narcissistic water insects jump, absorbed, not to mention the mysteriously alluring pool by which Apu keeps his vigil, are part of the gluey, non-linear substance of modernism, its flow and pattern of consciousness. We don't need to decide, for now, whether or not the pond sequence in Ray's *Pather Panchali* is "faithful to the Indian sense of time," or is another instance of "transplantation and indigenisation." I see it as a "fruition" of something, giving way to a moment of recognition that undermines these polarities, and ramifying into an awareness of other moments and histories available to us in modernity, which we didn't necessarily think of until that moment. Renoir's own shots of the river, too (in a film based on a Maupassant story that comes from a different impulse: to narrate the arc of a lifetime without abandoning economy and compression), I'm sure, must have appeared to Ray a "culmination, a fruition, rather than a beginning."

It's interesting, though, that, when Ray worries briefly about whether Kurosawa's predilection for "action" comes out of a "strong Occidental streak" in the filmmaker, or whether it arises from "within the Japanese artistic tradition," he doesn't mean by the latter the work of Ozu and Mizoguchi, or the constituents of a "film making nation," but an older, perhaps a purer, tradition. Yet, barely a paragraph ago, when speaking of the "culmination" that *Rashomon* is, he'd appeared to be locating that film (and, by implication, his encounter with it), in a context more complex, more impinging, and less pastoral than a Japan seen through the eyes of Lafcadio Hearn. In fact, it was *Rashomon* that had led Ray to the idea of a modern Japanese cinema, and to discover and uncover the different perspectives and convergences that Ozu and Mizoguchi represented. If we take stock today, we see that Kurosawa is still the best-known Japanese filmmaker outside of Japan; and, almost as well-known in the West, but certainly a slightly larger presence in Japan than outside it, is Yasujiro Ozu. What's noticeable about this confluence – between Ozu and Kurosawa – is how it brings into play two very distinct styles of seeing, two different approaches to time and movement, with the flow of the confluence weighted more in one direction – Kurosawa's – than the other. And, because of this difference of temperament (Kurosawa's polyphonic, sometimes mythopoeic; Ozu's urbane, quiet, and still), and also because, for a long time, we'd come to identify Kurosawa with Japanese cinema – for these reasons, Ozu must, for us, even now retain the air and freshness of a secret, of a personal discovery: almost as much as, in fact, he would have for Ray. He is the hidden co-ordinate in that "fruition" and "culmination," the one that lies behind the revaluation and opening that *Rashomon* involves, implicating us in a sense of the modern that is deceptively simple and immediate but far-reaching. To contain this pairing by saying that Kurosawa is less Japanese than Ozu is to miss the many-sided way in which we receive and interpret modernity. If we look at the countries I've cited in the course of this essay – Iran and India – we see how this pattern, in the context of film, repeats itself strangely but tellingly, and even, sometimes – challenging our preconceptions about cultural authenticity – inverts itself. In India, for instance, Ray himself is part of a pair, and the other half of the pair is the prodigiously gifted, but self-destructive, Ritwik Ghatak, who died in the Seventies probably as a result of his alcoholism. There are many ways in which this pairing could be described and contrasted; one could call Ray a classicist, and Ghatak the possessor of an operatic sensibility. One could also describe Ray as a progeny of the Enlightenment and its flowering in Bengal, and Ghatak as an errant son, someone who turned the Enlightenment inside out in his movies. More characteristically, however, Ray's temperament has been called "Western" by some Indian critics, and Ghatak the more genuinely "Indian" of the two, and for reasons completely opposite to those pertaining to Ozu and Kurosawa. I think that, in this formulation, Ray's slowness, which in Ozu is a mark of recondite "Oriental" stillness, his air of "calm without, fire within," is seen as a kind of European reserve, and associated, in particular, with Western-derived realism; while Ghatak's narrative energy, his melodrama, his fascination with mythic grandeur (all of which in Kurosawa can be seen to be driven by a "strong Occidental streak" that prefers declamation to suggestion, "action" to stillness), is, in the Bengali filmmaker, often supposed to emanate from authentically Indian, and oral, modes of storytelling. One can imagine a parallel planetary configuration in which Ghatak is more famous in the West than Ray, and Ozu than Kurosawa, and sense that, in that universe, the terms would be adjusted, and mirror each other, accordingly, and essentially remain unchanged.

Similarly, Iran: the two major filmmakers from that country, Abbas Kiarostami and Mohsin Makhmalbaf, have strikingly contrasting sensibilities, the former presenting a very interesting development on neorealism, where nuance, bourgeois ordinariness, and leisureliness, along with odd but rich self-reflexivity, create the lens through which Iran appears; the latter, Makhmalbaf, making use of folklore, bright colours, and fairy tales. This sort of dichotomy rehearses one that's been familiar to us for more than twenty years now: the one that identifies suggestiveness, compression, and realism with canonical Western traditions, and storytelling, fantasy, orality, and passion with post-colonial ones. When we are viewing Ray or Kurosawa or Kiarostami, however, we are really witnessing a "fruition" which always suggests more, which, at that moment, we are capable of sensing but not grasping. Not necessarily more of the same – other Kiarostamis and Rays and Kurosawas, confirming, thereby, these filmmakers' traditions and cultural identities – but of their opposites and others: Ozu and Makhmalbaf and Ghatak. All these form the hidden co-ordinates of what that moment of "fruition" gestures towards. They make, in a sense, the old opposing categories of "East" and "West" seem cumbersome and even redundant.

References

Satyajit Ray. "Calm Without, Fire Within." *Our Films Their Films*. New Delhi: Orient Longman, 1976. 152-161.
Sengoopta, Chandak. "Apu-In-The-World. Fifty Years After the Apu Trilogy, The West Still Misreads Ray." www.outlookindia.com-/article.aspx?262710

Falstaff in Switzerland, Hamlet in Bavaria: Expatriate Shakespeare and the Question of Cultural Transmission

Michael Dobson

This paper considers some of the consequences of the late eighteenth-century canonization of Shakespeare as an indigenously British writer for the performance of his plays in Continental Europe, particularly their hitherto under-studied history of non-professional anglophone performance among expatriates. It examines the conflict between two principal ways of understanding the workings of cultural transmission (essentially, between the notion of Shakespeare as belonging genetically to the English-speaking peoples, and a notion of Shakespeare as amenable to naturalization regardless of ethnicity), as it plays itself out during two periods of international conflict: that of Romanticism and revolution, and that of Modernism and world war. Drawing on diplomatic memoirs, geography textbooks, prologues, vanity-published journals and military archives, it looks particularly at Shakespearean performances by English expatriates and Swiss Anglophiles in Geneva in the aftermath of the Napoleonic wars, and at productions of Shakespeare mounted by Allied prisoners of war in Bavaria during World War Two. Whose different notions of high culture, ethnic identity and national heritage did these different mobilizations of Shakespeare serve?

Few questions have caused quite so much conflict in Europe as those concerning the nature of communal identity. The little matter of whether we are who we are because of ethnicity, or religion, or geography, or all or none of the above – and whether that "we" is first and foremost national or transnational or local – was already a vexed one in

Performing the Self. SPELL: Swiss Papers in English Language and Literature 24. Ed. Karen Junod and Didier Maillat. Tübingen: Narr, 2010. 101-125.

Tudor times, as any student of Shakespeare's history plays knows. The question, in particular, of whether distinctive national cultures are primarily founded on genetics or on some more accidental confluence of ideas and practices has haunted the reception of Shakespeare both within Europe and beyond, ever since he was canonized as a national figure in the Romantic period. Since the eighteenth century, Shakespeare's plays have been regarded by his compatriots as intensely native, indeed as paradigmatic expressions of the national character: generously irregular and socially inclusive; deeply attached to the countryside but thriving on the commercial energies of the city; clear-sighted about the deficiencies of monarchy as a political system but heavily invested in the institution regardless. I want to look in what follows at some instances of how an argument about whether the imputed Britishness of Shakespeare is based on biological heredity has played out around the performance of the plays on the European mainland during two periods of conflict, that of Romanticism and revolution, and that of Modernism and world war. I'm going to be looking in particular at theatrical productions staged in two mountainous and un-Warwickshire-like regions, Switzerland and Bavaria. They are productions which have been overlooked in accounts of Shakespeare's European canonization to date, for two main reasons: firstly, none was given by a professional company, and secondly, despite taking place in the heart of the Continent, all were given in English.

There have been two main accounts to date of how Shakespeare came to participate in global culture, and neither, I hope to show, is quite complete. One concentrates on how Shakespeare's plays were taken around the world as part of the cultural baggage of British imperialism. That story begins in Shakespeare's lifetime with the crew of the East India Company ship the *Red Dragon*, who performed *Hamlet* and *Richard II* off what is now Sierra Leone while en route for the East in 1607-8 (Taylor 223-48). In this account, the transmission of Shakespeare is largely a matter of genetics, with performances of his work spreading across the map along with the English-speaking peoples. The great expert on theatre in the nascent British empire, Kathleen Wilson, has researched a history of when different colonized territories right around the world were first treated to the spectacle of Anglophones staging Nicholas Rowe's *The Fair Penitent*, a play she associates with the policing of sexuality required to guarantee which children would count as British citizens (Wilson 240). The exercise would work just as well with Shakespeare's history plays, which helped to keep a sense of legitimate heritage and national identity alive in unfamiliar surroundings: *Richard II* off Sierra Leone, 1607; *Richard III* in New York, 1752; *Henry IV part 1* in Sydney, 1800; *The Merry Wives of Windsor* in the Windward Islands, 1842.

And so on; and that's without listing countless garrison and shipboard performances of *Henry IV* and *The Merry Wives of Windsor* in Ireland, Wales, Madras, Chatham, and elsewhere. Once Shakespeare was felt to speak for the native soil, then Falstaff in particular, as the Shakespearean character most often associated with that soil – identified with roast beef and plenty, and destined to go to Arthur's bosom babbling of green fields – seems to have become a necessary extra passenger on any homesick imperial voyage into terra incognita.

The other account of the globalization of Shakespeare looks instead at how the plays came to migrate not into newly-established colonies but into other languages and cultures entirely, starting in Europe. This process again dates back to Shakespeare's lifetime, when the English Players took their repertory on tour around the Low Countries and the Baltic adapting it to the needs of local audiences as they went, and gathered ever greater momentum as translations into local vernaculars proliferated in the eighteenth and nineteenth centuries. Between them, these two narratives suggest that Shakespeare has been taken all over the English-speaking world in English, as part of what "home" and "origin" are supposed to mean, and all over the rest of the world in translation, as a naturalized honorary local. But this is a simplification which leaves out a third aspect of Shakespeare's global transmission, the untranslated performance of Shakespeare in countries which nobody imagined were ever going to adopt the Bard's mother tongue as a lingua franca. A striking case-study is provided, for instance, by Switzerland.

1. Falstaff in Switzerland

Promulgating an affection for Sir John in anglophone camps and colonies is one thing; what about his own grandiloquent claim to be "Sir John with all Europe" (*2 Henry IV* 2.2.125)? If it was ever going to achieve any truth, then it was surely during the heyday of Romanticism, and in the country which the British at the time found most congenial [Figure 1].

Figure 1. "Swiss Peasants", from Jehoshaphat Aspin, *Cosmorama: a View of the Costumes and Peculiarities of All Nations*. London: Harris, [1827], plate 7. [Property of the author]

This illustration comes from Jehoshaphat Aspin's schoolroom text-book *Cosmorama: a View of the Costumes and Peculiarities of All Nations* (1827). Aspin helpfully articulates what at the time was the standard English view of Switzerland:

> This country lies on the east of France, and is the seat of honest simplicity and invincible attachment to liberty . . . [T]he Swiss have distinguished themselves in almost every branch of literature and science . . . [They] are generally tall, well proportioned, active, and laborious; distinguished for their honesty, steadiness and bravery . . . [They] also display a fund of original humour, and are remarkable for great quickness of repartee and sallies of wit, which render their conversation agreeable and interesting . . . In the Plate . . . a young herdsman of the Alps is supposed to have just descended from the mountain, on a Sunday morning, carrying some rich cream for his wife's breakfast. (106-7, 108)

How true it all still sounds; and how very unlike, for example, nearby Bavaria:

> [L]iterature and science have made no progress here; and travellers agree in representing the Bavarians as among the most phlegmatic and sensual of the German nations . . . Many of the court ladies know of no other employment than playing with their parrots, their dogs, and their cats. Some keep a hall full of cats, and have several maids to attend them; they spend half their time with them, and serve them with coffee, &c. dressing them, according to their fancy, differently every day. (74-5)

As for the men, although they can be "brave and patriotic" (77) they display "an extraordinary degree of bigotry . . . upheld with a ferocity that frequently gives rise to scenes of blood" (75-6).

Aspin's explanation for the differences in national character he describes is largely ethnic, but significantly it is also in part cultural. The Swiss not only come from good Helvetian stock, but they have lived for years in a republic, and a mainly Protestant republic at that. The brutality of the Bavarians, by contrast, is the result of their having lived for generations under an absolutist Catholic monarchy. This means that for Aspin there is always the hope of progress: if the Bavarians would only catch up with the Reformation and the Enlightenment, in time they too might become civilized. Then again, the gloomy Prussians are Protestants, and even so they live under "a military despotism," where "[l]iterature is much neglected" in favour of "military parade" (61-2). Doubtless what they too need is that encouragement of debate, enterprise and eccentricity which the English find in their great traditions of literature and theatre.

The English were already showing these traditions off to the Swiss – or at least to the Genevans, who would join the confederation in 1814 – a century before this. Live English-speaking Shakespeare first reached the shores of Lac Leman in the 1730s, in a context not of insular home-sickness or self-assertion but of aristocratic cosmopolitanism. As an important stopping-off point for those taking the Grand Tour southwards into Italy, excitingly francophone but reassuringly Protestant, Geneva was a place where cultured young Englishmen abroad might meet people of their own rank, and preferably not just from their own country. Richard Aldworth Neville, for example, stayed in the city from 1738 to 1742, socializing not only with compatriots such as Lord Brook, William Windham, and the poets Benjamin Stillingfleet (later an associate of the important Shakespearean critic Elizabeth Montagu) and Charles Churchill (future author of *The Rosciad*), but with other visiting Europeans such as the Comtes de la Lippe, and with the Genevois themselves: indeed, Neville went on to marry the daughter of a local grandee, Madelaine Calandrini (Galiffe vol. 2, 557). This group engaged heavily in amateur dramatics: in 1738 they staged John Hughes' congenially anti-Catholic tragedy *The Siege of Damascus*, and on 15 January 1739, before an invited audience including most of the governing Conseil, they performed an abbreviated and slightly simplified all-male *Macbeth*, with Neville in the title role, and George Hervey, son of the bisexual Lord Hervey pilloried by Pope as "Sporus," playing Lady Macbeth. Further to accommodate the non-Anglophones in their audiences, Neville and his friends gave out printed texts of key extracts from the scripts, and on each of these ambitious bills literary tragedy was counterbalanced by a wordless comic pantomime (Stillingfleet vol. 1, 73-81). As Syndic François Calandrini's own diary records, Neville's future father-in-law was impressed – "les seigneurs étrangers," he wrote, "ont joué leurs comédies avec beaucoup de succès" – and that was clearly much of the point (Engel 3). Much as he functions for Parson Yorick in Sterne's *A Sentimental Journey* (1768), this was Shakespeare as passport to the right European connections.

After Waterloo, however, when British military power and diplomatic leverage had helped to install reactionary governments right across Europe, live Shakespeare on the Grand Tour became something altogether less tentative. In the 1820s, one palazzo in Florence declared itself to be *de facto* British soil by mounting a series of untranslated productions of Shakespeare, including that garrison favourite, *Henry IV part 1*. The presiding actor-manager was a diplomat, Constantine Phipps, 1st Marquess of Normanby, author of *The English in Italy* (1825). He had always been stage-struck, and only the threat of being disinherited had prevented him, while still a Cambridge undergraduate, from marrying the actress Eliza O'Neill. Normanby's rank made these performances a suitable topic for sycophantic comment by society journalists, significantly not just in the local English newsletter but back in London:

> English theatricals in Florence. Extract from a letter dated Florence, December 8, 1829 . . . Last evening Lord Normanby opened the tasteful little Theatre he has had constructed in the Palazzo San Clementi [*sic*] which was filled by 400 persons of rank and fashion. Shakespeare's Historical Play of *King Henry the Fourth* (the first part), and the Farce of *Simpson and Co*, constituted the evening's entertainment . . . (NYPL)

The cast's status, furthermore, guaranteed that their performances would be unctuously well-received by those keenest to boast that they had been present:

> Where each filled his part so well it would be invidious to particularize. Lady Normanby [Lady Percy] acted delightfully . . . Lord Normanby [Hotspur], Mr Craven [Prince Hal], and Mr Mathews [Falstaff] evinced the greatest talent . . . the whole performance went off with the greatest *éclat*.
> (NYPL)

Transforming the British present into the natives and construing everyone else present as foreign wannabes, these performances predictably infuriated the most articulate non-British member of Normanby's invited audience, the American novelist James Fenimore Cooper. To the author of *The Last of the Mohicans*, they amounted merely to mediocre and parochial transplants from the stately homes of England, produced with an insolent disregard for their Italian surroundings. "We have seen Shakespeare in the hands of these noble actors once or twice," he wrote in *Gleanings in Europe: Italy*,

> and found the representation neither quite good enough to please, nor yet bad enough to laugh at. . . . It was like all private theatricals, good enough for a country house, but hardly in its place in the capital of Tuscany.
> (Cooper 24-5; see also Beard 346; Dentler 188; Garlington 87)

Despite this discouraging review, however, in 1830 another such group performed another *Henry IV part 1* in English, this time back on the far side of the Alps, in Geneva.

The big difference with the 1830 *Henry IV* – and part of what makes it a particularly intriguing and conflicted specimen of expatriate Shakespeare, divided between seeing Shakespeare as innately British and as eminently transplantable – is that its instigator and moving spirit was not English but a native Genevois, the bilingual Charles Michel Lullin.

After his patrician family were ruined by the French revolution, Lullin, able to pass as either English or French, was recruited by the spymaster William Wickham in 1793 to infiltrate and monitor possible political conspiracies among French émigrés in London (see Galiffe vol. 1, 110; Wickham esp. vol. 2, 145). Away from his desk at the Aliens Office, he became a passionate theatregoer, and a friend of the thoroughly counter-revolutionary Shakespearean actor-manager John Philip Kemble (see Jones). Combining work and play, Lullin kept an eye on London's French community by engaging key members in amateur dramatics, including a production of his own French verse translation of *Richard III* in 1799, apparently at his own house in Stafford Place, Pimlico. This show, based on Kemble's acting text of the Cibber adaptation, is memorably described in the memoirs of the Vicomte Gauthier de Brécy, a keen amateur actor who also took part in the Margravine of Anspach's Anglo-French private theatricals at Brandenburgh House in Hammersmith. Lullin's double casting of this exiled aristocrat cannily made Shakespeare's play encode the perfect royalist fantasy of vindication and restoration: in the first scene of the play de Brécy played Henry VI, the rightful king martyred by the usurper, and in the last he played Richmond, the exile who returns to avenge him and claim the crown from the usurper (Brécy 282-4). Lullin and his English wife Nancy staged other plays too: they were condescendingly described as "Swiss refugees and semi-gentlefolks" by the future Countess Canning when they later performed Racine's *Mithridate* before the exiled dukes of Berri and Angoulême at 3 St James' Square (Hare vol. 3, 385), but they were more warmly received when they and another cast of expatriates performed Racine's *Bérénice* at the home of an exiled Swiss doctor in Bloomsbury. (This was 23, Russell Square, subsequently the offices of Faber and Faber, just opposite what is now Birkbeck College). Joanna Baillie's friend Mary Berry, for instance, among an appreciative and fashionable audience, was delighted to have this rare opportunity to "admire the beauty of Racine's most French tragedy" (Lewis vol. 2, 476-7).

A sort of cross between Nick Bottom and the Scarlet Pimpernel, Lullin clearly knew all about the potential cultural cachet to be gained from being the right kind of foreigner in the right wrong place at the right time: as the old maxim has it, "when in Rome, do as the Greeks do." Having performed Shakespeare and Racine in French in London, when Lullin returned home to Geneva on a British government pension after the defeat of Napoleon he took to performing in English instead. Dedicating himself to providing hospitality to British visitors (among them Kemble, who retired to Lausanne), founding an Anglican church, and arranging performances of English plays at a purpose-built music room and expatriates' club known as "the Cassino", Lullin became

known in his homeland as "Lullin l'Anglais" (Offord 5-6). Augustin
Pyramus de Candolle, for instance, writing to Madame de Circourt on
13 July 1831, reported that Geneva was having a particularly brilliant
summer of culture: "d'un côté Mlle Duchesnois joue au théâtre, et Mr.
Lullin donne au Casino ses representations anglaises" (de Candolle 14).

In 1830 Lullin's English offerings were Otway's *Venice Preserv'd*, an
unnamed farce, and *Henry IV part 1*. Colonel Thomas Bradyll, already
famed for his performances at Wellington's headquarters during the
Peninsular War (Fletcher 88), played Falstaff: along with Nancy, Lullin's
fellow-actors also included his sister Anna and her politician husband
Jean Gabriel Eynard, both of whom had performed in scenes from
Shakespeare in Madame de Staël's salons, and who built private theatres
of their own in their apartment on the Cour St Pierre, at their country
house at Beaulieu outside Lausanne, and later in their commanding
Genevan town-house, the Palais Eynard (Alville 98-103). Lullin, like
Normanby, probably took Kemble's old role of Hotspur. He added further Anglophile credentials to this season by commissioning prologues
from Geneva's resident English poet: sadly, he had missed Byron and
Shelley by more than a decade, and now had to resort to the notorious
old bibliophile and snob Sir Samuel Egerton Brydges (see Maginn).
Brydges had been acquainted with Byron, and was still in correspon-
dence with major poets such as Southey, Wordsworth and Walter Scott.
He would have to do.

A decade of exile had at least compelled Brydges to give the question
of national identity some serious thought. Having bankrupted himself
making unsuccessful claims to be the rightful Baron Chandos, Brydges
had settled in Geneva in 1821, where he continued to dilate on his life
and opinions, especially in a magazine which he grandly called *The Anglo-
Genevan Critical Journal*. Disappointed to find that earlier English settlers
had made little impact on the Genevan gene-pool, Brydges was acutely
conscious of the collective insularity of his fellow expatriates. "It is the
fault of the English . . . when they come abroad," he wrote,

> still to live too much with one another. As islanders, it is long before we en-
> tirely abandon our strong peculiarities, and our conceit of the exclusive su-
> periority of all our own modes and customs and ideas. The English are [not]
> only esteemed proud by other nations, but really are so. The consequence
> is, that though they are feared, they are little loved by them.
>
> (Brydges *Autobiography* vol. 2, 102-3)

Brydges was suitably gratified, then, to be made much of by Lullin,
whom he praises in his poem *The Lake of Geneva* both as one "renown'd
upon the private stage, – / The oracle, thro whose lips miraculous

Shakespeare / Speaks" and as the "warmest in friendship and in hospitality" of all the many local patricians he catalogues (Brydges *Lake of Geneva* vol. 1, 129). A report on his work in progress for Lullin is full of self-congratulation: "I have written 4 Prologues for some intended Private Theatricals here," he wrote to a friend in London, "– Two for Venice Preserved – One for Henry IV. One occasional . . ." (Jones 328). Ever keen to name-drop, Brydges went on to remember the previous occasion on which he had been similarly employed:

> You will observe that I never wrote but one Prologue before, and that was 44 years ago for a private Theatre in Hampshire at Mr Austen's, the father of Jane Austen, author of *Pride and Prejudice* – *Northanger Abbey*, etc. See *Quarterly Review*. (Jones 328-9)

Brydges was sufficiently pleased with these latest efforts to publish them repeatedly, at first printing only his *Prologue for Shakespeare's Henry IV, Written for a Private Theatre at Geneva*, then publishing all *Four Prologues for a Private English Theatre at Geneva*, 1830, which then reappeared in *The Anglo-Genevan Critical Journal for 1831*.

These eloquent and largely incoherent pieces of verse demonstrate if nothing else how badly-suited the British nativist tradition of Bardolatry was to the task of presenting Shakespeare to non-British audiences. In his "Prologue. For Shakespeare's Henry IV. Written 13 Jan. 1830," for instance, Brydges instinctively adopts the rhetorical mode of David Garrick's Jubilee ode (1769), which commits him to an opening gambit of celebrating Shakespeare as utterly indigenous. *Henry IV* is initially offered as the expression of a British national character acquired primarily through genetics:

> IN every Land the sages say we trace
> Th'hereditary feature mark the face.
> But not alone distinct their outward forms;
> Their nobler part distinctive genius warms.
> With scornful pride each Nation boasts its Muse,
> Whose rays are tinted with unrival'd hues!
> Let but a Briton step upon the stage,
> Whence will he draw the glass for every age?
> To one lov'd fount of magic he will go;
> With one lov'd name his head and heart will glow;
> One only volume will his hand unroll;
> SHAKESPEARE, the mighty master of the soul!
> Him, with one voice whom varying critics praise;
> Him, the great theme of every poet's lays!
>   (Brydges *Anglo-Genevan* vol. 1, 303-5)

That's all very well for the British, clearly, but what about the Swiss? It is telling that Lullin had to ask Brydges to rewrite his prologue to *Venice Preserved* to include some remarks addressed specifically to a Genevan audience, and it looks as though the *Henry IV* prologue may have undergone the same process. Turning as if in embarrassment to apostrophize Falstaff at first instead of the Genevois, Brydges rather awkwardly and alienatingly classifies the fat knight's local spectators as "foreign":

> O soul of wit and humour, that attest
> The genuine sunshine of the social breast;
> Unseen before, unimitated since;
> Yet where each word, each look of life convince;
> Rare FALSTAFF, in the drama of life's stage
> Unique; to youth surprising; – new to age;
> Let foreign eyes thy form of fun behold;
> And foreign ears attend thy vein of gold!
> (Brydges *Anglo-Genevan* vol. 1, 303-5)

When it comes to actually speaking to these foreign ears, Brydges finds himself perversely having to argue that it is because the Alpine landscape is so unlike that of Shakespeare's England that its inhabitants should appreciate his work. Since the Genevans inhabit a romantic landscape, he claims, they should be ideally susceptible to the romantic magic of Shakespearean nostalgia:

> Ye, whom the blue Lake, clos'd by mountains hoar,
> Whispers to love all grand and genuine lore,
> Gaze on the glories of a British spell;
> Let your hearts on his vanish'd heroes dwell . . .
> (Brydges *Anglo-Genevan* vol. 1, 303-5)

In his thoroughly convoluted peroration, Brydges takes this idea further, suggesting that since the liberty-loving Swiss take their character from a sublime natural landscape, they may be able to appreciate Shakespeare's sublime genius, even in Geneva.

> Mid rocks and mountains and the torrent's roar,
> And cataracts that down precipices pour,
> If aught sublimer from the outward forms
> The spirit, that presides within us, warms,
> Here mayst thou have the seat of thy sublime!
> Here mayst thou listen to the noblest rhyme!
> Children of Freedom, born amid the show
> Of Nature's grandest works, may learn to glow

With strains, from Nature's loftiest Bard that flow!
(Brydges *Anglo-Genevan* vol. 1, 303-5)

The problem of offering what he still regards as innately British national culture to a European audience, clearly, deeply puzzles Brydges – hence the big "if" in that last passage. In the last of these prologues, indeed, contradicting his introduction to *Henry IV*, Brydges is forced to admit that national difference did nothing to prevent Byron and Rousseau being spiritually akin. As a result he ends up suggesting that the Swiss may enjoy Shakespeare and his literary compatriots not because of their excitingly foreign landscape, but despite it:

> What then is MIND? does climate, image, lot,
> Or form of government, or choice of spot,
> Wealth, poverty, or joy, or grief, bestow
> The breath that bids the flame of genius glow?
> Ah, not confin'd to climate, country, state, –
> MIND is above all fortune, and all fate!
> Rousseau and Byron, sons alike of fire,
> In their own flames were fated to expire!
>
> Here then congenial is the generous breast;
> Tho' mountains, with eternal snows opprest,
> Hang on thy walls, and suns of rosy ray
> Unfelt upon thy cloud-capt mountains play, . . .
> Here may the land of Avon's matchless Bard
> Claim for its golden tales the fair reward!
> (Brydges *Anglo-Genevan* vol. 1, 306-8)

Sadly, the sole extant contemporary comment on the performances introduced by these prologues, – in the *Dublin Literary Gazette, or Weekly Chronicle of Criticism, Belles Lettres, and Fine Arts* (Feb 1830 no 6, 140) – records only that the decor of these productions was more impressive than their acting. As far as I have been able to discover, Brydges' rhetorical efforts to present Falstaff to the Genevois as the perfect ambassador for British culture produced no long-term effects whatsoever: when it came to drama, the city still belonged to Voltaire rather than to Shakespeare. (Indeed, even when Geneva finally did acquire a permanent Geneva English Drama Society in 1933, it refused to perform any Shakespeare at all for the first forty years of its existence.) But then, why would a francophone city be interested in an exclusively anglophone Shakespeare anyway, save for reasons with little to do with its own dramatic traditions and everything to do with cultivating a nascent world power? (When Charles Kemble's company performed *Romeo and Juliet* and *Hamlet* in Paris in 1827, they had the sense to supply their audiences with crib-translations of the script). What European romantics more interested in their own cultures needed from Shakespeare was a source and stimulus for their national theatres and literary canons, not further advertisements for Britain's.

From this perspective, Brydges, unfortunately, was at the wrong end of the country. Shakespeare's most important Swiss admirers had already been busily laying the groundwork for his naturalization into their own drama-poor language for decades, but they had been doing so in Zurich, the city of Wieland, Eschenburg, Bodmer and Fuseli; and Fuseli, who had been painting the fat knight for years, certainly didn't need any prologue by Brydges to introduce him to Falstaff (see Stadler). But all this had been happening neither in English nor in French, and the really significant event of the 1830s for the subsequent development of European Shakespeare would not be these Genevan performances of *Henry IV* in English but the completion of the Schlegel-Tieck translation of the Complete Works into German. In practice when it came to live Shakespeare, much of Switzerland would remain a province of Greater Germany, presenting the plays not in English or French or *Schweizerdeutsch* but in *Schriftdeutsch*. As in other parts of Europe, in Switzerland Shakespeare would appear on stage not as Britain's national poet but as the third German classic.

2. Hamlet in Bavaria

This is not to say that English-language productions of Shakespeare haven't occasionally visited German-speaking regions of Europe too, nor that some haven't even originated in them. Some of the most surprising and little-known Shakespearean revivals to have been mounted by English performers in Germany proper, for instance, took place after Bavaria, Prussia and other neighbouring regions had already been enjoying the civilizing benefits of English drama in translation for a century and a half. In this second case-study, I want to examine the surviving traces of some of these shows, uneasy hybrids between the garrison model of expatriate theatre and the diplomatic, produced during a period when the Bavarians had other things on their minds than the pampering of cats. I want to examine the sometimes troubling ways in which these more recent expatriate Shakespeares bring together questions of national identity and questions of sexual identity, and consider how far it is theatrical patronage and censorship which decide whose notion of cultural transmission any given performance serves. These more modern expatriate productions may at first glance look as insular as Lord Normanby's *Henry IV* in Florence, but that isn't the whole story.

By the middle of the twentieth century, as the foundation of the Geneva English Drama Society suggests, the voluntary, non-commercial British theatre was experiencing something of a boom. This was true both at home and abroad. One especially fine non-professional *Hamlet*, for example, elegantly dressed and superbly photographed, was welcomed by eager capacity audiences of expatriates at every single one of its performances. (For surviving images, see Goodliffe; Loder). Michael Goodliffe, admittedly, who directed and took the title role, had formerly been a professional actor, who had appeared with Laurence Olivier in Tyrone Guthrie's production of *Othello* at the Old Vic. He had also seen Olivier play Hamlet there for Guthrie in 1937, and something of Olivier's celebrated feeling for visual line is surely imitated in the careful poise of Goodliffe's silhouetted fingers in the photograph depicting Hamlet's audience with the Ghost. Goodliffe's Ophelia, by contrast, had no professional stage experience at all: he was a junior British army officer called John Dixon. This *Hamlet* was first staged at Oflag VIIIB prisoner-of-war camp in Tittmoning, Bavaria, in early 1941, and it was then repeated with a different supporting cast after Goodliffe was transferred to Oflag VIIC at Eichstätt later in the war.

Although this is one aspect of prisoner-of-war life which has been kept well out of British popular memory, Axis camps like these in occupied Europe played host between 1940 and 1945 to what was easily the largest flowering of English single-sex theatre since Shakespeare's own time. Nor should this particularly surprise us. Even if the recent conscripts and volunteers who found themselves in captivity after Dunkirk hadn't included a few ex-professional actors and a far larger number of amateurs with experience in the amateur groups which flourished between the wars, many imprisoned servicemen would probably have picked up a taste for dressing up anyway from the seasoned career officers in their midst. In both the Navy and the Army, as in other all-male institutions such as boys' schools, in-house communal theatre had remained socially important. It had also, necessarily, remained single-sexed, just as on board the *Red Dragon* in 1607 or in Geneva in 1739, so that the armed forces provided one haven in which some of the conventions of the Renaissance stage had never quite died out. Lord William Lennox, writing in 1878, describes a standard practice of co-opting "beardless ensigns" to play female roles in the amateur performances which "in almost every garrison town, in our colonies . . . enliven the monotony of winter quarters" (Lennox vol. 2, 100-1). In this single-sexed thespian army, then, it's no wonder that in 1940 Michael Goodliffe, as the only fully-qualified actor in the camp to which he was sent after being captured during the fall of France, should have been seized upon at once by its senior British officer, General Victor Fortune, who in the interests of morale ordered him to "Put on some shows as soon as you can" (Goodliffe). Even with clothing in desperately short supply as the winter of 1940 set in, the quest for promising cross-dressers was on.

What might surprise us more than its scale or its enforced transvestism is that in an age of mass entertainment and mass conscription any of these captive military theatricals should have involved Shakespeare. It's true that during the First World War a group of aesthetes among the internees at Ruhleben camp in Berlin had staged an all-male *As You Like It*, and that this incident had been cited by some Old Vic supporters between the wars when arguing, rather in the manner of Brydges, for Shakespeare's status as the supreme and natural exemplar of disinterested British culture. At the time, however, other Ruhleben prisoners had been scathing about this enterprise, much preferring their home-grown theatrical repertory to revolve around musical comedy and revue (see Hoenselaars), and even the ambitiously high-minded Goodliffe produced sketch shows and a Christmas pantomime before undertaking his *Hamlet* in 1941. As a number of military archives show, that's much more what PoWs generally staged, when left to their own devices: revues and pantos, with occasional forays into recent middlebrow plays and popular musicals. A whole troupe of brassiered Geordies, the "Northern Lights" company, performed an item called "Perchance in Greece" in one of their revues at the large Stalag 383 camp at Hohenfels in Bavaria, where they were by no means the only purveyors of such entertainment, and the camp's Christmas pantomime for 1942, *Aladdin*, contained even more male-to-female cross-dressing than did its counterparts in the commercial theatre at home. (The following Christmas they put on *Dick Whittington*, complete with added mermaids). The same fat album in the National Army Museum in London which documents these shows, compiled by one R. J. Duncan, records that this theatre's finest hour was its production of Gilbert and Sullivan's *The Mikado*, which apparently so delighted the camp's commandant that he cancelled roll-call for three days as a reward (McKibbin 84; Duncan). Other such establishments too, even those reserved for hardened would-be escapees, showed similar theatrical tastes. The first show mounted at Colditz, in November 1941, was a revue called *Ballet Nonsense*, dominated by the display of home-made tutus (Mackenzie 210), and the establishment's thespians rarely ventured into anything more highbrow than Noel Coward thereafter.

The style of cross-dressed performance required by a successful male Gertrude or male Gertrude Lawrence, however, is obviously different to

the burlesque manner favoured in a sketch show like *Ballet Nonsense*, and
Goodliffe for one recognized that if he was to produce "straight" drama
at all with all-male casts his audiences were going to have to unlearn
their modern understanding of what stage drag meant. In the face of a
conditioned reflex of giggling, he later remembered, "we soon found
that unless the presentation of female roles was intelligently tackled, any
serious productions were impossible" (Goodliffe). It may be significant
here that despite staging two *Hamlets* and a *King Lear*, among many other
shows, Goodliffe's most elaborate Shakespearean revival was the *Comedy
of Errors* he mounted at Eichstätt in December 1943 (see Goodliffe;
Mansel 136). Although in this PoW context the frame-narrative of the
play must have been especially poignant – dramatizing as it does
Egeon's captivity in a hostile country and his ultimate release and reun-
ion with his family – the main plot was handled very lightly, the cast
dressed in comic and sometimes mildly salacious Regency costumes
which included a split red satin skirt for the Courtesan capable of being
detached from her dress to reveal elaborate lingerie. The play was entirely set to music, like a Viennese operetta, and was billed as that year's
Christmas pantomime. Despite this ultimate concession to the panto
tradition, however, Goodliffe claimed after the war that in his serious
productions, especially his Shakespeares, the cross-dressing conventions
of the Renaissance had been fully recovered: "Two or three clever actors solved this problem [with the female roles], so that our audiences
accepted them exactly as the Elizabethans accepted their boy-actors"
(Goodliffe).

In certain respects, the subculture which grew up around these prisoner-of-war playhouses did indeed hark back to Shakespeare's own theatrical world. As Stephen Orgel has shown, one of the reasons the early
modern English had all-male theatre companies was a belief that males
were simply better at performing, including performing as women; and
this belief surfaced once more during the war. Describing the 1942
Eichstätt pantomime in his diary, for example, John Mansel was especially impressed by Brian McIrvine, who had played Gertrude for Michael Goodliffe:

> Citronella (Brian McIrvine) is staggering and in a dance with the Prince,
> himself quite excellent, performs a dance at which the average girl would
> make a poor attempt. There is graceful movement accompanied by perfect
> control . . . (Mansel 68)

Such specialists in female roles, moreover, like Stalag 383's "Pinkie"
Smith, attracted cult followings of which seventeenth-century boy-
players like Solomon Pavey or Edward Kynaston would have been

proud: according to one prisoner, they "really needed protection going 'home' to their barracks after the shows" (Palmer 179). "Of course lots of the fellows have done this stuff previous to the war & we have some celebrities to be sure!", wrote one captured bombardier in a letter home about the theatrical scene at his own camp in Italy, ". . . some of the fellows have to take girls' parts & they are real knockouts . . ." (Good). Adulation of the beardless-ensign-come-boy-actor seems to have been especially marked at Stalag VIIIB, at Lamsdorf in Silesia, where an impressive *Twelfth Night* was staged in 1943 [Figure 2].

Figure 2. *Twelfth Night*, Stalag VIIIB, Lamsdorf, 1943. Bequest of Corporal Peter Peel (Sebastian, left). Courtesy of Second World War Experience Centre, Leeds.

This group picture was taken at the dress rehearsal, with a home-made camera. On the left, playing Sebastian, is Corporal Peter Peel, who saved this photo; and on the right, playing Viola, is a young RAF wireless operator called Denholm Elliott. Elliott seems to have enjoyed a level of idolization at Lamsdorf after which his post-war stage and screen career could only be an anticlimax. "Any person who played the [female] lead role in the camp theatre was considered to be a heart-throb," remembered his fellow-inmate George Moreton. "'She' had more fans and more people dreaming about 'her' than 'she' would ever imagine. When 'she' walked down the road, eyes would follow 'her' adoringly" (Moreton 96). This is borne out by a sailor called Andrew Macdonald-Bell, who recalled Elliott's Viola with the understated lyricism of the time:

> Spellbound, we watched and listened as first he presented as a girl, then as a girl pretending to be a youth, then again as a girl . . . [The following morning], [q]uite on impulse, I walked over to the slim lad who had been Viola, and I thanked him for his marvellous performance. Denholm smiled, a long-lipped Irish sort of smile. "Glad you liked it," he said, while his quiet eyes drifted shyly away from mine and his hand went up to finger back a flopping wing of dark hair. (Elliott 44-5)

As in the Elizabethan age, too, these latterday boy-players attracted some equally passionate anti-theatrical sentiment, both secular and religious. The Lamsdorf camp newsletter *Stimmt*, for instance, ran a sustained editorial campaign against "theatre 'pansies' and their bitchy admirers" (Mackenzie 212), while the diary of Ellison Platt, the Methodist padre at Colditz, is full of more pious outrage about the criminally tempting defiance of God's prohibition against cross-dressing, Deuteronomy 22:5, which he was compelled to witness in *Ballet Nonsense* and its successors.

As Marjorie Garber has pointed out, however, troubled attention to the transgression of gender boundaries represented by cross-dressing is always liable to represent the displacement of anxieties about different border transgressions entirely (Garber ch. 10). In the case of the born-again Renaissance boy-players of the Oflags and Stalags, what may be much more disturbing than their potential for sexual ambiguity is an ambiguity as to whose larger cultural and national agenda their transvestite performances were really serving. After all, these theatres were actually German, and even the revues mounted in them sometimes betrayed as vivid an engagement with German culture as with British. In Stalag 383, for instance, the revue "Bally Who" included a skit on Goethe called "Soust" (see Duncan). Did such Allied actors as these really perform strictly as homesick warriors, bravely sustaining their comrades' national identity in the interests of combatant morale, or were they for the time being good puppet citizens of Fortress Europe, entertaining their captors and keeping their colleagues from more belligerent thoughts? Theatre as elaborate as this would have been impossible without at the very least the toleration of the Nazi authorities, and this toleration often extended to actual assistance when it came to procuring make-up, lighting equipment, photographic facilities, printed programmes, and so on. As long as prisoners did not attempt to abscond in the civilian clothes they were allowed to wear in modern plays, camp guards were generally more than happy to see their charges occupied with theatricals, not only because such activities kept the Red Cross happy too, but because they usefully distracted many inmates from their professed military duty to escape. Given good enough productions of *Hamlet*, it appears, some prisoners could have been bounded in a nutshell and counted themselves kings of infinite space. "The entertainments as a whole, after [escape attempts], were the most important part of Camp life," recalled one of Goodliffe's actors, Robert Loder. "Some officers, not interested in escape work, used to get exceptionally annoyed if their regular entertainment was disrupted [by escape alerts]." (See the Loder papers, which also preserve several commercial make-up catalogues).

General, pragmatic toleration extended to definite patronage, however, when it came to camp performances of Shakespeare. As far as I have been able to tell, whenever Allied prisoners of war staged Shakespeare in Europe they did so with the active sponsorship and encouragement of the German authorities. Just as Shakespeare's company had operated under conditions provided and dictated by the Master of the Revels, so Goodliffe and his peers were ultimately working for the Master Race. It can't be accidental that Goodliffe didn't produce *Henry IV* as his first Shakespeare play, never mind *Henry V*, but instead offered a play which his captors regarded as a supreme triumph of Aryan high art. *Hamlet* had of course been the most important Shakespearean play for any self-respecting German since before young Werther got sorrowful (the Nazis' chief legal theorist, Carl Schmitt, would even publish a whole monograph about it after being deprived of his Berlin professorship in 1945), and Goodliffe's two productions were duly provided with costumes specially obtained for him from the Munich opera house: so was his Strauss-like *Comedy of Errors*. In a regime otherwise committed to extirpating all signs of sexual deviation in the interests of normative reproduction, cross-dressing by Englishmen performing in Shakespeare could apparently be permitted and even encouraged. Perhaps for the camp authorities the practice offered antiquarian glimpses of that odd offshore pre-history Shakespeare had enjoyed in the bad old days before he became German.

As in the case of this *Hamlet*, professionally-made costumes were also procured, from the Breslau opera house, for the Lamsdorf *Twelfth Night* – not coincidentally, the Shakespearean comedy revived most frequently in Germany during the 1930s, when a ban on decadent modern drama made Shakespeare more prominent than ever in the generously state-funded playhouses. The Germans, amazingly, even took this *Twelfth Night* on tour to other camps, transporting its cast around the country in Wehrmacht lorries which might otherwise have been moving supplies to the Eastern front. But then the Third Reich was serious about Shakespeare. In 1830 Brydges had seen Shakespeare as part of the genetic make-up of the English, and by 1911 Arthur Buckley could describe Stratford as "a temple dedicated to the genius of the Anglo-Celtic race" (Buckley viii). In 1940 the German writer Hermann Burte, delivering a lecture in Weimar on the eve of the Battle of Britain, similarly saw Shakespeare as part of an ethnic inheritance, albeit one which in his erstwhile homeland had now been fatally contaminated:

> Shakespeare ist der Unsere so gut wie der seiner Engländer, ja, wir kennen und spielen ihn besser als jene und behaupten kühn, daß wir als Deutsche von 1940 dem Geist der elisabethanischen Engländer und ihrem Genius William in Warheit näherstehen als die Englischen von heute, hinter deren Thron jener Shylock steckt und herrscht, den Shakespeare erkannte und – verwarf!

> [Shakespeare belongs as much to us as he does to the English . . . We Germans of 1940 are in truth closer to the spirit of the Elizabethan English and their genius William than the Englishmen of today, behind whose throne lurks and rules that Shylock whom Shakespeare recognized and – rejected!]
> (Burte 20; and see Mosse 141-4; Symington 244; Heinrich 192-4)

This remark, I think, provides a useful gloss on one incongruous item in Stalag 383's otherwise studiously undemanding repertory. It's the sole Shakespeare play this theatre ever attempted, and one of the only plays on the list R. J. Duncan preserved of its productions from which no photographs are displayed in his album: *The Merchant of Venice*. It would be nice to be able to pretend that what was still at the time the most often-revived Shakespearean comedy among English professionals and amateurs alike (see Markús) had been chosen for revival at this camp in sheer crass obliviousness to what ideological charge the play might carry in Hitler's Bavaria. But the cheerful account of life at Stalag 383 published after the war by N. M. McKibbin sadly makes this impossible:

> One useful gesture the Jerries did make was to loan us the complete costumes for *The Merchant of Venice* from the State Theatre of Berlin; and though this was done simply because they considered it an anti-Jewish play, it was none the less welcome. A grand production was most enthusiastically received. . . (McKibbin 85)

It is true that McKibbin, writing in 1947, after the doings of Stalag 383 had been rather upstaged by revelations about what had been happening at another camp only fifty miles away, Dachau, was at pains to remember this production as having challenged Nazism rather than collaborated with it. "I remember few more impressive performances," he continues, "than that of Bob Jarvis, an Australian professional, who gave Shylock a fine dignity rather disturbing to the Germans in the stalls" (McKibbin 85-86). But he seems unnaturally keen, just as Garber might predict, to change the subject immediately to that of the camp's "fellows who could make up to look like girls – glamorous and sophisticated girls," our "female impersonators," or rather "actors taking female parts, which is quite a different thing." "Shylock's daughter," he recalls, "was played by a sergeant whose name escapes me . . ." (McKibbin 85-86). It doesn't appear, then, that this production adopted the change to Shakespeare's script followed by Nazi dramaturgs, whereby Jessica became an adopted Gentile so that Lorenzo could enjoy a miscegenation-free elopement, but for McKibbin the point here is not the defence of interracial marriage but the vindication of cross-gender casting: "Under the magic of the Theatre the character was just Jessica and it was as easy to accept her beauty as to accept Lorenzo and the moonlit bank the lovers sat upon" (85-6). According to McKibbin, it appears, thousand-year Reichs may come and go, but world-beating British military cross-dressing goes on forever. But which factor was uppermost in determining what this performance, and others like it, could mean – the transvestite skills of its cast, or the vested interests of its sponsors? Despite being staged in English to a mainly English audience, this surely was a genuinely European Shakespeare, serving a vision of a pan-European literary canon. Unfortunately it was a vision much more determined to explain European identity in exclusionary racial terms even than Aspin's *Cosmorama* a century earlier.

Posterity has not been kind to either Samuel Egerton Brydges or Michael Goodliffe. Brydges died in 1837 without having made Geneva into a hotbed of live Shakespeare, and he is now remembered primarily in the footnotes to biographies of Jane Austen, who thought his fiction was dire (le Faye 22). Michael Goodliffe, after having the ill fortune to give his greatest Shakespearean performances under the patronage of a German regime which saw no contradiction between supporting high culture and carrying out genocide, managed an inconspicuous post-war career, often in prisoner-of-war films, before committing suicide in 1976. Their respective forgotten ventures in expatriate English-speaking amateur theatre now look like dead ends, Goodliffe's a not entirely honourable one. Between the German prison guards anxious to disown their Nazi pasts and the British casts and audiences anxious to forget having just-about collaborated with them, it is quite possible that after the 1940s nobody was able to remember Goodliffe's productions of Shakespeare, brilliant as they clearly were, with any pleasure. Even any visiting Red Cross officials who may have seen them have recently had the tale of their own blamelessly humanitarian role in the war sullied by the revelation that their organization knew about the Holocaust as early as the summer of 1942 but remained silent on the subject (presumably under pressure from the Swiss government of the time), something for which they officially apologized only in 1996. Sadly, for some in Switzerland neutrality and a tradition of Anglophilia didn't preclude selling hi-tech weapons to Hitler and banking gold melted down from dental fillings (see Ziegler).

As an Elizabethan whose works have incongruously survived into the 21st century, Shakespeare is nowadays at least as much a foreigner in England as he is anywhere else: the past, too, is another country. But Romanticism, unfortunately, established so decisively at the Stratford jubilee in 1769, in the long term managed to export not only Shakespeare to other countries such as Switzerland and Germany but the idea of culture as the indigenous and exclusive voice of the native soil. It would be comforting, but misleading, I fear, to think of this too as a historic mistake now long-abandoned. As the worst recession since the 1930s deepens, extreme right-wing nationalism is again making gains across our continent, and in the summer of 2009 Britain managed to export two further commodities to Europe; two Members of the European Parliament representing the British National Party. As their manifesto shows, this organization believes – despite his own enthusiasm for the establishment of the European Common Market – that Winston Churchill is on their side. It would be a pity if the notion of Shakespearean drama as an indigenous genetically-transmitted heritage were still sufficiently prevalent for them to retain the idea that Shakespeare is too.

References

Alville [Alix de Wattewille]. *Anna Eynard-Lullin et l'époque des congrès et des révolutions*. Lausanne: Feissly, 1955.

Aspin, J. *Cosmorama; a View of the Costumes and Peculiarities of All Nations*. London: Harris, [1827].

Beard, James Franklin, ed. *The Letters and Journals of James Fenimore Cooper*, vol 1. Cambridge, Massachusetts: Harvard University Press, 1960.

Brécy, le Vicomte Gauthier de. *Mémoires véridiques et ingénus de la vie privée, morale et politique d'un homme de bien*. Paris: Guiraudet, 1834.

Brydges, Sir Samuel Egerton. *The Anglo-Genevan Critical Journal for 1831*. 2 vols. Geneva: Vignier, 1831.

———. *The Autobiography, Times, Opinions, and Contemporaries, of Sir Egerton Brydges, Bart*. 2 vols. London: Cochrane and M'Crone, 1834.

———. *The Lake of Geneva*. 2 vols. Geneva: Vignier, 1832.

Buckley, Reginald R. *The Shakespeare Revival and the Stratford-upon-Avon Monument*. London: Allen and Son, 1911.

Burte, Hermann. *Sieben Reden von Burte*. Strassburg: Hunenburg, 1943.

Cooper, James Fenimore. *Gleanings in Europe: Italy*. 1838. Ed. John Conron and Constance Ayers Denne. Albany, New York: State University of New York Press, 1981.

de Candolle, Roger, ed. *L'Europe de 1830: vue à travers la correspondence de Augustin Pyramus de Candolle et Madame de Circourt*. Geneva: A. Jullien, 1966.

Dentler, Clara L. *Famous Foreigners in Florence, 1400-1900*. Florence: Bemporad Marzocco, 1964.

Duncan, R. J. Album of theatrical records and photographs from Stalag 383. National Army Museum, London. NAM 1999-03-45.

Elliott, Susan, with Barry Turner. *Denholm Elliott: Quest for Love*. 1994. London: Headline, 1995.

Engel, Claire-Eliane. "Shakespeare in Switzerland in the XVIIIth Century," *Comparative Literary Studies* XVII-XVIII (1945): 2-9.

Fletcher, Ian, ed. *For King and Country: The Letters and Diaries of John Mills, Coldstream Guards, 1811-14*. Staplehurst: Spellmont, 1995.

Galiffe, J.A. and others. *Notices généalogiques sur les familles genevoises*. 6 vols. Geneva: Barbezat and others, 1830-92.

Garber, Marjorie. *Vested Interests: Cross-Dressing and Cultural Anxiety*. New York: Routledge, 1992.

Garlington, Aubrey S. *Society, Culture and Opera in Florence, 1814-1830: Dilettantes in an "Earthly Paradise."* Aldershot: Ashgate, 2005.

Good, George H. Letter, July 15 1943. National Army Museum, London. NAM 2001-06-224-73.

Goodliffe, Michael. *Memoirs*, quoted on www.mgoodliffe.co.uk

Hare, Augustus John Cuthbert. *The Story of Two Noble Lives*. 3 vols. London: Allen, 1893.

Heinrich, Anselm. *Entertainment, Propaganda, Education: Regional Theatre in Germany and Britain between 1918 and 1945*. Hatfield: University of Hertfordshire, 2007.

Hoenselaars, Ton. "ShakesPOW". Unpublished paper, SHINE conference. Iasi, Romania, 2007.

Jones, W. Powell. "Sir Egerton Brydges on Lord Byron." *Huntington Library Quarterly* 13:3 (May 1950): 325-37.

le Faye, Deirdre, ed. *The Letters of Jane Austen*. 1995. London: Folio Society, 2003.

Lennox, Lord William. *Fashion Then and Now*. 2 vols. London: Chapman and Hall, 1878.

Lewis, Lady Theresa, ed. *Extracts of the Journals and Correspondence of Miss Berry*. 3 vols. London: Longmans, 1866.

Loder, Brigadier Robert. Unpublished papers. King's College Archive Centre, Cambridge. GBR/0272/PP/Misc. 22/4.

Mackenzie, S.P. *The Colditz Myth: British and Commonwealth Prisoners of War in Nazi Germany*. Oxford: Oxford University Press, 2004.

Maginn, William. "Gallery of Literary Characters: Sir Egerton Brydges." *Fraser's Magazine* 9 (February 1834): 146.

Mansel, John. *The Mansel Diaries*. Ed. E. G. C. Beckwith. London: Wildwood, 1977.

Markús, Zoltán. *"Der Merchant von Velence: The Merchant of Venice* in London, Berlin, and Budapest during World War II." *Shakespeare and European Politics*. Ed. Dirk Delabastita, Jozef de Vos and Paul Franssen. Cranbury, New Jersey: Associated University Presses, 2008. 143-57.

McKibbin, N. M. *Barbed Wire: Memories of Stalag 383*. London: Staples, 1947.

Moreton, George. *Doctor in Chains*. London: Corgi, 1980.

Mosse, George. *Nazi Culture*. 1966. Madison, Wisconsin: University of Wisconsin Press, 2003.

New York Public Library: Unidentified contemporary press cutting, New York Public Library for the Performing Arts. MWEZ+nc.8748.

Offord, Valerie. "The Welcoming City." Exhibition catalogue, State Archives of Geneva, 2003: http://www.geneva-heritage.com-/ArchExhib/EngCat.pdf.

Orgel, Stephen. *Impersonations: The Performance of Gender in Early Modern England*. Cambridge: Cambridge University Press, 1996.

Palmer, Graham. *Prisoner of Death*. Wellingborough: Stephens, 1990.

Platt, Ellison. *Diary*. Imperial War Museum archive, London, 1941-1945

Stadler, Edmund, ed. *Shakespeare und die Schweiz*. Bern: Theaterkultur, 1964.

Stillingfleet, Benjamin. *Literary Life and Select Works of Benjamin Stillingfleet.* 2 vols. London: Longman, Hurst et al, 1811.

Symington, Rodney. *The Nazi Appropriation of Shakespeare: Cultural Politics in the Third Reich.* New York: Edwin Mellen, 2005.

Taylor, Gary. "*Hamlet* in Africa, 1607." *Travel Knowledge: European "Discoveries" in the Early Modern Period.* Ed. Ivo Kamps and Jyotsna Singh. London: Routledge, 2001. 223-48.

Wickham, William. *The Correspondence of the Right Honourable William Wickham, from the Year 1794 . . . , Edited, with Notes, by his Grandson, William Wickham MA.* 2 vols. London, 1870.

Wilson, Kathleen. "'Rowe's Fair Penitent as Global History: Or, a Diversionary Voyage to New South Wales." *Eighteenth-Century Studies* 41:2 (Winter 2008): 231-251.

Ziegler, Jean. *La Suisse, l'or et les morts.* Paris: Seuil, 1997.

Language, Ideology, Media and Social Change

Nikolas Coupland

Social change is rarely treated in sociolinguistics, even though other perspectives on change, and the specific interpretation of language change developed in variationist traditions, are fundamental. A concept of "sociolinguistic change" should be able to embed analyses of language change, taken to include change in the ideological loadings of linguistic varieties, within accounts of social change. The mass media, generally precluded from analyses of language change, are a powerful resource promoting and disseminating sociolinguistic change. "Standard" and "non-standard" language, interpreted as ideological attributions, are reassessed in relation to social change in Britain over the last 50 years, particularly changes in the constitution of social class. The framing and significance of class-related voices are then briefly explored in a sequence from the popular-culture, high-reach, British TV show, *Strictly Come Dancing*. Conventional sociolinguistic accounts of "standard" and "non-standard" speech fail to capture the characterological work done in the TV performance, and arguably much more generally in the less socially structured and more multi-centred and globalised circumstances of late modernity.

The main traditions in the study of dialect have had plenty to say about language change but little to say about *social* change, even though the two sorts of change are necessarily inter-related.[1] The very possibility of construing linguistic and social dimensions of change separately comes

[1] I am grateful to Justine Coupland, Peter Garrett and particularly Adam Jaworski for comments on an earlier draft and to Elen Robert, Janus Mortensen and Charlotte Selleck for their many contributions to discussions of these issues. An earlier version of this text was presented as a tribute to Tore Kristiansen on the happy occasion of his 60th birthday.

Performing the Self. SPELL: Swiss Papers in English Language and Literature 24. Ed. Karen Junod and Didier Maillat. Tübingen: Narr, 2010. 127-151.

about because the linguistic has often taken precedence over the social in dialect research, rather than language and society being seen as mutually constitutive entities, and indeed processes. Let us initially take a quick and sketchy tour around three broad approaches to dialect.

The approach commonly referred to as traditional dialectology, associated in England, for example, with Harold Orton's work on the *Survey of English Dialects* (Wakelin; Chambers and Trudgill) seemed to freeze both linguistic and social change. Dialect surveys sought to capture the forms and patterns of the rural speech of older people, and therefore the sociolinguistic norms of earlier generations – earlier relative to the moment of the research survey. This was a dialectology of the *pre-modern*, redolent with "folk" values and interests. The concerns of traditional dialectology were certainly connected with historical linguistics, opening a window on the speech of the rural English past and aiming to preserve what it found. This "traditional dialect geography" had a strong social and cultural leaning, in the sense that older linguistic forms bore witness to older cultural practices. But processes of social change were not of interest in themselves. Social change was simply the underlying force that was undermining traditional dialects.

Urban variationist sociolinguistics (Chambers, "TV makes people sound the same;" Labov, *Pattern*; *Principles*) majors on linguistic change. Variation in speaker age has been a key methodological resource, but this time in order to study language change in "apparent time," across different age-cohorts in the same locality, where cohort differences at one sampling time are assumed to stand proxy for changes across "real time." The time that matters most for the apparent time method is the end of the critical period for language acquisition, when people's vernacular speech norms are, it is argued, consolidated, allowing young adult speech patterns across a range of familiar social categories such as gender and class to stand for their cohort types. There is no interest in how any particular historical configuration, in a socio-cultural sense, might shape the forms or functions of the speech varieties or systems in question. Time in variationist sociolinguistics is operationalised as a series of sampling points for the measurement of how language varieties, viewed as autonomous systems, are changing. Social class at time 1, for example, is theorised to be the same as social class at time 2. In variationism there is no attempt to understand how language variation and use are embedded in changing socio-cultural ecosystems. Variationism's rather sparse social theory has been a common criticism (Coupland, *Style*). This approach to dialect is rooted in *modernist* assumptions about society, assuming relatively fixed models of gender, class and age.

More recent, social constructionist approaches to dialect often claim some sort of warrant in the circumstances of late modernity, and I have made this claim myself. The argument runs that the social conditions of late modernity (taken to mean post-industrial, fast-capitalist, globalising modernity – see Giddens) require a more fluid approach to sociolinguistic and semiotic function. When researchers approach "dialect" and "standard" language in this framework, they are sceptical about what these terms can actually mean in late modernity, both in general and then in any specific context of linguistic performance. The social categories that variationists have mainly relied on are argued to be becoming unreliable; identities are more contextualised and ephemeral, more amenable to agentive construction – the social through the linguistic (Coupland and Jaworski). Social change is certainly on the agenda here in a couple of different respects. But critics can correctly say that constructionist sociolinguistics has not adequately demonstrated the connection between micro acts in discourse and anything we might take to define the current historical moment. It is fair to say that the link between language use and late modernity often tends to be presumed in dialect-focused research (although Rampton, *Language in Late Modernity* is an important exception).[2]

So, as a broad generalisation, each of these three approaches to dialect engages only in very limited ways with social change. But there are plenty of prima facie reasons to take social change seriously in sociolinguistics, and in the analysis of what we call "standards" and "dialects"[3] as part of that. To put it negatively, it is inconceivable that the social values that attach to "standard speech" are the same today as they were 50 or 60 years ago. Take for example the Queen's speech in a British context. Studies have shown how it has changed over time (Harrington; Harrington, Palethorpe and Watson; Wales 1994) and they help make the point that change in speech norms over the adult lifespan is far from impossible. But it is also true that "the Queen's speech" – especially if we understand that phrase in the determinate sense of her annual Christmas TV "broadcast to the nation" – operates in a different sociolinguistic environment today from earlier decades. I am thinking of how these broadcasts, in the earliest years of Queen Elizabeth's reign

[2] Non-dialect sociolinguistics is, on the other hand, increasingly interested in the relationship between language and social change – see, for example, Chouliaraki and Fairclough.

[3] I persist in putting "standard" and "non-standard" in quotation marks firstly because these default terms in sociolinguistics have not been subjected to enough critical consideration; and secondly because whatever relationship they originally pointed to between language and society now needs to be reassessed. We need to reassess these terms in the light of social change processes, as I suggest below.

(crowned 1953), were received by a relatively dutiful and royalist public, many of whom would stand in silence in front of their radios or TV sets when the (so-called) "British" (so-called) "national" anthem was played over the airwaves.[4] The Queen's speech still features in Christmas Day television schedules, although 2008 saw the 15th alternative Christmas message being broadcast by Channel Four, an event that previously featured speakers including Brigitte Bardot, Ali G (the satirical comedian) and Marge Simpson. The British media and many British people's orientation to "the Queen's speech" in the winter of 2008 clearly differed from earlier decades, and several interlinked dimensions of social change are relevant to this shift.

What are these dimensions of change? Let me propose – overconfidently, no doubt – a list of general observations about social change in Britain over the last 50 years. This is the sort of list that people born in the middle of the 20th century will, I am assuming, recognise as part of their own experience, as I do myself. The list refers to different sorts of change, some more material, some more ideological:

Social change in Britain, 1960-2009: A tendentious list

Increasing mediation of culture and greater cultural reflexivity
The proliferation and speeding up of communication technologies
A shift towards multi-modal textual representations
A shift from manufacturing to service sector work
The decline of the Establishment
Failing trust in professional authority
The growth of the middle class but the accentuation of the rich/poor divide
Greater subservience to market economics, in the face of its demerits
An upsurge in consumer culture and new forms of commodification
A shift from group-based to individual-based rights and obligations
Some blurring of the distinction between private and public spheres
A reduction of the grosser inequalities by gender and sexual orientation
The pursuit of body projects and a stronger economy of personal appearance
Developing ethnic pluralism, especially in urban settings
The development of a post-retirement life-stage
The slow dawning of a more liberal politics of ageing
Massively increasing geographical mobility
National boundaries becoming in different ways more permeable
Reframing and rescaling of local-global relationships

---

[4] This further rash of hedging, through scare-quoting, is meant to imply that there are important challenges to any claim that Britain is a "nation" (see below) and that the anthem in question unequivocally represents or iconises Britain.

Different observers would construct different versions of this list and argue about its contents and emphases and about the status of the evidence. Evidence is patchy but significant – I shall refer to some of it shortly. Many elements of the list cohere into broader-based patterns of social change, summarised by tricky and potentially over-reaching concepts like *globalisation*,[5] *individualisation* and *commodification*. For all their trickiness, these are themes I want to engage with in what follows. While debates are raging in social science about how we should define and nuance these and related concepts, very few if any social scientists feel we should dismiss them altogether, so neither should sociolinguists dismiss them. My argument is that, if we assume that Britain and not-too-dissimilar countries have been experiencing social change of the above sorts, then it is inconceivable that language use and language ideologies have not been reshaped by it, whether or not we use the short-hand term "late modernity" in reference to where we are now.

Incidentally, we should note that 1960 – the notional first date in the caption to the above list – coincides more or less with the birth of sociolinguistics. So what is at stake here is how a more contemporary sociolinguistics might need to break its ties with some of the discipline's foundational assumptions about social organisation, social identity and the meanings of dialect variation. As an effort towards this sort of reorientation, I shall enlarge on three more particular themes relevant to the list of change processes – *social class, national identity* and *mass media* – and try to anticipate how our understanding and analysis of "standard language" and the complementary concept of "dialect" might need to be adjusted in the light of ongoing social change.

Social change, social class and the attribution of "standard"

Social class has been the focal social dimension of modernist, structuralist, variationist sociolinguistics since the 1960s. Sociolinguistic variables have generally been defined by how their variants index social class, in the sense of marking class differences in frequencies of use between class groups. A common social-evaluative gloss has been that "standard" speech variants or speech styles "have high overt prestige" while their "non-standard" counterparts "are socially stigmatised." Variation in relation to style/situation is then modelled as a secondary dimension,

---

[5] It might seem blinkered, in the early weeks of 2009, to point to continuing globalisation, when much of the world is having to retrench and restructure under the body blow of "the credit crunch." But I am taking a longer view here, and there is no evidence that the world is ready to "de-globalise," particularly in cultural and linguistic dimensions.

overlaid on "social" (social class-related) variation (Labov, *Patterns*). Gender-related variation is modelled as the relative frequency of use of class-salient speech variants, and so on, confirming that social class sits at the heart of social explanation in variationism. But the most important, if obvious, point here is that *the terms "standard" and "non-standard" are themselves ideological value-attributions.* Yet sociolinguists often take them to be primes, as if we could identify what a "standard" variant is, independently of social judgements that are made about its use or its users. The term "standard" in the variationist paradigm, and in most of sociolinguistics, is taken to be a linguistic reflex of high social class: the assumption is that "standard language" is what "educated people" use when they write (in accordance with grammatical, lexical and orthographic norms), and in a different sense what people at the top of the social hierarchy use when they speak (according to grammatical, lexical and phonological norms). The problems of definition here are obvious: Is class that stable? Is educatedness a reasonable proxy for class? Is sociolinguistic indexicality that direct? But social change is making these problems of interpretation even more acute.

Sociolinguistics has come to accept a particular account of the concept of "standard" and of the process of linguistic standardisation, for example in the authoritative account given by James Milroy and Lesley Milroy (Milroy and Milroy). In a clear summary text, James Milroy writes that "standardization consists of the imposition of uniformity upon a class of objects" so that "the most important property of a standard variety of a language is uniformity or invariance" (133). Milroy then gives us good news as well as bad news about standardisation. On the one hand he equates the drive to standardise language with the drive to standardise weights and measures, and he suggests there are social advantages in the process:

> The availability of a standard variety is in fact highly functional in human affairs, just as standardized weights and measures are so obviously functional. Standard varieties are comprehensible much more widely than localized dialects are. Furthermore, elaboration of function is one of the characteristics of a standard language; it can be used in a wide variety of different spheres of activities. (134)

But he is also clear that there are restrictive, judgemental and discriminatory aspects of standard language ideology that are operative in "standard language cultures" (such as Britain):

> In standard-language cultures, virtually everyone subscribes to the idea of "correctness" with some forms being considered right and others wrong . . . a person who uses non-standard linguistic forms will often be from a minority ethnic group or a lower social class. (134-5)

The apparently positive "weights and measures" reading of "standard" is in fact a quite different reading from the "standard as correct" reading. There is no process of social discrimination (and Milroy uses the term "discrimination" himself in the bad news part of his account) in establishing standard units of length, weight or currency. Is any person or group who is committed to using alternative units discriminated against or disenfranchised by standardisation in this regard? In what ways is linguistic standardisation functional? It is conceivable that a linguistic "standard" *could* be constituted on this "weights and measures" principle. But if discrimination (in Milroy's bad news account) is structured into standard language ideology, then to posit a supposed neutrality in the (good news) definition of a linguistic "standard" comes close to accepting the arguments of language ideologues, who have seen "standard English," usually very poorly defined, as "obviously functional." I have suggested that when "standard language" has been revered, this stance is rationalised by the claim that it is the only *authentic* language, according to criteria including historicity, coherence and value (Coupland, *Authenticities*). That is, standard language ideology has involved de-authenticating "non-standard" language on the basis that it supposedly lacks a dignified history, is opportunistic or chaotic or worthless.

Even so, we have to ask how pervasive and persuasive standard language ideology actually is. Milroy goes on to make familiar points (following the classic sociolinguistic treatment by Einar Haugen) about the "selection" of a standard variety being an arbitrary process, but in the gift of people in authority who impose their interpretation of correct usage on others, the majority, particularly through the education system. The oppressed then "accept" and "implement" the standard (Milroy 135-6). But in what sense is "standard language," for example in contemporary Britain, a continuing imposition by elites on the disenfranchised masses, whose speech is by implication "non-standard" and systematically devalued and stigmatised? Is there so much bad news?

We know that speakers of linguistic varieties conventionally called "non-standard" sometimes do judge themselves inferior to speakers of varieties called "standard," along the lines of Labov's vivid early characterisation of New York City as "a sink of negative prestige" (*Patterns*). In Britain, Received Pronunciation (RP) is often felt to be a prestigious way of speaking, and non-RP speakers sometimes even find RP intimidating.

But there are also domains where speaking RP is impossible or marginal or even risible. It is remarkable how uncritical linguists have been in interpreting the co-variation of class and "standardness" that survey research into linguistic variation has thrown up, as if the general patterns of co-variation that we find are sufficient to validate theoretical assumptions around "standardness" and the empirical procedures used for defining and operationalising social class. There are several potential *non sequiturs* here. Class stratification has never been a universal of social organisation in all regions and communities in Britain or elsewhere, and class is constituted differently in the different social settings in which it functions.[6] Judgement/attitudes research has always shown that the social meanings of linguistic varieties are complex and multi-dimensional, and (as Tore Kristiansen's research clearly shows, e.g. Kristiansen, "Language Attitudes"; "Norm-Ideals") contextual factors impinge crucially on which social meanings are attributed to linguistic varieties. Although this is not the place to attempt a full review, sociolinguistics has often over-simplified its account of the ideological loading of linguistic varieties. So any analysis of contemporary "de-standardisation" (see below) should be wary of assuming that standard language ideology (SLI) was ever as fully consolidated as many have assumed.

Of more direct relevance to my argument here is that the meaning of social class itself, in Britain and no doubt elsewhere, has not been constant *over time*. The most extreme and most contentious claims in this area have been made by Ulrich Beck, for example in the assertion that social class has become a "zombie category" in late modernity – a category emptied out of any contemporary relevance, an idea circulating in the social twilight despite being to all intents and purposes dead (Beck, "Brave New World;" Beck and Beck-Gernsheim). Beck builds a thesis

---

[6] In Coupland ("Speech Community") I reconsider sociolinguistic theorising of speech community, community of practice and "the authentic speaker." "Communities" can be class-structured in radically different ways, not least from one time period to another. For example, the South Wales Valleys have seen extreme and damaging de-industrialisation with the demise of coal-mining, compromising the tight work-based social networks and communal norms that distinguished the working Valleys for much of the 19th and early 20th centuries. In consequence, older indexical associations of Valleys ways of speaking, centred on communal pride, resilience, socialist politics and resistance, traditional masculinities, and so on are called into question. Aggressive social change has, we might say, cast Valleys voice and identities adrift from their anchoring social forms and practices. It is also important to note that social class in the Valleys never existed as a full, incrementally graded hierarchy, and there was no normative aspiration to a "high-prestige" speech variety such as RP. In the Valleys as in much of Wales, RP primarily means "English" and "not us", where the perceived outgroup by no means has unquestioningly attributed "prestige."

around individualisation. He says that contemporary education, legal and welfare systems "presume the individual as actor, designer, juggler and stage director of his or her own biography, identity, social networks, commitments and convictions" (Beck, *Reinvention of Politics* 95). He argues that in late modernity individuals are disembedded from historically prescribed social structures, and therefore disembedded from social class hierarchies; individualisation is a change-process that has stripped away the relevance of class. Many sociologists have resisted or qualified this claim (e.g. Atkinson; Skeggs; Walkerdine), but Beck's ideas have stimulated significant reconsiderations of class in contemporary sociology and triggered empirical research on the nature and extent of related changes. There is evidence to support milder and better-contextualised versions of Beck's individualisation thesis.

To take one instance, research by Tilley and Heath, using a self-report survey method, has assessed whether and to what extent social class and other "traditional identities" such as religiousness and Britishness in Britain have been reconfigured in the last 40 years. They found that the proportion of British people who claim adherence to a religious identity has declined markedly over four decades (28), although those who say they are religious do prove to have normative (conservative) moral views that differ considerably from non-religious people's views. With social class, Tilley and Heath found that Britons are still on the whole prepared to ally themselves with different social class groups, but that social class categories have ceased to be indicative of any great differences in personal values. Class belonging in Britain, Tilley and Heath argue, now has little influence on attitudes and behaviour:

> There has been little, if any, decline in class identity, but nowadays, at least, differences in class values are relatively small compared with differences in religious values – and appear to have declined quite considerably over the last two decades. While people may still think of themselves to belong to a particular class, social classes do not seem to act as distinctive normative reference groups in the way they once did. (28)

For example, self-ascribing social class groups were formerly quite sharply divided on the politics of economic redistribution, with strong views in favour of redistribution being held by working class people. Tilley and Heath show that such value differences between classes have now largely lapsed. Class is not dead, but there *is* evidence of the implications of class having waned, in the sense that it nowadays fails to divide groups politically and ideologically. Neo-liberalism has swamped working class ideological politics.

Another study where survey research fails to find close relationships between social class and social attitudes, values or preferences is Chan and Goldthorpe who studied the relationship between social stratification and patterns of cultural consumption in England, with particular reference to people's engagement with different genres of music. They found a tendency for working class people to be more "univorous" (listening to and consuming only one genre of music – pop and rock) than people in the highest social strata. But their main findings are that *all* social classes share this tendency and that there is nowadays no "music-consuming elite," because people in the high social classes simply tend to be rather more "omnivorous" – more wide-ranging in their tastes – than others. There is no evidence of a "dominant class" whose "class conditions" predispose them to consume "high culture," in the way that Bourdieu's analysis of taste and distinction suggests (Bourdieu).[7] What might the social change towards relative classlessness or towards more omnivorous cultural consumption mean for a sociolinguistics of "standardness"?

In purely distributional terms, we would expect an expanded self-ascribing middle-class to be more diffuse in their overall speech styles in any given region than previously. The smaller, more structurally distinct middle-class of earlier times would have had more potential to cohere around "standard language." Dialect levelling (Britain, Vandekerckhove and Jongburger) will have reduced the gap between working-class and middle-class norms, but the new middle class is likely to contain people whose speech spans a wider range of styles than the old middle class. But also, even where patterns of linguistic variation persist across class-indexed groups (as of course they do, despite degrees of linguistic levelling), we would expect the sociolinguistic indexicality of class – the value associations of "standard" and "non-standard" speech – to be weaker and less significant. This might be part of a more general waning of senses of social superiority and inferiority – democratisation of a sort, then – but it would more specifically relate to a weakening semiotic of "sociolinguistic taste," including as regards "prestige" and "stigmatisation." We would expect that people at the top of the social scale, however this might be measured, or claimed by people themselves, will have become more sociolinguistically "omnivorous", as they are with musical taste, in their willingness to "consume" (to accept and possibly even positively value) a wide range of language varieties.

---

[7] It is likely that the 25 years since Bourdieu's text have seen significant social change.

We need to explore new possible configurations where linguistic differentiation at the level of usage persists, but where the social meanings of variation change. In some cases, these meanings may be blunted and more obscure. In other cases, earlier meanings may be reallocated as demands on speaking and performing change. If, for example, there are greater demands on more speakers to self-present as "socially attractive" more than "competent," then the evaluative and ideological architecture of "standard language" will have changed. Shifts of this sort would indicate that Britain was becoming, or had already become, less of a "standard language culture" in Milroy's sense. At the risk of overemphasising the central point here, the core process of change here is not language change but language-ideological change, embedded in wider processes of social change.

Other demonstrable social changes in Britain are consistent with shifts of this sort. The ideology of "standard as correct" that Milroy describes is in fact located in "Establishment" values rather than in social class hierarchies in general, and "the Establishment" is certainly not co-terminous with (all of) "the middle-class" (Milroy's educated people) or even "the upper-class" (to the extent we have one in Britain). The Establishment is, or was, a highly conservative body of policy-making and opinion-forming people in Britain, with influential roles in military, religious (Church of England) and political life. Harold Macmillan, elected Prime Minister in 1959, and earlier, Lord John Reith, general manager of the BBC, 1922-1927, can stand as historical prototypes of the Establishment. But the British Establishment has been in retreat for decades, under the forces of internationalism, secularisation, popular culture displacing high culture, plus a good deal of media exposure, criticism and ridiculing of elites. There are certainly relic features of the Establishment to be found in contemporary Britain; we might think of the gentrified demeanour of some members of the House of Lords, or self-styling elites in some private schools, cricket clubs or sailing clubs. Some English towns, like Marlborough, style themselves as retainers of conservative, elite values. The Establishment has arguably "gone heritage" in such places, packaged for late-modern consumption by people whose speech, dress, lifestyles and possessions are strikingly and self-consciously "old school."

However, in relation to spoken "standard language" and Received Pronunciation (RP), Mugglestone writes about a long shift, which she sees as having begun in the 1960s, whereby "talking proper" in Britain (according to Establishment standard language ideology as promoted by Lord Reith at the BBC, for example) has come to be construed as "talking posh."[8] The attribution "posh" entails a certain *lack* of respect for a "high" dialect/accent variety, or at least the acknowledgement that its claims to superiority are not fully credible. Posh cuts away the ideological underpinnings of the concept of "standard," as it has been uncritically used in sociolinguistics. It also undermines the relic-Establishment semiotic, where it persists or where it is recreated as a would-be elite form. Posh de-natures the Establishment voice, cutting through its links to authenticity (which are as spurious as those of other claimed sociolinguistic authenticities, as with the notion of "the pure vernacular" – Coupland, "Authenticities").

Following arguments like these, there are reasons to suppose that the conventional class-based sociolinguistic conceptualisation of "standard" and "non-standard" speech is becoming out-dated; it starts to appear modernist from a late-modern perspective. Blommaert's idea (following Silverstein) of "orders of indexicality" can be invoked here, referring to competing and potentially shifting value systems around language use. Older indexical orders, such as Establishment SLI, have given way to newer ones, where posh speakers are quite commonly laid open to ridicule, and under some circumstances start to feel "insecure," where the social meaning of voice is less determinate, and where backing social class winners and losers is not the only game in town. There is therefore an increasingly urgent need for contextual sophistication in accounts of social meaning, although it has *always* been the case that SLIs have successfully colonised *particular* speech genres, social domains and social groups, *and not others*. To take one example, Ben Rampton's research gives us access to the particular domain of secondary school education and multi-ethnic urban youth in two British cities. He concludes from his ethnographic research (Rampton, *Crossing*; *Language in Late Modernity*) that posh is indeed structured into the social experience and imaginings of the British youngsters he studies, but that its meanings are diffuse and, once again, at a much more micro-level, highly contextualised. Rampton argues that his informants are *not* subordinated by oppressive meanings of class that limit their life chances. Although it would be unwise to generalise from these specific data to broader patterns of

---

[8] "Posh" is far from being a recent coining and today there are other ways of lexicalising inter-class relations, including "ra." "Ra," said (and commonly stylised) with a long open back vowel, is mainly used in reference to young females, their voices (selectively conservative RP), their taste in clothing (e.g. pashminas) and their taste in alcoholic drinks (e.g. Lambrini). The long open back vowel picks up on the long-standing short/long contrast between southern (RP) and northern pronunciation in the word set that includes *class, dance* and *fast*. But it is in stylised performances of "ra," with hyper-backed and open vowel quality, that the class stereotype and the speaker's stance towards it are conjured.

change, Rampton's research emphasises that we need to move on from received assumptions about indexical orders.

Social change, national identities and "standard language"

Globalisation is widely held to be destabilising nation-states and national identities, to the extent that some social theorists want to dispense with the concept of national identity. Some of them want to dispense with appeals to identity altogether (Brubaker and Cooper; Hastings and Manning). Beck's claims (see above) pattern with other influential treatises on new global inter-dependencies (e.g. Bauman, *Liquid Modernity*; *Individualized Society*; Giddens), all of which point to the decline of national political autonomy under globalisation. The relationship between language and globalisation urgently needs to be reassessed (see Fairclough; also Coupland "Sociolinguistics and Globalisation;" *Handbook of Language and Globalisation*) and, once again, it needs to be nuanced and contextualised. There are some clear sociolinguistic trends that need to be studied and theorised, including the onward march of "world languages," the linguistic consequences of increased trans-national migration and influence, new core-periphery arrangements, etc.

Several of the ideas I drew on in relation to social class have a clear trans-national dimension. Blommaert, for example, applies his concept of orders of indexicality mainly across cultural zones, implying that when people and linguistic varieties "travel," they are potentially subject to very different and often very damaging value re-orderings. He gives the example of when an English text authored by a middle-class person in Nairobi, and judged to be an instance of elite practice there, is judged sub-standard in London (Blommaert 4). Nairobi and London are, to that extent, different "centres" of authoritative judgement, yet texts and varieties increasingly have to function across national boundaries where new globalised inequalities lie in wait. Rampton's multi-ethnic student groups are of course a demographic product of earlier trans-national flows, and Rampton interprets the young people's shifts in and out of ethnic as well as class voices as the working through of new inter-ethnic and inter-class relationships.

Issues of "standard and non-standard language" relate very directly to the structural integrity of nation-states, because SLIs, where they function convincingly, derive their authority from state institutions. The decline of the Establishment, which we considered in relation to changes in social class in Britain, began with the loss of empire. It is continuing alongside the waning of British influence in the world and a massive upsurge in transnational exchange – economic, communicative and cultural. James Milroy makes the point that, in a "standard language culture," people assume that language is a cultural artefact, owned by the cultural group and both needing and meriting protective action (136). In contemporary Britain it is impossible to hold to these principles of ownership and purity for English, or to see "standard English" as the property of "the English" or "the British," let alone "the English/British Establishment."

We can once again turn to recent sociological surveys in Britain for evidence of a decline in "Britishness" as a meaningful and valued self-attribution since World War II. McCrone argues that this decline was, as I suggested just-above, in the first instance a post-empire phenomenon, but the rise of Scottish and Welsh nationalism[9] and political devolution in its varying degrees and contexts are certainly further considerations. Tilley and Heath's study, which I drew on earlier, also points to immigration and ethnic pluralisation, and to three factors underlying the decline of Britishness: (a) increasing cosmopolitanism, which tends to downplay the importance of the nation state; (b) the impact of particular events over recent decades, such as political devolution; and (c) generational change, in that people who grew up in a time of "national solidarity" (epitomised by World War II, although Britain has never truly been a single "nation") developed lasting "national" (British) identities that appealed less to more recent generations.

Tilley and Heath's main conclusion from this dimension of their empirical work is that there has indeed been a decline in British national pride. Data across the period 1981 to 2003 revealed, for example, that 57% of respondents surveyed in 1981 said they were "very proud" to be British, a percentage that had declined to 45% by 2003, but with strong birth-cohort effects too. The authors also show that Welsh and Scottish groups were (stepwise) lower in expressed British pride in 2003, and that their values fell more dramatically over the period after 1981 than those of English groups. Young Scots expressed least pride in being British. Tilley and Heath say that those who claim British identity nowadays do *not* have very distinctive views or attitudes from those who don't. Britishness is therefore another candidate for being considered something of a "zombie category," even when it is invoked.

Our own sociolinguistic survey results point to patterns of social evaluation where Scottish and Welsh people attribute significantly more prestige and social attractiveness to their "home" varieties, while attributing less prestige and social attractiveness to varieties labelled "standard

---

[9] These "nationalisms" are not easy to sum up and do not closely parallel each other.

English" and "the Queen's English" than many other groups do (Bishop, Coupland and Garrett; see also Coupland and Bishop). In that study, although the "standard" varieties presented for assessment still generally remained in the ascendancy, there was intermittent evidence of a weakening of support for "standard English." Younger informants, for example, regularly attributed more positive values to conventionally low-prestige varieties than older informants did, and this might indicate generational shift over time (as opposed to intrinsically age-graded difference). Also, we argued that the survey method and the use of conventional labels for accent varieties were likely to have predisposed conservative ideological stances. The general point is that we should expect the declining appeal of Britishness to be freeing up particular "non-standard" varieties to function as targets (or "norm-ideals" in Kristiansen's sense) in particular domains, as new evaluative "centres" (in Blommaert's sense) come to prominence. Some of these centres are already apparent in the mass media.

Mass media, social change and the meanings of dialect

The mediatisation of late-modern life is probably the best evidenced social change of the last fifty years, in Britain and globally (but of course with hugely variable rates of change and levels of impact in different places). Sociolinguistic interest in change and the media has been dominated by the assertion that systemic linguistic change is *not* directly influenced by television as a "social factor" (Chambers, "TV Makes People Sound the Same;" Labov, *Principles*), although there have also been some efforts to reassess this claim (Stuart-Smith). But if we cast the net wider, as we surely must do, and ask what impact the broadcast media have on the evaluative and ideological worlds in which language variation exists in late modernity, then it is inconceivable that the "no media influence" argument can hold. Mass media are changing the terms of our engagement with language and social semiosis in late modernity, and with linguistic variation and dialect as part of that.

TV in particular has put mediated linguistic diversity in front of the viewing public far more pervasively and with much richer and more saturated indexical loading than face-to-face social reality can achieve. TV representations have confirmed, but also challenged, social stereotypes attaching to dialect varieties in Britain, in highly complex patterns. If we look for TV's role in confirming traditional sociolinguistic stereotypes, we can confidently point to ways in which, since the 1960s, TV's high-reach channels have often represented structured urban speech communities. For example, two long-running soap operas based in

London (*East Enders*) and Manchester (*Coronation Street*) have imaged close-knit, working class communities sharing lifestyles, social problems, hardship and resilience narratives, each of them powerfully articulating a distinctive sense of place through voice. TV shows of this sort have consolidated regionalised versions of urban working class lifestyles and ways of speaking, in stark opposition to the old institutional voice of public broadcasting. There is no major urban or regional British vernacular that does not have a ready sociolinguistic prototype in a TV soap opera or in some high-profile celebrity. British radio has also contributed to a sociolinguistic stratification effect, in the hierarchy of "serious" to "popular" broadcasting roles. Conservative RP has often been associated with the voices of "serious" news readers (particularly on BBC Radios 3 and 4), and "non-standardness" has been ideologically confirmed in the voices of not only TV and radio soap stars but also stand-up comedians, footballers, snooker players and vox pop street interviewees. Radio 1, the youth-oriented pop and rock BBC channel, aligns very much with the popular culture vernacular norm, to the extent of being one of those environments where RP is not only non-functional but risible.

But these implied hierarchies – which they are only from selective viewpoints – are only a part of the sociolinguistic order that television and radio portray. The mass media also pose powerful *challenges* to traditional sociolinguistic orders. One key consideration here relates to ways of experiencing and consuming the mass media, over and above the sociolinguistic forms and styles that the media represent. The social reflexivity of the mediation process is what changes our terms of engagement with mediated voices. Dialect on TV is, as variationists rightly point out, "not real," and as viewers we do not orient to it or to media performers in the same way as we do to co-participants in face-to-face social interaction. But the mediation gap encourages critical reflexivity around dialect performance, particularly across the vast and growing range of available representations. At the very least, as we consume diverse media images of sociolinguistic types, we cannot avoid construing alternatives, seeing performances that could have been quite different, built from different semiotic indexicalities. It is this contrastive bricolage effect, the complex but condensed admixture of linguistic styles and meanings, that the mass media uniquely provide, for example when we hop channels or simply wait for the next half-hour slot to bring around a fresh mix.

Contrastive dialect semiosis is in fact the basis of a particularly striking recent trend in British TV. This format involves disembedding speakers with strongly resonant "regional and social dialects" from the social matrices that might appear to provide their distinctiveness. A

clutch of new popular TV formats are built on the design of mixing social types in the same social settings and exploiting the social disso-
nances between them. The most obvious instances are the "lifestyle exchange" shows that, for example, put posh people into menial work
roles, or give people "makeovers" that disrupt their physical and social
identities (see J. Coupland on the *Ten Years Younger* format). In one sense
these disembeddings *confirm* the traditional sociolinguistic order, as people often flounder in their newly contrived social contexts. But the audience has nevertheless been led into reflexive appraisal, to construe alternatives to the traditional, modernist order based on gender, age or class
principles. Audiences see the process of recontextualisation as well as
the social structure that is recontextualised. This meta-level resource
encourages consumers to "see through" the dialect hierarchies that persist – to hear "standard and nonstandard voices" as stylisations of class
language (Coupland, "Dialect Stylisation").

Many other contemporary British TV shows are premised on strong
typological contrasts in voice and demeanour. In the Christmas 2008 TV
schedules the BBC's most-watched show was an episode of *Strictly Come
Dancing*. The show positions people who have succeeded in very different walks of life (an international rugby player, a TV soap star, a pop
singer, a TV political commentator, and so on) as celebrity members of a
dance competition. Their dancing skills, which are often implausibly
good, are progressively honed over the TV series and aired in weekly
performances of different demanding dance styles. Performances are
picked over and assessed by a resident team of judges and also by the
general public who vote by telephone. In any traditional framework, the
sheer range of social and sociolinguistic types here is bewildering. The
four judges, three males and one female, are themselves typologically
dispersed. Each one is easy to define in a series of reductive social cate-
gorisations: "the tall, serious, posh male judge," "the sharply critical
London-sounding female judge," "the tall, avuncular, London-sounding
male judge," and "the wacky, short, second-language, Italian-sounding
male judge." These are (my own) highly essentialising descriptions, but
they are the categories worked into and exploited in the show itself.
Each judge plays up to his or her stereotyped persona, and some of the
social attributes I have just listed are routinely mentioned in the show's
discourse.[10]

---

[10] Craig Revel Horwood is constructed as the posh judge, even though his speech is not
consistently RP. The gap between his relative RP and slightly camp self-presentation and
the more vernacular styles of the other judges is sometimes parodied by the show pre-
senters.

Strictly therefore presents sociolinguistic bricolage, but another aspect of this is to break up the predictable associations of "standardness" and status – to render traditional orders incoherent. The judges are mostly a pretty vernacular bunch who pass judgement, often derisorily, on the more "socially accomplished" dance trialists. The show is hosted by Bruce Forsyth, an elderly doyen of British TV game-shows, known for his silly humour, his long chin, his tap-dancing, his catch phrases and his London voice. The other host is Tess Daley, whose reductive typological description might be "the tall, beautiful, working-class, northern-sounding former model" – Tess's attributes are, from a conventional socio-structural viewpoint, internally complex and (in modernist conceptions) incoherent in their own right. The level of *individualisation* in this persona formatting is remarkable – characters are quickly pulled away from any residual social matrices. The "Italianness" of the fourth judge is not salient in ethnic or national terms, but his linguistic quirkiness and ebullience probably are. Tess Daley is not meaningfully "northern" in the social configuration of *Strictly*, as the show creates its own principles of social contextualisation. There might be residual semiotic values of "northern unpretentiousness" in Tess's manner, but Tess Daley is . . . simply Tess Daley, just as "Brucie" (Bruce Forsyth) is his own auto-iconic individual self. *Strictly* generates a cast of individualised celebrities who are played off against each other. The dance competition scrutinises the individual competences of performers, and there is only one winner.

We should also recognise another basic quality of TV semiosis, and that is its multi-modal framing.[11] *Strictly* is once again a revealing case, when we consider its kinetic and bodily dynamism, the startling colours of performers' dance costumes and the visual extravagance of its sets. *Strictly* is undoubtedly an extreme case, but the social meanings of voice *per se* are further complicated when voices work alongside the semiotics of movement, body shape and stature, physical and physiognomic beauty, clothing, and so on. TV "personalities" and "celebrities" (Turner) are constructed at the intersection of multiple semiotic modalities, and this is another key consideration in how mass-mediated late modernity is repositioning "dialect." While a movement towards study-

---

[11] I am grateful to Adam Jaworski for this observation. AJ also notes that it is easy to be too generous in assessing the media's affordances and representational openness. The media exercise their own versions of gate-keeping and censorship (cf. Blommaert's discussion of evaluative "centres," earlier). AJ also cautions that mass-mediated individualisations are often *aspirational*, "working alongside the upsurge in consumer culture and the growing importance of market economies, which precisely depend on aspiration as the main motive for consumption because it's inexhaustible" (personal note).

ing "dialect in discourse" is in evidence in sociolinguistics, there is as yet no concerted project of studying how voice "means" in relation to concurrent non-linguistic parameters.

Discussion

In this paper I have entertained several claims about how linguistic varieties referred to as "standards" and "dialects" are coming to hold different, generally less determinate and more complex, values in a late-modern social order. I have had Britain in mind, although the social changes I have been referring to are far from unique and much of the social movement in question is globally based. I have pointed to several sociolinguistic assumptions that have remained largely unchallenged since the early years of the discipline, particularly assumptions relating to a fixed and meaningful class order, operating through a relatively isolated and intact national framework, where linguistic indexicalities are formed and maintained in warm-bodied social exchanges but under the ideological control of dominant social groups. My conclusion is that this is, nowadays, an account in need of revision. It is true that there is a risk of swimming with a critical tide of grand-theory revisionist claims (e.g. that class and national identities are no more, although these are not the positions I have argued), but there is a comparable risk of acquiescing to conventional dogma.

The concept of *de-standardisation* does seem appropriate to alert us to many of the relevant language-ideological changes, although it clearly needs specifying and evidencing. A first step is to blend the concepts of linguistic change and social change into a unified notion of *sociolinguistic change*, broad enough to conceptualise the interplay between the existing variationist field and changes in the structure and application of beliefs and social evaluations of language varieties. Sociolinguistic change will study language-ideological change in the context of social change, and refer to changes in linguistic usage within that broader matrix. If we try to theorise de-standardisation, this would refer to the whole of the matrix, not merely loss or distributional reduction of the use of high-status varieties over time as one form of linguistic levelling. Whether or not linguistic repertoires change substantially over time, we have to ask how individuals and groups perceptually segment those repertoires at any given point in time and in different social contexts, and how they may reallocate values and meanings to existing styles and valorise new ones.

Kristiansen ("Language Standardisation and Standard Languages") suggests a distinction between linguistic *de-standardisation* and *demotisation*. In this opposition, de-standardisation is a type of value levelling that washes out status meanings formerly linked to "standard" and "non-standard" varieties. Demotisation refers to continuing investment in a "standard" or "best" variety of speech, but where a formerly popular or more vernacular variety rises to take the place of the earlier "standard." The shifts I have discussed above appear to sit better under the rubric of de-standardisation than demotisation. In Britain at least, it is very difficult to point to any one vernacular that is rising to be treated as "the best way of speaking." So-called Estuary English is sometimes discussed in these terms in popular media, but there is no evidence of a coherent new variety – a demoticised RP – coalescing around London-influenced features and being used in the prototypical domains where old RP held sway. It is more a matter of "locally distinct dialects . . . being replaced by supralocal or regional koines, which are characterised both by the levelling of marked or minority features and by interdialect caused by imperfect accommodation between speakers of different dialects in contact" (Britain 149). But also, there is informal evidence of RP increasingly failing to unquestioningly attract attributions of power, status and authority, and the result is indeed a sort of democratisation. One problem here is, however, that we know from attitudes research that RP rarely ever had this unquestioning support. The "superiority" of RP was often a two-edged sword in social-evaluative terms.

But de-standardisation need not be simply a neutralisation of indexical meaning, a bleaching-out of socially attributed values. I have argued that the mass media have increased our level of sociolinguistic reflexivity, and dialect difference, at least in Britain, is very much alive as a productive source of meaning-making, albeit in shifting value systems. Some of the emotional heat and prejudice around class does appear to have dissipated, and to that extent we might suggest that class is becoming, if not a "zombie" category, a more "banal" dimension of social life, in the same way that Michael Billig suggests has happened with nationalism in Britain). A more banal social class ideology would involve less overt conflict over taste and socio-economic resources, even though social groups would still be distinguishable by virtue of their semiotic markers. We might look for evidence of "class games" through language in late modernity, as opposed to the class wars of modernist Britain, even though we should not underestimate the potential for social inequality to be linguistically focused *in particular contexts*. Vernacular speech retains its potential to evoke regional and social affiliations, and under globalisation, "the local" often acquires new positive value as an antidote to "the global familiar." We need to look for signs that the old sociolinguistic association of vernacular speech with social stigma is breaking down, as well as being selectively maintained. As with RP, many vernacular speech styles in Britain have had multi-dimensional evaluative profiles. The language-ideological shift I am speculating about here might therefore be best described as a reconfiguring of evaluative profiles in particular contexts, rather than a wholesale democratising shift. In this reconfiguring, long-standing stereotyped attributes of vernaculars, such as personal attractiveness and unpretentiousness, come more to the fore, under changed social priorities.

As the (relative) national consensuses about class and "national" British identity break down, we would expect to see a more multi-centred sociolinguistic culture being affirmed. This is a society where singular value systems, including those for ways of speaking, are being displaced by more complex and, once again, more closely contextualised value systems. We might be seeing a *relativisation* (rather than a neutralisation) of sociolinguistic values. The broadcast media are far more diverse in their formats and genres than they were, so there has been substantial expansion of both "dialect" and "style" dimensions of variation, classically conceived – we engage with people who "are from" hugely disparate social enclaves but also with people who "are doing" hugely disparate things, sociolinguistically. However unfashionably in the discipline, I think we are bound to seek connections between these changes in the mediated world and the world of "everyday language." With the growth of service-based employment, there are greater demands on people to be able to self-present "attractively" as well as (in other situations) "competently," and we might expect the performative range of "everyday" language use to be broadening in response.[12] The old sociolinguistic dimension of stylistic "formality" has proved to be far too restrictive to capture the range of self-presentational resources that recreational talk and talk-at-work nowadays demands (Coupland, *Style*). In some accounts we are living in an increasingly ironic world where, consistent with a culture of increased sociolinguistic reflexivity, we are expected to be able to perform ourselves with considerable metalinguistic sophistication. Neo-liberalism prioritises what we can "bring off" and earn in local markets, not what we are structurally limited to or entitled to. The resources of "standard" and "dialect" presumably have to be deployed in new acts of identity within such markets.

---

[12] Scare-quoting of "everyday" here is to suggest that the mass media are very much part of most people's "everyday" experience, just as many people transact large parts of their "everyday" lives via mediated communication.

Finally, on the theme of how to approach change, it is interesting to return to how sociolinguistics has built change into its paradigms. Variationists regularly try to distinguish "age-grading" effects (linguistic changes linked to individuals growing older) from "language change" effects (linguistic changes that show the speech system evolving). The evidence for systemic change in a speech system is what social theorists and gerontologists call a cohort effect, where researchers can hope to distinguish the linguistic consequences of advancing years (ageing effect) from the linguistic consequences of cohort membership (cohort effect, based on the likelihood that the individual has gone through life sharing historical experiences with a wider group of people born into the same circumstances at the same time). But there is a well-established *tripartite* model of change (see Mason and Fienberg) that recognises not only "ageing" and "cohort" effects, but also "period" effects, and the theoretical assumption is that all three corners of the change triangle and their interactions need to be borne in mind. Sociolinguistics have generally not considered "period effects," which we could interpret sociolinguistically as how language use and language ideologies settle into specific patterns during any one historical epoch. The point, then, is that any ageing individual and any particular cohort will need to come to terms with (tune into or resist) the dominant socio-cultural ethos at any one time. The challenge for sociolinguists working with an expanded concept of sociolinguistic change is to interpret synchronic data in relation to a more rounded model of diachronic processes.

References

Atkinson, Will. "Beck, Individualization and the Death of Class: A Critique." *British Journal of Sociology* 58: 3 (2007): 349-366.

Bauman, Zygmunt. *Liquid Modernity*. Cambridge: Polity Press, 2000.

———. *The Individualized Society*. Cambridge: Polity Press, 2001.

Beck, Ulrich. *The Reinvention of Politics: Rethinking Modernity in the New Global Social Order*. Cambridge: Polity Press, 1997.

———. *The Brave New World of Work*. Cambridge: Polity Press, 2000.

——— and E. Beck-Gernsheim. *Individualization: Institutionalized Individualism and its Social and Political Consequences*. London: Sage, 2002.

Billig, Michael. *Banal Nationalism*. London: Sage, 1995.

Bishop, Hywel, Nikolas Coupland and Peter Garrett. "Conceptual Accent Evaluation: Thirty Years of Accent Prejudice in the UK." *Acta Linguistica Havniensia* (The Linguistics Circle of Copenhagen) 37 (2005): 131-154.

Blommaert, Jan. "Sociolinguistics and Discourse Analysis: Orders and Polycentricity." *Journal of Multicultural Discourses* 2:2 (2007): 1-16.

Bourdieu, Pierre. *Distinction: A Social Critique of the Judgement of Taste*. Cambridge, Massachusetts: Harvard University Press, 1984.

Britain, David, Reinhild Vandekerckhove and Willy Jongburger, eds. "Dialect Death in Europe?" *Thematic issue of International Journal of the Sociology of Language* (2009): 196-197.

Brubaker, Rogers and Frederick Cooper. "Beyond 'Identity'." *Theory and Society* 29 (2000): 1-47.

Chambers, J. K. "TV Makes People Sound the Same." *Language Myths*. Ed. Laurie Bauer and Peter Trudgill. London: Penguin, 1998. 123-131.

——— and Peter Trudgill. *Dialectology*. Cambridge: Cambridge University Press, 1998.

Chan, Tak Wing and John H. Goldthorpe. "Social Stratification and Cultural Consumption: Music in England." *European Sociological Review* 23:1 (2007): 1-19.

Chouliaraki, Lilie and Norman Fairclough. *Discourse in Late Modernity: Rethinking Critical Discourse Analysis*. Edinburgh: Edinburgh University Press, 1999.

Coupland, Justine. "Time, the Body and the Reversibility of Ageing: Commodifying the Decade." *Ageing and Society* 29:6 (2009): 953-976.

Coupland, Nikolas. "Dialect Stylisation in Radio Talk." *Language in Society* 30 (2001): 345-375.

———. "Sociolinguistic Authenticities." *Journal of Sociolinguistics* 7:3 (2003): 417-431.

——, ed. "Sociolinguistics and Globalisation." *Thematic issue of Journal of Sociolinguistics* 7:4 (2003): 465-472.

——. *Style: Language, Variation and Identity*. Cambridge: Cambridge University Press, 2007.

——. "Speech Community and the Authentic Speaker." *Language and Identities*. Ed. C. Llamas and D. Watt. Edinburgh: Edinburgh University Press, 2009. 99-112.

——, ed. *Handbook of Language and Globalisation*. Oxford: Wiley-Blackwell, 2010.

—— and Hywel Bishop. "Ideologised Values for British Accents." *Journal of Sociolinguistics* 11:1(2007): 74-103.

Fairclough, Norman. *Language and Globalization*. London: Routledge, 2006.

Giddens, Anthony. *Modernity and Self-Identity: Self and Society in the Late Modern Age*. Cambridge: Polity Press, 1991.

Harrington, Jonathan. "An Acoustic Analysis of 'Happy-Tensing' in the Queen's Christmas Broadcasts." *Journal of Phonetics* 34 (2006): 439-457.

——, S. Palethorpe and C. Watson. "Does the Queen speak the Queen's English?" *Nature* 408 (December 2000): 927-8.

Hastings, Adi and Paul Manning. "Introduction: Acts of Alterity." *Language and Communication* 24 (2004): 291-311.

Kristiansen, Tore. "Language Attitudes in a Danish Cinema." *Sociolinguistics: A Reader and Coursebook*. Ed. N. Coupland and A. Jaworski. Basingstoke: Palgrave, 1997. 291-305.

——. "Social Meaning and Norm-Ideals for Speech in a Danish Community." *Metalanguage: Social and Ideological Perspectives*. Ed. A. Jaworski, N. Coupland and D. Galasiński. Berlin: Mouton de Gruyter, 2004. 167-192.

——. "The Nature and Role of Language Standardization and Standard Languages in Later Modernity." *Orientation paper for the Copenhagen Planning Workshop, February 2009*, 2008.

——, Frans Gregersen, Shaun Nolan and Jacob Thøgersen. "The Nature and Role of Language Standardisation and Standard Languages in Late Modernity." Unpublished keynote paper for the Copenhagen workshops on *The nature and role of language standardisation and standard languages in late modernity*, 2008.

Labov, William. *Sociolinguistic Patterns*. Philadelphia: Pennsylvania University Press, 1972.

——. *Principles of Linguistic Change. Vol. 2 Social Factors*. Oxford: Blackwell Publishers, 2001.

Mason, W. and S. Fienberg. *Cohort Analysis in Social Research: Beyond the Identification Problem*. New York: Springer-Verlag, 1985.

McCrone, David. "Unmasking Britannia: The Rise and Fall of British National Identity." *Nations and Nationalism* 3 (1997): 579-596.

Milroy, James. "The Ideology of the Standard Language." *The Routledge Companion to Sociolinguistics*. Ed. Carmen Llamas, Louise Mullany and Peter Stockwell. London: Routledge, 2006. 133-139.

—— and Lesley Milroy. *Authority in Language: Investigating Standard English*. London: Routledge, 1998.

Mugglestone, Lynda. *"Talking Proper": The Rise of Accent as Social Symbol*. Oxford: Clarendon Press, 1995.

Rampton, Ben. *Crossing: Language and Ethnicity among Adolescents*. Cambridge: Cambridge University Press, 1995.

——. *Language in Late Modernity: Interaction in an Urban School*. Cambridge: Cambridge University Press, 2006.

Silverstein, Michael. "Contemporary Transformations of Local Linguistic Communities." *Annual Review of Anthropology* 27 (1998): 401-426.

——. "Indexical Order and the Dialectics of Sociolinguistic life." *Language and Communication* 23 (2003): 193-229.

Skeggs, Beverley. *Class, Self, Culture*. London: Routledge, 2004.

Stuart-Smith, Jane. "The Influence of the Media." *The Routledge Companion to Sociolinguistics*. Ed. Carmen Llamas, Louise Mullany and Peter Stockwell. London: Routledge, 2006. 140-148.

Tilley, James and Anthony Heath. "The Decline of British National Pride." *British Journal of Sociology* 58:4 (2007): 661-678.

Turner, Graeme. "The Mass Production of Celebrity: 'Celetoids', Reality TV and the 'Demotic Turn'." *International Journal of Cultural Studies* 9 (2006): 153-165.

Wakelin, Martyn. *English Dialects: An Introduction*. London: The Athlone Press, 1977.

Wales, Katie. "Royalese: The Rise and Fall of 'The Queen's English'." *English Today* 10 (1994): 3-10.

Walkerdine, Valerie. "Reclassifying Upward Mobility: Femininity and the Neo-Liberal Subject." *Gender and Education* 15:3 (2003): 237–248.

"There are many that I can be": The Poetics of Self-Performance in Isak Dinesen's "The Dreamers"

Barbara Straumann

This paper looks at issues of identity in relation to artistic performances of the feminine self. Isak Dinesen's story "The Dreamers" from her collection *Seven Gothic Tales* (1934) is remarkably in tune with contemporary theories of identity construction, notably with Judith Butler's concept of gender performance. Pellegrina Leoni, the protagonist of Dinesen's tale, is an acclaimed opera singer who loses her voice in a tragic accident. After having herself symbolically buried, she assumes an infinite series of masks and masquerades. My reading demonstrates how by abandoning her rigid star persona, Dinesen's heroine comes to perform a far more mobile selfhood. Her relentless role-play stands in stark contrast to a narrative desire which seeks to impose a stable identity upon her and by which she is eventually killed in a fatal scene of interpellation. By reading "The Dreamers" as a quasi-manifesto of Isak Dinesen's art, I argue that her poetic project feeds on a complex dialectics of self-masking and self-presentation. It is in and through her masquerade that this modernist writer develops a compelling form of feminine self-expression.

When Hannah Arendt reviewed a biography of Isak Dinesen for *The New Yorker*, she noted that, for Dinesen, "the chief trap in one's life is one's identity" (viii). But how is Arendt's statement to be understood? How does Dinesen's writing enact the vicissitudes of identity and, at the same time, create a poetics of resonant self-expression? In the following, I will examine these and related questions through a close reading of "The Dreamers" from *Seven Gothic Tales* (1934), the very first story collection by Karen Blixen, with which she established herself as the internationally renowned writer Isak Dinesen. As I shall argue, "The Dream-

Performing the Self. SPELL: Swiss Papers in English Language and Literature 24. Ed. Karen Junod and Didier Maillat. Tübingen: Narr, 2010. 153-163.

ers" suggests a paradoxical self-fashioning that hinges on a fragmentation and dispersal of the self. The protagonist of the story, the opera singer Pellegrina Leoni, abandons her role as a public performer and dissolves herself so as to reemerge and turn all the world into a stage for her protean performances. The poetics thus developed by Dinesen's writing foregrounds issues of identity that bear on the self-presentation of the woman artist in critical ways.

Dinesen's self-fashioning as a public persona already indicates how important masks and masquerades are to her artistic self-expression. In a photograph taken in 1954, Baroness Karen Blixen adopts a particularly remarkable pose: the writer can be seen to wear a black headdress topped by a black feather together with a pierrot costume she already possessed in her youth.[1] She fixes the viewer with her alert look and smiles enigmatically. Her heavy make-up and the spectacular way she is lit underline the theatricality and flamboyance of Blixen's self-dramatization, while at the same time her thin figure almost disappears under the ample folds of her white costume and the semi-transparent fabric framing her face. Her photographic portrait and her masculine pen-name Isak Dinesen, under which she published her English texts,[2] both suggest a complex dialectics of self-presentation and self-masking, and they also refer us to the multiple artistic self-transformations that characterized her biography. It was after she had to give up her African farm, described in her most famous text, *Out of Africa* (1937), and return to her native Denmark that Blixen reinvented herself and began to write professionally. As well as writing literary tales, she fashioned herself as a highly fictionalized persona by claiming, for instance, that she was three thousand years old and had already dined with Socrates (Thurman 331; Brantly 66). Indeed she repeatedly asserted that she had promised her soul to the devil so that she could turn her life into tales (Thurman 140, 258, 337; Brantly 66).[3]

---

[1] This photograph is reproduced in the illustrated biography by Frans Lasson and Clara Svendsen (181).

[2] Blixen's *nom du plume* is, strictly speaking, a half-pseudonym. Dinesen was her maiden name, while the assumed Hebrew name Isak means "the one who laughs." Blixen had several nicknames such as Tanne and Tania and she acquired a number of further pseudonyms, including Osceola and Lord Byron. On Blixen's names and pseudonyms, see Judith Thurman (5).

[3] Blixen felt that she had been cut off from life after realizing that she had contracted a severe form of syphilis from her husband Bror von Blixen-Finecke and after having lost both her farm and her lover Denys Finch Hatton in Africa. It was against this backdrop that she turned to a second life in her writing and, as part of her artistic practice, fashioned herself as a living artefact. For a detailed account of Blixen's life, see Judith Thurman's standard biography *Isak Dinesen: The Life of a Storyteller* (1995).

Dinesen's myriad self-stagings are remarkably in tune with contemporary notions of performance and performativity. It is no doubt as a result of Judith Butler's seminal work on gender performance that critical attention has increasingly shifted to the performative character of identity. At the same time, the work of Dinesen can also be seen to resonate with an earlier and, in fact, contemporaneous text by Joan Rivière. In her essay – entitled "Womanliness as Masquerade" and published in 1929, that is, one year after Virginia Woolf's novel *Orlando*, another literary example that highlights performative aspects of identity – Rivière argues that gender and masquerade are "the same thing" (38). By drawing on Rivière's notion of gender masquerade, J. L. Austin's performative speech act theory but also on Louis Althusser's concept of interpellation and Michel Foucault's work on discursive power, Butler calls attention to a fundamental ambivalence of identity. On the one hand, we are interpellated as subjects and have to subject ourselves to cultural codes and social norms that curtail and injure us. On the other hand, if identity is performative, there is, according to Butler, scope for resignification, reiteration or renegotiation. Sedimented codes and norms are both affirmed *and* defied as subjects reiterate them with a difference.

My wager is not simply that Dinesen anticipates contemporary notions of identity as a series of performative acts. Rather, what I want to highlight is the feminine self-articulation enacted by Dinesen's poetics. "The Dreamers," with which she launched her literary career, is particularly pertinent to a discussion of artistic performances of the feminine self. The story revolves around a female performer, the spectacular opera singer Pellegrina Leoni whose voice serves us a powerful means of self-construction. However, when Pellegrina loses her professional singing voice, the emphasis of the text shifts from the stable persona of the prima donna to a self-performance that is more mobile, fluid and plural.

Who is the singer Pellegrina Leoni? How is her voice described? And how does she construct herself through her role as a singer? As observed by her impresario, the old Jew Marcus Cocoza, the operatic star performer Pellegrina Leoni "'had in her life two great, devouring passions, which meant everything to her proud heart.'"

"The first was her passion for the great soprano, Pellegrina Leoni. [. . .] In her relation to this idol she had no forbearance and no rest. [. . .] She worked in the service of Pellegrina Leoni like a slave under the whip, weeping, dying at times, when it was demanded of her.

"She was a devil to the other women of the opera, for she needs must have all the parts for Pellegrina. She was indignant because it was impossible for her to perform two rôles within the same opera. [. . .]

"And the other great passion [. . .] of this great heart was her love for her audience. And that was not for the great people, the proud princes and magnates and the lovely ladies, all in jewels; not even for the famous composers, musicians, critics, and men of letters, but for her galleries. Those poor people of the back streets and market places, who would give up a meal or a pair of shoes, the wages of hard labour, to crowd high up in the hot house and hear Pellegrina sing, and who stamped the floor, shrieked and wept over her – she loved them beyond everything in the world. [. . .] And she was adored by the people." (Dinesen 402-405)

Remarkable in this characterization of Pellegrina Leoni is the mutual implication of the individual and the collective dimensions of the singer's voice. It is in dialogic exchange with her rapt audience and the operatic system as a whole that the protagonist constitutes herself as a star performer. She sings for the "poor people," who in turn confirm her in her social role as a celebrated public voice. But not only this. Driven by her boundless love for her audience and her unconditional commitment to her star persona, Pellegrina sacrifices herself in order to turn her own figure into an object of quasi-religious devotion, which is worshipped by her audience and herself alike.

On the one hand, the voice of Pellegrina Leoni is composite, multiple and plural because she performs various operatic roles. When necessary, that is, "'when it was demanded of her,'" Pellegrina will weep and die. She undergoes the numerous deaths demanded by the operatic scripts and scores only to constantly resurrect herself on stage. On the other hand, the passage implies that her voice becomes monologic in so far as she privileges one single role. As mentioned by Marcus, "'she needs must have all the parts for Pellegrina.'" Rather than actually transforming herself into the various operatic figures she enacts, she claims all parts so as to use them as her own vehicle and subsume them under her one superlative role, "'the great soprano, Pellegrina Leoni.'"

When a fire breaks out during a performance of Mozart's *Don Giovanni* at the opera house in Milan, the singer is hit by a falling beam. She makes a narrow escape from death, but loses her voice as a result of the shock. How is this near-fatal accident to be read? Dinesen's tale can be seen to rewrite nineteenth-century narratives in which female figures performing in public such as, for example, the improviser and genius Corinne in Germaine de Staël's novel *Corinne ou l'Italie* (1807) tend to eventually lose their voice.[4] Seemingly in this tradition, "The Dreamers"

---

[4] Further examples include the demonized diva Alcharisi in George Eliot's *Daniel Deronda* (1876) or the political speaker Verena Tarrant in Henry James's *The Bostonians* (1886). For a reading which connects "The Dreamers" to *Corinne ou l'Italie* and other female *Künstlerromane* from the romantic period, see Kari E. Lokke (150-162).

reverberates with a tragic sense of loss. The singer leaves the stage never to be heard again. However, by using what would be a classic ending in a nineteenth-century text as her point of departure, Dinesen reshifts the narrative argument. The accident of Pellegrina Leoni can be seen to point to a deadlock in her persona as a singer. Investing everything in one single role, the incident suggests, is fatal.

Dinesen's protagonist loses her professional voice and her public acclaim as a singer, but she gains access to a different form of self-expression. After the star soprano Pellegrina Leoni has been buried at a public fake funeral, she explains to her former impresario: "'There are many that I can be. [. . .] I will not be one person again, Marcus, I will be always many persons from now. Never again will I have my heart and my whole life bound up with one woman, to suffer so much'" (Dinesen 417-418). What Pellegrina opts for is a protean performance of the self. Having recognized the lethal effects of a single self-construction, she fragments her former persona into a myriad of masks and masquerades: "'I will not be one person again,'" and "'there are many that I can be.'" Following her wish never again to be trapped and caught up in one single role, Pellegrina not only turns into a traveller but also adopts a new mask for each lover she encounters on her journey. To the Englishman Lincoln Forsner in Rome, she presents herself as the courtesan Olalla, to Friedrich Hohenemser in Lucerne as the milliner and revolutionary Madame Lola, and to Baron Guildenstern in Saumur as the saint Rosalba. Even while these roles suggest images of femininity that are flagrantly stereotypical, Pellegrina is, significantly enough, in control of their performance. Moreover, her radical role-play suggests at once a critical distance from and a vibrant expression of the self. It is by adopting multiple masks and personas that she can articulate herself.

The actual theatre may have burnt down, but for Pellegrina, the wanderer, all the world becomes a stage. The self-dramatizations on which she embarks after the symbolic burial of her singer persona follow a typically modernist project. By transposing her theatrical scenarios into everyday life, she recreates herself as her own work of art. As an arch-performer, she keeps transforming herself not unlike Virginia Woolf's cross-dressing and sex-changing Orlando, who becomes a purely aesthetic sign of writing and, in so doing, blurs any boundaries between text and self. Although, or rather because Pellegrina has lost her voice as a singer, she has a "voice" of her own, and this time her self-expression is indeed multiple. In keeping with the theatricalization of her masks and disguises, her self-performances do not give expression to any psychological interiority. Instead Pellegrina can be described as the sum of the effects which her vibrant vitality and her star-like luminosity have on her various lovers. Significantly enough, she lacks a shadow but has herself perpetually "shadowed" by Marcus. Whenever she starts to feel tied down to a particular role, Marcus helps her disappear without a trace and adopt a new mask. As a result, her self-performance is one of fleeting evanescence, of continual disappearance and reemergence.

Pellegrina serves as a figure who reflects Dinesen's aesthetics. She refers us to a voice which disappears and then resounds as pure text. Her voice can no longer be attached to a person but instead dissolves into writing. Moreover, it is important to note that her impersonal "voice" is mediated by the narration of other character voices. Her stellar career, the loss of her voice and her adoption of multiple roles are the chronological events of the story we can reconstruct once we reach the end of "The Dreamers." The actual structure of the text, however, consists of several narratives that frame Pellegrina, who is almost the only figure not to tell a story: a first-level narrative of the authorial narrator frames a second-level narrative, that is, the story that Lincoln Forsner tells to the "much renowned" but weary storyteller Mira Jama on a full-moon night, whilst their ship is sailing off the East African coast on the Indian Ocean (Dinesen 328). According to Lincoln, he was searching for the prostitute Olalla, who had made him a dreamer, when he met his two friends Hohenemser and Guildenstern, who, in turn, told him their stories about Madame Lola and Rosalba.

Dinesen's text works with two different modes, both of which are important to our discussion of identity and performance: Pellegrina's mobile enactment on the one hand and the narrative frames of the three men on the other. There is tension not just between the various male narrators, all of whom derive a narcissistic sense of identity from their beloved object. The fiercest conflict can be observed between their narrative desire and Pellegrina's protean performances. While Pellegrina keeps reinventing herself so as to avoid being read and appropriated, each of the three men seeks to reduce her to the particular figure she represents in his story.

This conflict comes to a climax on a stormy winter night. The three men have just finished telling each other their stories about Olalla, Madame Lola and Rosalba in a hotel in the Swiss Alps when, all of a sudden, they catch sight of a veiled woman. They all believe to recognize their respective object of desire and chase the woman as she is running towards the liminal scene of a mountain pass. Because Pellegrina eludes any single role, the question Lincoln asks her, when he finally catches up with her, is inevitable. Yet it also turns out to be fatal.

"...Who are you?"

She did not turn, or look at me. But the next moment she did what I had always feared that she might do: she spread out her wings and flew away [. . .] she threw herself from the earth clear into the abyss, and disappeared from our sight. [. . .]

I thought then of how it had been my question to her which had driven her into this great white full-moon death, in the end.   (Dinesen 395-397)

Pellegrina refuses to answer and attempts to escape from this scene of interpellation altogether. However, as suggested by the lethal injuries which she suffers in her failed flight, she is literally killed by the question which would pin her down to one single identity.

What then is the poetics of "The Dreamers"? The narrative mode of Dinesen's text, I suggest, presents a critique of the way in which the female figure is reified. It shows, and actually performs, the violence implicit in the narrative framing of the male characters. Significantly enough, it is only as the woman lies dying that Marcus tells the name and story of the great soprano. In a deft gesture, Dinesen has his belated commentary on the stable persona of the singer coincide with the actual death of the woman. Or put differently, the text implies that death is brought about by a narrative desire that seeks to reduce her to one single identity.[5]

Yet the feminine, or perhaps feminist, mode of Dinesen's text goes further than that: shortly before Pellegrina's death, her narrative containment is disrupted by a strange voice effect.

Her whole body vibrated under her passion like the string of an instrument.

"Oh," she cried, "look, look here! It is Pellegrina Leoni – it is she, it is she herself again – she is back. Pellegrina, the greatest singer, poor Pellegrina, she is on the stage again. To the honour of God, as before. Oh, she is here, it is she – Pellegrina, Pellegrina herself!"

It was unbelievable that, half dead as she was, she could house this storm of woe and triumph. It was, of course, her swan song.

"Come unto her, now, all, again," she said. "Come back, my children, my friends. It is I – I forever, now." She wept with a rapture of relief, as if she had in her a river of tears, held back long.

The old Jew was in a terrible state of pain and strain. [. . .]

Of a sudden he took up his little walking stick and struck three short strokes on the side of the stretcher.

"Donna Pellegrina Leoni," he cried in a clear voice. "*En scène pour le deux* [sic]."

---

[5] Also note Elisabeth Bronfen (1986), who shows that in Dinesen's tales narrative closure often means death.

Like a soldier to the call, or a war horse to the blast of the trumpet, she collected herself at his words. Within the next minute she became quiet in a gallant and deadly calm. She gave him a glance from her enormous dark eyes. In one mighty movement, like that of a billow raising and sinking, she lifted the middle of her body. A strange sound, like the distant roar of a great animal, came from her breast. Slowly the flames in her face sank, and an ashen grey covered it instead. Her body fell back, stretched itself out and lay quite still, and she was dead. (Dinesen, 426-427)

Initially Pellegrina's famous singer persona seems to be reconstituted by the cue given by her impresario. She slips into her former symbolic role, ready to resume her part of Donna Anna in Mozart's *Don Giovanni* at precisely the point at which she had been interrupted by the near-fatal accident. The accumulation of the words "she," "herself," "Pellegrina Leoni" and "I" in her speech suggests unreserved identification with the role of the singer: "'It is Pellegrina Leoni – it is she, it is she herself again [. . .]. Oh, she is here, it is she – Pellegrina, Pellegrina herself! [. . .] It is I – I forever, now.'" Yet ironically Leoni, a figure to whom she refers almost exclusively in the third person, is just as much a mask as any of her other roles. Rather than coming back to the stage, Pellegrina has actually never left the theatrical boards. And, indeed, while the three men seek to demask her, this last performance shows not just the fatality but also the inherent impossibility of their attempt to lay bare and thus expose her identity.

What is, however, even more disruptive is the culmination of Pellegrina's swan song in a monstrous utterance towards the end of the passage – "a strange sound, like the roar of a great animal." The sheer sound of her non-verbal voice disrupts not just the narrative desire and fantasy of the three men. It also undercuts all symbolic and imaginary codes, and hence all social identities. The sublime song Pellegrina used to produce as a singer allowed her and her audience to mirror themselves in each other. Her swan song refers her listeners to the very reverse: an articulation of radical alterity.

As a quasi-manifesto of Dinesen's art, "The Dreamers" demonstrates, and indeed performs, a radical dispersal of identity into a multiplicity of masks. Or as Kari E. Lokke puts it in her reading, Dinesen's text "explodes, in explicit and spectacular fashion, all received notions of a coherent, individual self in favor of an imaginatively constructed collective selfhood that comes into being through performance" (151). As I have been arguing, the disappearance of Dinesen's protagonist from the opera stage effects a resonant self-creation, at least as long as Pellegrina can continually renew herself in and through her perpetual performance. It is because she abandons her monolithic star persona that she can articulate herself through her myriad masks.

On the one hand, Dinesen's text accentuates the subversive elusiveness of its protagonist who cannot be pinned down to a single role. On the other hand, the story of Pellegrina does carry a tragic note – not just because she cannot sustain her protean performance and dies in her failed attempt to escape from her symbolic interpellation. What is also sad is the fact that she is able to fashion herself as a star singer but has to exit the public arena, which is a fate she shares with many earlier female performer figures featured in nineteenth-century texts.[6] In contrast to Woolf's Orlando, who gains a voice in English literature as a woman writer by eventually publishing the poem she has been rewriting for centuries, Dinesen's Pellegrina has to fall silent in order to express herself and eventually dies in her effort to escape from fixed identity constructions. However, as pointed out by Kari E. Lokke (158), the tale does not end quite as tragically. In the closing narrative frame, Lincoln and Mira Jama both affirm that Pellegrina may not be dead after all. They claim that she survives as a "'pretty little jackal'" and reasserts the potential of multiplicity and metamorphosis by barking "'I am not one little jackal, not one; I am many little jackals.' And pat! in a second she really is another, barking just behind you: 'I am not one little jackal. Now I am another'" (Dinesen 429). The fatal interpellation of the singer may thus ultimately be counteracted by her transformation through yet another series of masquerades.

Dinesen had long turned herself into an iconic figure and cultivated her legendary status when she visited the United States towards the end of her life. During her trip her many activities included a lunch given in her honour. One of the pictures taken on this occasion shows her together with two American authors, namely Carson McCullers and Arthur Miller on the one hand and the tragic star Marilyn Monroe on the other.[7] Like Monroe, who is looking at her, Dinesen is immediately recognizable. Marked by age and illness, she looks frail and fragile. However, if Monroe stands for the lethal logic of the single star image she came to enact over her body, Dinesen refers us to a resilient modulation and expression of the self. Seen in profile, her made-up face looks like an elegant mask, which puts the existence of a real Karen Blixen into question and simultaneously proclaims the presence of a fictionalized Isak Dinesen.

---

[6] See again the tragic silencing of the female performers in novels such as Germaine de Staël's *Corinne ou l'Italie*, George Eliot's *Daniel Deronda* and Henry James's *The Bostonians*.

[7] A reproduction of the image can again be found in the illustrated biography by Lasson and Svendsen (198).

As Susan Hardy Aiken points out, Dinesen's fusion with her writing "was never more poignantly enacted" (255) than in the last years of her life, when she seemed to literally die into her art as her already emaciated body withered to merely skeletal dimensions. However, as my reading has shown, it is already in "The Dreamers," the first tale written at the very beginning of her literary career, that she develops a complex dialectics of disappearance and reemergence. Similar to her literary alter ego Pellegrina Leoni, Dinesen modulates her voice as a storyteller by always speaking through her consciously staged masks. In contrast to her fictional character, she succeeds in sustaining both her artistic voice and self-performance.

References

Aiken, Susan Hardy. *Isak Dinesen and the Engendering of Narrative*. Chicago: The University of Chicago Press, 1990.

Arendt, Hannah. "Foreword: Isak Dinesen, 1885-1962." 1968. Isak Dinesen. *Daguerrotypes and Other Essays*. Chicago: The University of Chicago Press, 1979. vii-xxv.

Brantly, Susan. "Isak Dinesen: The Danish Scheherazade." *Scandinavian Review* 90:2 (2002): 58-66.

Bronfen, Elisabeth. "'Scheherazade sah den Morgen dämmern und schwieg diskret': Zu der Beziehung zwischen Erzählung und Tod in den Geschichten von Isak Dinesen (Karen Blixen)." *Skandinavistik* 16:1 (1986): 48-62.

Butler, Judith. *Gender Trouble: Feminism and the Subversion of Identity*. New York, London: Routledge, 1990.

———. *Bodies That Matter: On the Discursive Limits of Sex*. New York, London: Routledge, 1993.

Dinesen, Isak. "The Dreamers." *Seven Gothic Tales*. 1934. London: Putnam, 1969. 327-430.

Lasson, Frans and Clara Svendsen. *The Life and Destiny of Isak Dinesen*. Chicago: The University of Chicago Press, 1970.

Lokke, Kari E. *Tracing Women's Romanticism: Gender, History and Transcendence*. London, New York: Routledge, 2004.

Rivière, Joan. "Womanliness as a Masquerade." 1929. *Formations of Fantasy*. Ed. Victor Burgin, James Donald and Cora Kaplan. London, New York: Routledge, 1986. 35-44.

Thurman, Judith. *Isak Dinesen: The Life of a Storyteller*. New York: Picador, 1995.

Woolf, Virginia. *Orlando: A Biography*. 1928. Ed. Rachel Bowlby. Oxford: Oxford University Press, 1992.

Constructing Identity on Facebook:
Report on a Pilot Study

Brook Bolander and Miriam A. Locher

In this paper we examine the construction of identity on the social network site (SNS) Facebook. We thereby focus on the language use in personal profiles and status updates (SUs) of ten individuals from Switzerland. This paper thus presents the results of a pilot study, which is part of a larger project on language and identity in Facebook. Drawing on previous work on SNSs by Zhao et al. and Nastri et al., this paper highlights that Facebookers use a variety of strategies to construct their identities, i.e., visual, enumerative, narrative (cf. Zhao et al.) and self-labelling practices, as well as what we term "Creative language usage." Results show that identity construction on Facebook tends to be mediated more extensively via implicit identity claims than explicit ones, which corroborates the results of Zhao et al. We hypothesize that this may be related to the fact that individuals in Facebook tend to have "anchored relationships" (cf. Zhao et al.), which means their Facebook relationships are grounded in offline life. The paper also points to particular factors relating to the medium and the social context of interaction which appear to influence language use in this SNS, and which will need to be studied in further depth as the project proceeds.

1. Introduction

This paper explores identity construction on the social network site (SNS) Facebook (cf. Section 3 for more information on SNSs) and presents the results of our pilot study of the personal profile pages and status updates of ten Facebookers living in Switzerland. Personal profile

Performing the Self. SPELL: Swiss Papers in English Language and Literature 24. Ed. Karen Junod and Didier Maillat. Tübingen: Narr, 2010. 165-187.

pages give individuals the possibility to "type [themselves] into being" (Sunden 3, quoted in Boyd and Ellison) through a process of self-labelling and description, or enumeration, of hobbies and interests. Example 1 shows the information provided by one woman on her personal profile page:

Example 1:
<F-7> is a "woman," "engaged," "interested in men," "looking for friendship," provides details of birthday, college education and job situation.

From this particular individual's personal profile page, we learn about F-7's sex ("woman"), her marital status ("engaged"), sexual orientation ("interested in men"), motivation for using Facebook ("looking for friendship"), birthday, college background and employment situation. This information is the result of F-7's practice of self-labelling and enumeration, whereby she selects options (such as "woman") from pre-existing lists of traits and characteristics (such as "man" or "woman"), and describe her hobbies and interests in spaces provided by the site for this purpose (cf. Section 5 for more detail).

The practice of self-labelling can be seen to constitute a relatively explicit form of identity construction. It is seen as explicit since individuals choose labels to describe themselves, thereby straightforwardly and unambiguously placing themselves in categories (e.g., the category of sex/gender) and positioning (Davies and Harré) themselves within the categories (e.g., by selecting from the options "man" or "woman" within this category). The enumeration of hobbies and interests, on the other hand, is a less explicit form of identity construction, since there is a less straightforward connection between statements about one's hobbies and interests, for example, listening to music, reading books or going on holiday, and the type of identity one constructs for oneself through such a claim (cf. Section 5.1 for more detail).

Through the status updates we gain insight into other processes of identity construction, both explicit and implicit, i.e., processes of identity construction which see a more or less straightforward connection between the language used and the type of identity claim made (cf. Section 6 for more detail). Status updates are texts written by Facebook users in which they share information about what they are doing at the present moment (through the system prompt "What are you doing now"),[1] or other information with their Facebook friends, for example,

---

[1] At the time we collected the data for this project this was the system prompt for status updates. In the interim, the prompt has changed, and now reads "What is on your mind."

pertaining to how they are feeling, what they did in the past or plan for the future. In Examples 2-4 we see three status updates, in which the Facebook user constructs her identity as an employee (Example 2), and as a student (Examples 3 and 4).

Example 2:
<F-7> ordered 15,000 paper towels by accident! My boss' face: priceless!

Example 3:
<F-7> has got to start writing her first assignment for university now :-(.

Example 4:
<F-7> is at work and starting to get nervous about tomorrow! University will rule my life once again!

While we do not see explicit identity claims, since F-7 does not explicitly state that she is an employee and student, information on identity is nonetheless conveyed through the language of the status updates, e.g. through the nouns "boss," and "university." This implicit means of identity construction is clearly different to the explicit form evident in the self-labelling on the profile pages.

Taking these examples as a starting point, we wish to explore how users of the SNS Facebook employ language to create identities in this virtual world. Our research questions are thus:

1)   How and to what extent do the participants in our pilot study make use of the information categories provided on the personal profile pages?
2)   In what ways does the language used in the status updates contribute to identity construction?

These two questions are explored for ten individuals from Switzerland, who form a group of friends, and whose profile pages and status updates have been analyzed for the purposes of this study.

The structure of the paper is as follows. In Sections 2 and 3 we outline previous work on identity and language, and social network sites (SNS) and Facebook, so as to be able to contextualize our research within a wider framework of research on Computer-Mediated Communication (CMC). In Section 4, we briefly describe the data, before turning to the personal profiles in Section 5 and the status updates in Section 6. In both sections 5 and 6, we first outline the method and then the results and discussion. The paper concludes in Section 7 and points to implications of the results of this pilot study for further research.

2. Language and identity

Our individual identities are shaped by numerous factors, including age, gender, class, ethnicity, upbringing, profession, hobbies and regional loyalties. However, our identities are not simply the sum of these factors. In this paper, we adopt a definition of identity as "the social positioning of self and other" (Bucholtz and Hall 586; cf. also Mendoza-Denton; Locher). This points to the importance of the intersubjective and the interactional, i.e. to the fact that we position ourselves and others in and through interactions with others. Thus, identity "is intersubjectively rather than individually produced and interactionally emergent rather than assigned in an a priori fashion" (Bucholtz and Hall 587).

In other words, identity is constructed in and through interpersonal relationships and social practice, or through the performance of "acts of positioning," where positioning can be defined as follows:

> Positioning [. . .] is the discursive process whereby selves are located in conversations as observably and subjectively coherent participants in jointly produced story lines. (Davies and Harré 46)

Thus, as the quote indicates, when we interact with others, we are underlining the existence of a particular self, which can be observed by others at a particular point in time. Within public spaces where there are witnesses to acts of positioning (like in Facebook), the positioning of self and others is particularly interesting, since by claiming I am a friend of X, for example, I am also positioning X as a friend of mine.

However, while endorsing a view of identity and identity construction which underlines that the process is dynamic and emergent, it is important to note that this does not mean that interactants reinvent themselves from scratch in every new interaction. Instead, they are embedded in their knowledge as social actors in their social world and they draw on expectations about identity claims and stereotypes derived from previous encounters in a process of analogy. While not the only means, language is one key way of constructing identity when we engage in social practice.

3. Social network sites and Facebook

Facebook is a social network site situated on the Internet. It was originally launched in early 2004 for Harvard students, and thus targeted "distinct college networks only" (Boyd and Ellison). However, since

2006 it has been open to everyone. Following Boyd and Ellison, we define SNSs as web-based services that allow individuals to

(1) construct a public or semi-public profile within a bounded system,
(2) articulate a list of other users ["friends"] with whom they share a connection,[2] and
(3) view and traverse their list of connections and those made by others within the system. (Boyd and Ellison)

Facebook can be classified as an SNS on these criteria. Individuals can construct a profile within the Facebook platform, and this profile can be more or less public depending on the privacy settings the user selects. They can become "friends" with other individuals on Facebook, to whose profiles they then have access.[3]

Recent work on CMC has underlined the need to emphasize "the role of linguistic variability in the formation of social interaction and social identities on the Internet" (Androutsopolous 421). This constitutes a clear move away from the *computer* or *technological determinism* which was pervasive to early work on CMC (cf. Androutsopolous, for example, for a criticism of the computer deterministic viewpoint). While the influence of the medium on language use should not be ignored, scholars argue for the importance of appreciating both medium and social/situational factors for language use.

This recognition of the potential role played by both medium and social/situational factors is most clearly expressed in Herring's faceted-classification scheme for computer-mediated discourse, a non-hierarchically ordered, open model which lists those factors which have hitherto been shown to influence language use in a variety of genres of CMC, while recognizing that others may well also play a role. The whole model cannot be presented here, yet it is worth emphasizing that the medium factors of "asynchronicity (M1)" and "message format (M10)" and the social factor "participant structure (S1)," which includes considerations about the degree of anonymity, have been seen to influence language use in our data (cf. Section 6).

Literature on Facebook thus far has tended to come from communication studies, sociology and network studies. Linguistic interest has been relatively limited. Two articles which demonstrate a linguistic interest are Zhao et al. and Nastri et al. The former explores identity con-

---

[2] It is worth noting that Facebook's slogan emphasizes notions of "sharing" and "connecting:" 'Facebook helps you connect and share with the people in your life [. . .]" (http://www.facebook.com/).
[3] As mentioned before, depending on the privacy settings, different friends of a Facebook user may have varying degrees of access.

struction in Facebook and demonstrates an interest in language, although language is not studied in its own right. It is an important text in relation to identity construction in SNSs, since, as Zhao et al. point out, "[i]dentity construction in a nonymous online environment has not been well studied" (1818). Nonymity (the opposite of anonymity) refers to the fact that Facebook users' relationships tend to be grounded in off-line life. In their study of 63 Facebookers, who were students at an American northeastern university, Zhao et al. found that: "Facebook users predominantly claim their identities implicitly rather than explicitly; they 'show rather than tell' and stress group and consumer identities over personally narrated ones" (1816). In light of our research, this is interesting, since it suggests that we can expect to find less self-labelling (which is a form of explicit identity construction) in the personal profiles, and more implicit identity claims made by individuals via their status updates. Nastri et al.'s paper, while neither concentrating on identity construction nor on Facebook *per se*, does focus on a linguistic analysis of the language of away-messages in Instant Messaging (IM), using Speech Act Theory. In Sections 5.2. and 6.2. comparisons between our own results and those of Zhao et al. and Nastri et al. are made.

4. Data

The participants in our data are ten Swiss individuals, who are in their late twenties and early thirties, nine of whom went to university. Eight know each other in offline life. They are thus part of the same social network, which is relatively loose-knit: some individuals have multiplex and dense ties, while others are only close friends with our anchor person,[4] and have only casual offline connections with the others (cf. Milroy and Milroy). For ethical reasons, we chose to obtain permission to use the data as part of our study (cf. Ess and the AoIR ethics working committee; Eysenbach and Till).

The data for our pilot study consists of the "personal profile pages" and the status updates on the so-called "walls" of the users. While the function of a wall in a physical context is primarily to enclose a space and/or to separate space, it can also be used to post messages on (notice board/pin wall) or to decorate (paintings, posters, etc.). "Walls" in Facebook constitute a space on the website where the owner of the wall and his or her friends can leave messages and where the acts they en-

---

[4] In order to find our ten participants, we focused on one person and chose those nine friends the majority of whom also know each other on Facebook.

gage in are documented. The acts (or "action types" as we have called them) individuals can perform on their walls are manifold. This is evidenced by Table 1, which shows the "action types" performed by the pilot study group (N=481). The time frame in question is from 1 December 2008 until 31 January 2009. It should, however, be noted that we collected our data in spring 2009 for this time frame, so as to avoid the observer's paradox. The action types were performed by the individuals at a time when they were not aware that their entries would later be used for research purposes.

Table 1: Action types

Action types:		Total #	%
SU:	status update	227	47
AP:	application activity	87	18
AC:	acceptance of a gift or similar item	51	11
PH-CO:	a comment on a photo	43	9
SQ:	a source or quote (from a newspaper, magazine, blog, etc.)	20	4
PH:	uploading of photo	14	3
FAN:	becoming a fan	12	2
GR:	creating a group	10	2
SQ-CO:	a comment on an SQ	11	2
EV:	announcing an event	4	1
REV:	writing a review	1	0
GA:	game move indicated by system	1	0
Total		**481**	**99**

As evidenced by Table 1, SUs were the most prominent action type, with 47%. Applications (AP), such as becoming a friend with someone, and the acceptance of a gift or something similar (AC) were also relatively common. Since this is a small sample, it remains to be seen whether similar patterns are observable for the other individuals in our wider study.[5]

While SUs were the most common action type, not all ten individuals wrote them. Indeed, as Table 2 shows, two individuals (F-1 and F-8)

[5] This paper reports on a pilot study on ten Swiss individuals within a corpus that contains 74 individuals in Switzerland, and 58 in England.

had none at all, and were virtually inactive on their walls, whereas F-7 and M-2 produced 55 and 45 status updates respectively.

Table 2: Participants and their extent of activity on the wall

Action types:	F-1	M-2	F-3	F-4	F-5	M-6	F-7	F-8	F-9	F-10	Total	%
SU		45	19	16	20	29	55		37	6	227	47
AP				3	1		6	4	35	38	87	18
AC			1	2			1	24	18	5	51	11
PH-CO		7	9	5			21			1	43	9
SQ		2	1		1	10	3		3		20	4
PH		1	4		2	1	3		2	1	14	3
FAN		9			1	1			1		12	2
SQ-CO		2				6	3				11	2
GR		0				1	1	1	4	3	10	2
EV		1				2			1		4	1
REV		0							1		1	0
GA		1									1	0
Total	0	68	34	23	27	51	93	29	102	54	481	99
%	0	14	7	5	6	11	19	6	21	11	100	

More generally, Table 2 highlights different degrees of activity on Facebook. While F-9 performed a total of 102 actions (21%) and F-7 93 (19%), F-4 performed 23 (5%) and F-1 zero. It is noteworthy that there is variation both in terms of general activity on the wall, and in terms of the types of activities performed on the wall. Again, further research will underline whether the same stands true for other groups of Facebook users.

5. Explicit and implicit identity labelling in the Facebook profile pages

In Sunden's words, "[p]rofiles are unique pages where one can 'type oneself into being'" (3, quoted in Boyd and Ellison). The personal profile page on Facebook invites users to provide information about themselves: The header "basic information" triggers self-labelling with respect to age, sex, relationship status, etc.; "personal information" invites enumerating activities, interests, favourite music, TV shows, movies, books and quotations and entails a section entitled "about me;" the headers "contact information" and "education and work" trigger further details. The ten individuals in the study varied in terms of the amount of personal information they chose to reveal to their friends, as will be shown shortly.

5.1. Method

As mentioned in Section 3, we rely strongly on Zhao et al. for the methodology used in this paper. Table 3 is adapted from their study and shows a continuum of identity claims, which ranges from implicit to explicit. These claims are linked to the Facebook categories within the profile pages.

Table 3: "The continuum of implicit and explicit identity claims on Facebook" on profile pages, adapted from Zhao et al. (1824)

	More implicit <-----------------------------------> More explicit			
Category	Visual	Enumerative	Narrative	Self-labelling
Type	Self as social actor	Self as Consumer	First Person Self	First Person Self
Category in Facebook	Pictures	Interests/ Hob-bies/ etc.	"About Me . . ."	Basic information

In the column "Visual," we have implicit identity claims. These claims are made through pictures.[6] Here, the self is described as a "Social Actor," since, "[i]t is as if the user is saying, 'Watch me and know me by my friends'" (Zhao et al. 1825). In other words, the identity claims here are made on the basis of showing not telling (cf. Zhao et al 1816).

In the column "Enumerative," the Self is described as a consumer, since he/she foregrounds interests, tastes, hobbies, favourite books, movies, etc; i.e., what she/he consumes, in the sense of "engages in" or "utilizes." This column describes more explicit identity claims than the visual one, but the acts are still indirect, since they are about "see[ing] what I like/do/read/listen to" (Zhao et al. 1825–1826).

More explicit still is the narrative column, which contains verbal descriptions of the self. These are explicit, since in the "About me" section in Facebook, individuals have the possibility of directly presenting themselves to their friends. Hence, the focus is on the "First Person Self."

---

[6] Facebook users can also upload pictures. This action will appear on the wall. This practice is not discussed in this pilot study.

Finally, the most explicit column within the personal profiles is the "Self-labelling" one, which we added to Zhao et al.'s original framework. Here, again, we can speak of a "First Person Self," since individuals have the option to label themselves. Mostly, they can do so by selecting from a series of options (e.g., "Relationship status," which provides options, such as "single," "engaged," "it's complicated"), and sometimes by providing a short text (e.g., relating to their religious views). This is to be regarded as more explicit than the "Narrative" column, since we are dealing with labels, which serve the function of categorizing individuals, in a means analogous to the social variables assigned to individuals in variationist sociolinguistic and sociological studies, such as "sex," "age" (through the "birthday" information), "education."

We analyzed the implicit and explicit identity claims in our data systematically according to the framework just presented in order to address research question 1, repeated here for convenience:

1) How and to what extent do the participants in our pilot study make use of the information categories provided on the personal profile pages?

This research question can be split into two sub-questions, namely:

a) To what extent do individuals make use of the information possibilities?
b) How can the observed practices be linked to identity construction?

5.2 Results and discussion

Tables 4 and 5, dealing with the "Visual," "Enumerative," "Narrative" and "Self-labelling" categories, present the results from the analysis of the personal profile pages (research question 1a), and in the following we will attempt to interpret these initial research results and relate them to identity construction (research question 1b). As evidenced by the tables, the results on identity construction in the personal profiles are mixed.

Zhao et al. report that their sample of 63 students is characterized by "the almost universal selection of dense displays of profile photos and wall posts, followed by highly enumerated lists of cultural preferences associated with youth culture, and finally the minimalist, first-person 'about me' statements" (1826). Their general conclusion is thus that "Facebook users predominantly claim their identities implicitly rather than explicitly; they 'show rather than tell' [. . .]" (1816). With respect to pictures, Table 4 shows that 9 out of the 10 Facebookers of our study also use a profile photo on their main profile page, which is a visual means of implicit identity construction.

Table 4: Visual, enumerative and narrative identity construction

Category	Present	Absent
Visual identity construction		
Profile photo	9	1
Identity construction through enumeration		
Interest types	3	7
Favourite music	3	7
Favourite TV programmes	3	7
Favourite books	3	7
Activities	2	8
Favourite movies	2	8
Favourite quotations	2	8
Political views	2	8
Networks type	2	8
Religious views	1	9
Identity construction through narrative		
"About me"	3	7

When we turn to identity construction through enumeration, we observe different frequencies from Zhao et al. (range from 48 to 73% presence). As Table 4 shows, for all of the categories the majority of users did not volunteer any information at all. Indeed, our individuals only present scarce information about themselves as consumers, by referring to their interests, favourite music, TV programmes, books and movies. Information on activities, favourite quotations, political and religious views, and network types is even rarer. This is interesting in light of the discrepancy in frequency between our results and those of Zhao et al., although one must note that only tentative conclusions can be drawn from this comparison, since our sample, as it stands, is simply too small. The results of Zhao et al. showed that most of the users in their study "provided highly elaborated lists of such preferences signaling precise cultural tastes" (1825). For them, this can be interpreted in light of the two potential audiences in Facebook, friends and strangers:

> What better way to personally convey "kool, hot and smooth" than to signal it through "kool, hot, and smooth" music. A better way to present oneself to strangers as well as to friends is therefore to "show" rather than "tell" or to display rather than to describe oneself. (Zhao et al. 1826)

Indeed, in their initial sample of 83 users, 63 students made a large part of their accounts visible to both friends and non-friends. However, in our study, this does not apply, since none of the ten individuals seem to have made their profiles visible to non-friends. The relative lack of listings in our sample may have to do with the nonymity of the relationships between our informants. Thus, the particular participant structure (and one of the social factors described in Herring's model) of our group influences the practice.

Like in Zhao et al.'s study (42 / 67%), a smaller number of participants chose to make use of the "About me" option in Facebook (3 / 10; Table 4) in comparison to the picture information. Moreover, these three texts are very short, M-2 writes the word "mehl," (German "flour"). M-6 writes "hello. i like." and F-9 writes a German proverb "Hunde, die bellen, beissen nicht," which is equivalent to the English "a dog's bark is worse than its bite."

In all three cases, it is not immediately evident how this can be linked to the "First person self" we expect to see when we read the "About me" section. Despite the scant amount of data, it is interesting that the individuals chose to make these claims as a response to the "About me" system prompt. For this reason they deserve to be considered as potential identity claims, albeit opaque ones. Thus, in the case of F-9, one could argue that the German proverb constitutes an identity claim, since the individual might be saying this about herself. She may be constructing her identity as an individual who sometimes "barks," or gets loud, but is not actually someone to be feared. Even more opaque are M-2's "mehl," and M-6's "hello. i like." However, we can argue that the intent is to be humorous. Indeed, for both M-2 and M-6 this can be backed up by the fact that out of the ten pilot study participants they use humour the most in their status updates: M-2 uses humour in 24.4% and M-6 in 17% of his status updates.[7]

While a full 67% of the users in Zhao et al.'s study made use of the "About me" option, 37% of these only wrote 1-2 short sentences. The authors thus conclude that "this category tended to be the least elaborated of the identity strategies" (1826). However, those identity claims made were of a more explicit nature. Thus, claims, such as "I'm a laid back type" (Zhao et al. 1826) are described as "typical example[s] of these brief 'about me' statements" (1826). We did not find any of these in our data.

---

[7] Further research on the "About me" sections, the types of claims made and their potential functions in light of identity construction is needed to provide a fuller picture of the relevance of this part of the personal profile for identity construction (see Section 7).

Finally, at the other end of the continuum, we find explicit identity construction through self-labelling. This is a category not directly included by Zhao et al. in their figure, although it is addressed in their paper. In our study, we added it to Table 3, since we are convinced that self-labelling is an explicit form of identity construction. Table 5 shows that the use of this form of identity construction is mixed.

Table 5: Identity construction through self-labelling

Category	Present	Absent
Birthday	9	1
Relationship status	7	3
Job	5	5
Sex	4	6
College	4	6
Hometown	3	7
Interested in	3	7
Looking for	2	8
High school	2	8

Most individuals included information about their birthday and their relationship status, and half provided insight into their job. For the other categories, we find under half of the users self-labelling themselves as being either male or female, and providing information about their colleges, hometowns, what they are interested in, looking for, and where they went to high school.

Again, this result may be linked to a variety of factors, for example, the participant structure and the nonymity of the relationships, or the purpose of using Facebook. For example, all seven participants who provide information about their relationship status are in a relationship (i.e., five have a boyfriend or girlfriend, one is engaged and one is married). They may thus be constructing their identities as "taken" or simply expressing pride in their partners. This is especially the case if one considers that five of the seven provide the name of their partner. By doing this, we can argue that not only are these individuals positioning themselves as being in a relationship with their partners, they are also positioning their partners as being in a relationship with them (cf. Section 2).

Regarding information on one's birthday, it is hard to say whether this labelling is motivated by an identity act, in the sense of claiming to be part of an age cohort. It may have more to do with the fact that individuals want to let others know when their birthday is, so that they can be congratulated, which indeed is a common practice on Facebook walls when someone celebrates their birthday.

Why the other categories tend to be left open, could be connected to the nonymity of the relationships (i.e. to the participant structure), or the fact that there are various possibilities of constructing one's identity on Facebook. This is notably the case on the wall and through status updates, so that individuals may more readily make use of this latter option of identity construction, thereby opting to underline what is relevant for a specific point in time, as opposed to utilizing more static labels. Furthermore, in the case of "sex," many may have selected not to use the self-labelling route, since the visual component (i.e., the profile photo) and the fact that our informants know each other offline and have subscribed with their real names make this kind of information redundant.

In sum, our results generally support Zhao et al.'s, particularly regarding the "visual" and "narrative" elements. Further results will be needed to better be able to reflect upon the differences regarding the "enumeration" and to comment on the "self-labelling" component in more detail.

6. Status updates and the creative usage of language for identity construction

The research question at the centre of this section of the paper is the following:

2) In what ways does the language used in the status updates contribute to identity construction?

What we find in the status updates is termed "Creative language usage," since individuals can use language without restrictions.[8] While they are prompted by the general system prompt "What are you doing," there are no options to choose from, or specific prompts, relating to religious, or political interests, the way there are on the profile page. Thus, status updates invite individuals to share snippets of their lives with others, and by doing so they construct their identities.

In order to account for this creative use of language, we have adapted Table 3 by adding two columns at both ends of the continuum of implicit to explicit identity claims; in addition, we have specified whether the practice witnessed occurs on the profile page or on the wall (Table 6).

---

[8] There is a length restriction of 420 signs.

Table 6: "The continuum of implicit and explicit identity claims on Facebook" on profile pages and the Wall, adapted from Zhao et al. (1824)

More implicit <------------------------------------> More explicit

	Creative L-usage	Visual	Enumerative	Narrative	Self-labelling	Creative L-usage
Type	Actions	Self as social actor	Self as consumer	First person self	First person self	Actions
Category in Facebook	See Table 1	Pictures	Interests/ Hobbies/etc.	"About Me ..."	Basic information	See Table 1
Location	Wall	Profile/wall	Profile	Profile	Profile	Wall

We are thus focusing both on implicit and explicit identity claims: implicit, in the sense that statements like Example 2 (<F-7> ordered 15,000 paper towels by accident! My boss' face: priceless!) indirectly construct the individual's identity as an employee in this specific instant. On the other hand, we can also find explicit identity claims, along the lines of "F-7 is engaged to [name]! yay!." The latter constitute examples of "self-labelling," yet without the system prompt "Relationship status," and thus are still regarded as within the framework of "Creative language usage."

As outlined in Section 4, we are focusing on 227 status updates. Overall, they add up to a corpus of 1,984 words. On average these were 7.7 words long (minimum 2; maximum 29; SD 4.6). If we think back to the length of the three "About me" narratives (one word, three words, five words), it becomes evident that individuals write longer SUs, i.e., employ language in a creative way within this interactional context, more so than they do as an explicit presentation of the "First person self." The self here is described as a "social actor," yet unlike the social actor in the visual element of the profile, this "self" also tells something. He/she uses language to engage socially with his/her friends.

6.1. Method

In addition to Zhao et al., Nastri et al. served as an inspiration for our method of analyzing the status updates. The latter analyzed 483 away messages in Instant Messaging (IM), produced by 44 US students, applying speech act theory and analyzing the use of humour. We thus systematically coded the status updates for speech acts and the occurrence of humour as well. Further analysis involved the use of metaphors, non-standard language, and the grammatical and syntactic realization of the status updates. In this paper, we can only report on the speech acts and the use of humour and their connection to identity construction.

6.2. Results and discussion

Table 7 presents the results of the speech act types used in the status updates. It shows that assertives were clearly the most common type of speech act in the SUs (177 / 59%), followed by expressives (78 / 26%) and commissives (27 / 9%). Examples are given in Table 7.

Table 7: Speech acts in status updates

Speech acts:		Total #	%
Assertive:	M-2 wonks around in lol-universe.	177	59
Expressive:	M-2 loves bass.	78	26
Commissive:	F-7 is off to Basel soon!	27	9
Directive:	F-7 [...] grow, my little green shrubs, grow!	7	2
Question:	F-5 is pan tan wan? san xang oder pak wando??	7	2
Quotation:	M-6 is easy like sunday morning.	2	1
Link posting:	M-6 google under attack: http://tinyurl.com/aa8c2q	2	1
Total		**300[9]**	**100**

Nastri et al. also found these three types to be the most frequent in their analysis of 483 away messages (68%; 14%; 12%). The functions of these messages in Facebook, as opposed to in IM are, however, different. Nastri et al. concur with Baron et al. when they argue that "[o]ne of the main functions of informational away messages is to convey that one is not in front of the computer or to otherwise signal unavailability for instant messaging at that time." Since IM is a synchronous medium, there may be communicative consequences if one does not signal that one is away from the computer and is hence no longer available to chat. While Facebook has both synchronous and asynchronous components, SUs are asynchronous, and one does not expect one's friends to be waiting online for a new update. What Herring calls the medium factor "asynchronicity (M1)" may partly explain why Facebookers use SUs dif-

---

[9] It should be noted that since some SUs constituted more than one speech act, we allowed for double-labelling, so that the total is more than 227.

ferently: we propose that the main function of Facebook SUs is to perform identity work. On the basis of this realization, we conducted a content analysis of the status updates in order to see what the Facebookers are doing when they use an assertive, or expressive, for example. These results are presented in Table 8.

Table 8: Content analysis of the status updates

Content analysis:	Total #	%
State of mind (happy, angry, ...)	88	25
Reference to action in progress	59	17
Reference to future action	50	14
Reflection on past events	24	7
State of body	20	6
Location (S is in ...)	18	5
Reference to completed action	18	5
Reference to likes	14	4
Expression of desire	13	4
Identity claim (S is somebody)	9	3
Request for help/advice	6	2
Offer recommendations/advice	6	2
Send wishes	7	2
Quotation	2	1
Response	2	1
Metacomment on SU	4	1
Advertising something	4	1
Express thanks/gratification	3	1
Apologise	2	1
Reference to dislikes	1	0
Total	**350**	**102**

This list is not exhaustive, and our continued analysis of newer data shows that other functions can also be fulfilled through the SUs (e.g., expression of love or friendship). However, the Facebookers in our study mostly used SUs to refer to their state of mind (25%), and to reference action in progress (17%) and future action (14%). It should again be noted here that the message format (Herring's category M10), i.e. the medium, may have played a role in influencing the frequency of references to action in progress, by virtue of the SU system prompt "What are you doing."[10] However, overall this influence seems to be rather small.

To illustrate these three most prominent actions and link them to creative language use for the purpose of identity construction, we will use Examples 5 and 6.

Example 5:
<F-4> is happy to stay with <F-10>.

Example 6:
<F-7> is in the office and trying to be as productive as possible so she can actually go out and have some fun tonight!

In Example 5, an expressive speech act, we have a reference to "state of mind," grammatically realized through the adjective phrase "happy to stay with <F-10>." On the level of identity construction, it highlights a relationship of friendship between two of the individuals of this pilot study. Thus, F-4 constructs her identity in this instant as a "friend" of F-10, although she does not explicitly state "I am friends with F-10." It is important to stress that this claim of friendship is done publicly, i.e. it is witnessed by their mutual circle of friends, which renders this act even stronger. Moreover, we again have an example in which the positioning of F-4 as a friend of F-10 simultaneously constitutes a positioning of F-10 as a friend of F-4 (cf. Section 2).

Example 6 is an assertive speech act and fulfils a triple function: F-7 specifies a location ("F-7 is in the office"), references an action in progress ("trying to be as productive as possible") and a future action ("so she can actually go out and have some fun tonight"). What she also does, in this instance, is construct her identity as an employee (notably through the specification of the location), and as someone who enjoys going out (notably through the reference to future action).

While the use of humour is not frequent in our sample, we argue that having "a sense of humour" is nevertheless an important identity claim in our data (this is in line with Nastri et al.'s[11] and Baron et al.'s findings). Individuals construct their identities as "amusing, funny people" in those moments when they update their status and share this informa-

---

[10] Indeed, this led us to expect a strong use, even overuse of the present continuous, which was, however, not confirmed by the grammatical analysis of our data. Only 20 % of the SUs were realized using "is + verb-ing."

[11] Nastri et al. report that one fifth of their data contained a humorous element. This frequency is much higher than ours.

tion with others. In 29 SUs we identified the occurrence of humour[12] in a variety of functions. Table 9 exemplifies the types of humour we coded.

Table 9: Types of humour in SUs (more than one type can occur in an SU)[13]

Humour type	Total #	%
Irony	14	37
Humour used to bond with in-group	8	21
Word play	7	18
Personification	3	8
Humour at the expense of others	2	5
Self-deprecation	2	5
Canned jokes	1	3
Hyperbole	1	3
Vulgarity	0	0
Total	**38**	**100**

As Table 9 shows, humour is predominantly used in an ironic and bonding way, as exemplified by Examples 7-9:

Example 7:
<M-2> ignores facebook by updating his status.

Example 8:
<M-2> has applied laser hair removal, botox and gallons of protein-enhanced smoothies.

Example 9:
<F-7> is tackling the books . . . and they are winning :-(.

Example 7 is clearly ironic, since M-2 is not ignoring, but using Facebook. In Example 8, we have a case of humour for the purpose of in-group bonding: M-2 received a trip to Miami as a present, and his friends know that he did not actually have his hair removed, nor did he get Botox, or drink smoothies. He is instead referring to practices one may stereotypically associate with the location. This is a case of in-group

---

[12] As humour is often subjective, we have labelled conservatively, that is only when we found clear evidence either through linguistic means or background knowledge that warranted the SU to be taken humorously (cf. Hay; Nastri et al.).
[13] It is for this reason that we have 38 occurrences of humour in 29 SUs.

bonding, since only those who know where he is, what he is doing (or not doing) there, and who have information about certain cultural stereotypes, will appreciate the humour of the update, and not take it literally. This is even more so the case, since there is no emoticon or other paralinguistic feature to highlight that he is "joking." Finally, in Example 9, we have a case of self-deprecation (because she puts herself in the position of the "loser" of the battle), irony (because she is not really tackling the books) and personification (of the books, since books cannot actually engage in battle), which is made humorous through the metaphor STUDYING IS WAR. This is evidenced by the combined use of the verbs "tackle" and "win," in relation to the practice of "studying."

7. Conclusion and suggestions for further research

In this section, we would like to draw two initial conclusions warranted on the basis of our pilot study of the Swiss group, point to what types of research we are in the process of conducting and outline what further research needs to be done in order to better understand language use and identity construction on Facebook.

Our first conclusion is that Facebookers in our pilot study used more implicit than explicit identity claims in their SUs and on their personal profile pages. As already mentioned, this may have to do with the participant structure relevant for our group, i.e., that they entertain relationships with one another which are grounded in offline life. Thus, identities on Facebook reinforce or add new elements to offline identities rather than creating them from scratch (cf. Zhao et al. 1830). Facebook is thus different in this regard to anonymous SNSs and other CMC interactions. Further study is obviously needed here.

Secondly, initial results show that both medium and social/situational factors influence language use on Facebook. In this paper, asynchronicity, participant structure and message format were highlighted. As our study progresses, we will investigate the effects of a whole range of further factors (for example, purpose of the group, purpose of the activity, filtering and quoting options, and persistence of transcript; Herring) which have been shown to influence language use in CMC.

Our next step in the analysis of our data is to study the profiles and SUs of ten individuals from England. We will systematically compare the results and will look for similarities and differences with the pilot study on Swiss individuals. The questions that will follow are (1) Are the similarities and differences between the two groups indicative of group-specific patterns or idiosyncratic usage?; (2) Do individuals who perform less explicit acts of identity construction compensate for these through the creative use of language in the status updates?; (3) Do the processes of identity construction in the profiles challenge or underline those in the status updates? It is only through research into these issues that we will better understand the processes of identity construction on Facebook. Furthermore, and this is our key desideratum for further research, we need to augment our catalogue of speech acts with a catalogue of acts of identity. This will entail categories, such as "employee," "student," "friend," etc. which have surfaced through the analysis of the status updates (and have been presented in this paper) and will include both implicit and explicit identity claims. By compiling such a catalogue we can better and more fully understand the processes of identity construction on Facebook and the language used by various individuals to construct their identities, or perform acts of positioning when interacting with one another and presenting themselves to their friends.

Finally, it should be noted that it was not our aim to pinpoint the sum of individual identity claims. This is connected to the theoretical approach to identity we have chosen to adopt. Nevertheless, future research would benefit from following a number of individuals and their implicit and explicit identity claims on Facebook in close detail, in order to better understand how the strategies work together. This research approach can be combined with more quantitatively oriented ones in an attempt to mix methodologies in order to circle in on such an elusive subject as linguistic identity construction.

Acknowledgments
We would like to thank Vera Mundwiler for her help in preparing the database for this pilot study and the anonymous reviewers for their constructive criticism.

References

Androutsopolous, Jannis. "Introduction: Sociolinguistics and Computer-Mediated Communication." *Journal of Sociolinguistics* 10.4 (2006): 419-438.

Baron, Naomi S., Lauren Squires, Sara Tench and Marshall Thompson. "Tethered or Mobile: Use of Away Messages in Instant Messaging by American College Students." *Mobile Communications: Re-Negotiation of the Social Sphere.* Ed. Rich Ling and Per Pedersen. London: Springer-Verlag, 2005. 293-311.

Boyd, Danah and Nicole Ellison. "Social Network Sites: Definition, History, and Scholarship." *Journal of Computer-Mediated Communication* 13.1 (2007). Available at: http://jcmc.indiana.edu/vol13/issue1/-boyd.ellison.html. Accessed on: 14 April 2009.

Bucholtz, Mary and Kira Hall. "Identity and Interaction: A Sociocultural Linguistic Approach." *Discourse Studies* 7.4-5 (2005): 584-614.

Davies, B. and R. Harré. "Positioning: The Social Construction of Self." *Journal for the Theory of Social Behavior* 20 (1990): 43-63.

Ess, Charles and the AoIR Ethics Working Committee. "Ethical Decision-Making and Internet Research. Recommendations from the Aoir Ethics Working Committee" (2002). Available at: http://-www.aoir.org/reports/ethics.pdf. Accessed on: 1 April 2009.

Eysenbach, Gunther and James Till. "Ethical Issues in Qualitative Research on Internet Communities." *British Medical Journal* 323 (2001): 1103-1005.

Facebook slogan (2010). Available at: http://www.facebook.com. Accessed on: 25 January 2010.

Hay, Jennifer. "Functions of Humor in the Conversations of Men and Women." *Journal of Pragmatics* 32 (2000): 709-742.

Herring, Susan. "A Faceted Classification Scheme for Computer-Mediated Discourse." *Language@Internet* 1 (2007). Available at: http://www.languageatinternet.de/articles/761. Accessed on: 28 August 2009.

Locher, Miriam A. "Relational Work, Politeness and Identity Construction." *Handbooks of Applied Linguistics. Volume 2: Interpersonal Communication.* Ed. Gerd Antos, Eija Ventola and Tilo Weber. Berlin: Mouton de Gruyter, 2008. 509-540.

Mendoza-Denton, Norma. 2002. "Language and Identity." *Handbook of Language Variation and Change.* Ed. J. K. Chambers, Peter Trudgill and Natalie Schilling-Estes. Oxford: Blackwell, 2002. 475–499.

Milroy, James and Lesley Milroy. "Social Network and Social Class: Towards an Integrated Sociolinguistic Model." *Language in Society* 21.1 (1992): 1-26.

Nastri, Jacqueline, Jorge Peña and Jeffrey Hancock. "The Construction of Away Messages: A Speech Act Analysis." *Journal of Computer-Mediated Communication* 11.4 (2006). Available at: http://jcmc.indiana.edu/vol11/issue4/nastri.html. Accessed on: 1 April 2009.

Sunden, Jenny. *Material Virtualities: Approaching Online Textual Embodiment.* New York: Peter Lang, 2003.

Zhao, Shanyang, Sherri Grasmuck and Jason Martin. "Identity Construction on Facebook: Digitial Empowerment in Anchored Relationships." *Computers in Human Behavior* 24.5 (2008): 1816-1836.

Notes on Contributors

BROOK BOLANDER is an assistant for English Linguistics at the University of Basel, Switzerland. Her research interests are in computer-mediated communication (CMC), sociolinguistics and discourse analysis. Within the field of CMC, she is particularly interested in language use and power in blogs, and identity construction/relational work through language in Facebook. At present she is working on a PhD project on the negotiation of power in blogs.

AMIT CHAUDHURI is, according to the *Guardian*, "one of his generation's best writers." His latest novel (his fifth), *The Immortals* (London: Picador, 2009), was a *New Yorker* Book of the Year, and Critics' Choice, Best Books of 2009, in the *Boston Globe* and the *Irish Times*. He is also an internationally acclaimed essayist, and a musician, having performed worldwide as a singer in the Hindustani classical tradition, and as an experimental musician at venues such as the London Jazz Festival and the Brecon Jazz Festival. Among the prizes he has won are the Commonwealth Writers Prize, the Society of Authors' Encore Award, the *Los Angeles Times* Book Prize, and the Indian Government's Sahitya Akademi award. He is Professor of Contemporary Literature at the University of East Anglia, and a Fellow of the Royal Society of Literature. He was one of the judges of the Man Booker International Prize 2009. He is also the first Indian writer to have had a *Guardian* editorial written about him, "In Praise of . . . Amit Chaudhuri."

NIKOLAS COUPLAND is an elected member of the UK Academy of Social Sciences and Research Director of the Centre for Language and Communication Research at Cardiff University. He was founding editor, with Allan Bell, of the *Journal of Sociolinguistics*, published by Blackwell. With Adam Jaworski he edits the Oxford University Press book series, *Oxford Studies in Sociolinguistics*.

MICHAEL DOBSON, Professor of Shakespeare Studies at Birkbeck College, University of London, has worked extensively in universities in Britain and the United States, and has held visiting fellowships in the USA and in China. He comments regularly on Shakespearean performance and criticism for the *London Review of Books* and the BBC, and has contributed programme notes for the Royal Shakespeare Company, Peter Stein, the Sheffield Crucible, and Shakespeare's Globe. As well as pursuing interests in textual, historical and biographical matters, his work on Shakespeare is particularly concerned with the stage and critical history of the canon from the Renaissance to the present. His publications include *Performing Shakespeare's Tragedies Today: The Actors' Perspective* (Cambridge: Cambridge University Press, 2006), *The Making of the National Poet: Shakespeare, Adaptation and Authorship, 1660-1769* (Oxford: Clarendon Press, 1992), *The Oxford Companion to Shakespeare*, co-edited with Stanley Wells (Oxford: Oxford University Press, 2001), and *England's Elizabeth: An Afterlife in Fame and Fantasy*, with Nicola Watson (Oxford: Oxford University Press, 2002), as well as many articles and book chapters. He is co-editor of the Palgrave Shakespeare Studies monograph series, serves on the editorial boards of *Shakespeare Survey* and *Shakespeare Quarterly*, and is a founder member of the European Shakespeare Research Association. At Birkbeck he is convener of the MA programme in Shakespeare and Contemporary Performance.

ANGELA ESTERHAMMER is Professor of English Literature at the University of Zurich. She works in the areas of English, German, and European Romanticism, performativity and performance, and philosophy of language. Her most recent book publications are *Romanticism and Improvisation 1750-1850* (Cambridge: Cambridge University Press, 2008) and the co-edited volume *Spheres of Action: Speech and Performance in Romantic Culture* (Toronto 2009).

KELLIE GONCALVES received her BA in German and Politics from New York University in 2000. Subsequent to teaching EFL to both children and adults in Voralberg, Austria, she came to the University of Berne and completed her Lizentiat in 2005. She completed her PhD in October 2009 entitled *Language and Identity Performance among Intercultural Couples: An Interactional Approach*. It is a localized qualitative study of Anglophones married to native Swiss German speakers residing in the geographic area of Interlaken. Her research interests include Sociolinguistics, English as a Lingua Franca, Historical Linguistics, Language Change, Discourse and Identity Construction and Narrative Studies. She has taught courses in Historical Linguistics, Macrolinguistics, Discourse and Identity and The History of the English Language.

CÉLINE GUIGNARD is currently a doctoral student and an "assistante diplômée" at the University of Fribourg, Switzerland. She took her master in English and History at the same university and wrote her master thesis on Ossianic poetry, pseudo-ancient literature of the eighteenth century and Gothic fiction. During the course of her studies, she studied Scottish literature and history, together with Celtic studies, at the University of Edinburgh. Her academic stay in Scotland awakened her interest in Scottish Gaelic and she returns yearly to the Isle of Skye to attend Gaelic classes at the Gaelic College of Sabhal Mòr Ostaig (Colaiste Ghàidhlig na h-Alba). Her doctoral thesis is a study of the representation of Scottish Highlanders, their language, culture and history, in the Scottish literature of the 1890s-1930s. Her interests encompass Scottish and Gaelic literatures, histories and languages, James Macpherson's Ossianic poetry, Gothic, fantasy and horror fictions, and Anglo-Saxon, Welsh and Irish medieval literatures.

MARC HAAS graduated from the University of Lausanne in 2009 (B.A. in Linguistics, English, Film Studies). He is currently doing work towards his MPhil degree in Linguistics at the University of Oxford, which he will complete in 2011.

MIRIAM A. LOCHER is Professor of the Linguistics of English at the University of Basel, Switzerland. Her work has been in the field of linguistic politeness and the exercise of power in oral communication (*Power and Politeness in Action*, Mouton, 2004) and advice-giving in an American Internet advice column (*Advice Online*, Benjamins, 2006). She has edited a collection of papers on impoliteness together with Derek Bousfield (*Impoliteness in Language*, Mouton, 2008), on *Standards and Norms of the English Language* (Mouton, 2008), together with Jürg Strässler, on interpersonal pragmatics with Sage L. Graham (Mouton, 2010) and on computer-mediated communication and politeness (Journal of Pragmatics, 2010). She is currently working on illness narratives in a joint project with the medical humanities of the University of Basel.

ADRIAN PABLÉ is Assistant Professor of Linguistics at the School of English, The University of Hong Kong. While his former interests included historical dialectology, sociolinguistics and literary linguistics, he is now publishing in the fields of integrationism and philosophy of mind. He is a member of the editorial board of the journal *Language & Communication*, as well as member of the Executive Committee of the International Association for the Integrational Study of Language and Communication (IAISLC).

BARBARA STRAUMANN is Senior Assistant in the English Seminar at the University of Zurich. Her research interests include literary and cultural theory, psychoanalysis, gender, film and visuality. She is the co-author, with Elisabeth Bronfen, of *Die Diva: Eine Geschichte der Bewunderung* (Munich: Schirmer/Mosel, 2002) and the author of *Figurations of Exile in Hitchcock and Nabokov* (Edinburgh: Edinburgh University Press, 2008) as well as a number of articles on masculinity, celebrity culture, Germaine de Staël, Henry James and Willa Cather. She is currently working on her *Habilitation* project on female performer voices in nineteenth and twentieth-century narrative fiction and another book tracing the cultural afterlife of Queen Elizabeth I.

ALEXA WEIK is an Assistante-docteure in the English Department at the University of Fribourg, Switzerland and currently also an International Fellow at the Rachel Carson Center for Environmental Studies in Munich. She earned her PhD in Literature at the University of California, San Diego in 2008 with a dissertation on cosmopolitan American literature. She has published articles on ethnic and transnational American literature, environmental justice, cosmopolitanism, and eco-cosmopolitanism in the *African American Review, The Journal of Commonwealth and Postcolonial Studies*, and elsewhere.

Index of Names

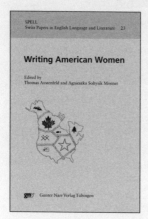

Thomas Austenfeld
Agnieszka Soltysik Monnet
(eds.)

Writing American Women

Swiss Papers in English Language and
Literature 23
2009, 232 Seiten,
€[D] 49,00/SFr 81,00
ISBN 978-3-8233-6521-1

The essays in *Writing American Women* offer a sustained investigation of what writing has meant for North American women authors from the earliest captivity narratives to Kym Ragusa's acclaimed recent memoir, *The Skin Between Us* (2006). By focusing on women rather than the more porous category of gender, contributors offer a meaningful survey of the issues that have shaped women's writing in America. Some of the questions that emerge with particular force include the fraught relationship of women authors to the institutions of literary production, their complex geographical and cultural self-definition, and the special place of autobiography in their work. Combining historical, literary, institutional, and theoretical considerations, this volume brings into focus the rich nuances and heterogeneity of contemporary American studies as well as the vital contributions of women writers to American literature.

Writers discussed in this book include Mary Rowlandson, Lucy Larcom, Amy Lowell, Louisa May Alcott, Edith Wharton, Kay Boyle, Nancy Huston and Lois-Ann Yamanaka.

narr
VERLAG

Narr Francke Attempto Verlag GmbH + Co. KG
Postfach 25 60 · D-72015 Tübingen · Fax (0 7071) 97 97-11
Internet: www.narr.de · E-Mail: info@narr.de

Indira Ghose
Denis Renevey (eds.)

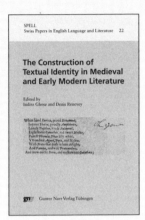

SPELL
Swiss Papers in English Language and Literature 22

The Construction of
Textual Identity in Medieval
and Early Modern Literature

Edited by
Indira Ghose and Denis Renevey

When kind Janus, proud Bituminis,
Iayster Thaise, proudly Amphitrite,
Lovely Psyches, trade Radamel,
Light from Cynothia, and sweet Music,
Pure & Wawela, Thae lilly white,
Wondred Aquol Pyra, and Rosea,
With Pruta that doth in loue delight,
And Pampa, and will Proteradaa,
And now merle Daea, and mischenhim Galatina;

The Construction of Textual Identity in Medieval and Early Modern Literature

Swiss Papers in English Language and
Literature, 22
2009, 222 Seiten,
€[D] 49,00/SFr 81,00
ISBN 978-3-8233-6520-4

This volume sets out to bridge the gap between medieval and early modern literary studies. It contains a selection of essays by both distinguished experts and young scholars in either field, and marks the foundation of the Swiss Association of Medieval and Early Modern English Studies. The contributions address the crucial issue of how texts engage with other texts. They do so in a variety of ways, focusing on pretexts, paratexts, and marginalia. What emerges is an insight into the way texts shape identity – be it that of the author, the readership, or the texts themselves.

Narr Francke Attempto Verlag GmbH + Co. KG
Postfach 25 60 · D-72015 Tübingen · Fax (07071) 97 97-11
Internet: www.narr.de · E-Mail: info@narr.de

narr
VERLAG